CONTEMPORARY INDIAN MIGRAT

CONTEMPORARY INDIAN MIGRATION IN THE GULF

Mohammed Taukeer

TRANSNATIONAL PRESS LONDON
2024

MIGRATION SERIES: 56

Contemporary Indian Migration in the Gulf

by Mohammed Taukeer

Copyright © 2024 Transnational Press London

First Published in 2024 by Transnational Press London in the United Kingdom, 13 Stamford Place, Sale, M33 3BT, UK.
www.tplondon.com

Transnational Press London® and the logo and its affiliated brands are registered trademarks.

Requests for permission to reproduce material from this work should be sent to:
sales@tplondon.com

Paperback
ISBN: 978-1-80135-313-7
Digital
ISBN: 978-1-80135-314-4

Cover Design: Nihal Yazgan
Cover Images are from Wikipedia

Transnational Press London Ltd. is a company registered in England and Wales No. 8771684.

CONTENTS

ABOUT AUTHOR

Mohammed Taukeer is a former research fellow at the International Institute of Migration and Development (IIMAD), Thiruvananthapuram, Kerala, India. He completed his D.Phil in Geography and M.Phil in Development Studies from G B Pant Social Science Institute, University of Allahabad. He also completed a Master's Degree in Geography from the University of Allahabad. His research area is labour migration, refugees and Diaspora studies in the context of rural-urban migration in India and Indian migration in the Gulf. He is also an expert in the study of undocumented migration from South Asia to European countries. He also qualified for the National Eligibility Test (NET) for research. He also worked as a Junior Research Fellow (JRF) and Senior Research Fellow (SRF) of the University Grants Commission (UGC), India. He is an expert in conducting research in India, Greece and the United Arab Emirates. He also participated in The Migration Conference (TMC) at Harokopio University, Athens, in 2017. He has 4 publications in the Journals of Transnational Press, London and 8 in UCG care journals of the University Grants Commission (UGC), India and the Government of India. He has also published chapters in edited books in Routledge publication. His hobbies are creative thinking, reading, writing, speaking and exploring the social science of the world with passion and curiosity.

ACKNOWLEDGMENT

This book is the result of my hard work with creative, innovative research thinking. I would like to give special thanks to my M. Phil supervisor Professor Bhaskar Majumder and PhD supervisor Professor Badri Narayan. Both motivated and inspired me for global innovative research. I would also like to thank the University Grants Commission for financial support. I also express gratitude to Professor S I Rajan, who gave me the opportunity to work as a fellow at the International Institute of Migration and Development, Thiruvananthapuram, Kerala, India. Apart from that, I also expressed special thanks to Professor Anisur Rahman, Centre for West Asian Studies, Jamia Millia Islamia University, New Delhi, India, for guiding me in completing the book. I would like to express a special gratitude and thanks to Professor Ibrahim Sirkeci at the International Business School, Manchester, who encouraged me to publish this book. Therefore, it is my first book and I would like to give my full appreciation to Professor Ibrahim Sirkeci and his team.

FOREWORD

Migration of people from one place to another has been happening since the dawn of human civilization.But now, it has becomeanimportant force in the world. Historically, it is noted that immigrant-receiving nations like Australia, Canada, and the United Stateshave had hugein-flow of migration especially from the Europe and their demographic size have changed significantly. Meanwhile, in European nations that had historically sent immigrants abroad abruptly changed to welcoming societies. Almost all the Western European nations experienced a large increase in the number of foreign workers after 1945. Many of the migrants arrived from developing nations especially from Africa, Asia, the Caribbean, and the West Asia by the late 1960s. It is further witnessed that the South Asian migration on the large scale began to the Gulf countries since the early 70s on account of oil price hike. Today the total number of international migrants has grown to 281 million globally.

It is evident that migration has emerged as a prominent issue in contemporary time as it is taking place in every part of the world. It is now the responsibility of the policy makers to deal with this issue at the national as well as at the global levels to leverage the benefits to the society at large. Owing to migration from developing countries to the developed nations, the inflow of huge amount of remittances are taking place in global south especially in South Asian countries. India is one of the leading countries in the world which receives the maximum volume of remittances from across the world, especially from the Gulf countries. The developing countries use these remittances for eradicating poverty, inequality, and unemployment from their respective countries. Several studies suggest that South Asian countries such as India, Pakistan, Bangladesh, Sri Lanka, etc., have used migration as strategy for social and economic development of their respective countries. Migration thus, has become the existing reality of 21st Century. But it is also evident that the violations of human rights of migrant workers are taking place in every migrant host country. Now the time has come to ensure the rights of the migrant workers so that they can contribute more for the growth and development of their home as well as host countries.

Dr Mohd Taukeer Khan, a bright scholar who is specializing on different facets of migration, made good attempt to explore several issues of Indian migrant workers who have migrated from India to Gulf countries. He has tried to trace the historical legacy of migration to the Gulf region. This book is mainly based on primary data collected from the field when he was doing his M. Phil and Ph. D. The studyis quite intriguing that deals with the contemporary challenges of the Gulf migration in the context of globalization and its sustainable implications on the ground level. It is in fact the outcome of deep analysis of the socio-economic and cultural paradigm of Gulf-based Indian migration by Dr Khan. It further provides detailed information about the process, determinants and consequences of Indian migration in the Gulf and its realities from the social science perspective.I do hope that this book will generate enormous interest not only amongst migration specialist and scholars but also amongst general readers and policy makers alike.

Prof. Anisur Rahman

Centre for West Asian Studies

Jamia Millia Islamia

New Delhi, India

CHAPTER 1

AN OVERVIEW OF LABOUR MIGRATION FROM INDIA TO THE GULF COUNTRIES: PAST AND PRESENT

1.1. An overview of migration in GCC states

"The Gulf Cooperation Council (GCC) was established on May 25, 1981 and economic cooperation agreement was signed on November 11, 1981, in Abu Dhabi, the capital of UAE. The Gulf Cooperation Council (GCC) comprises six oil-producing countries, located in the Arabian Peninsula between the north-east border of the African continent and the Persian Gulf. It is a political and economic organization of six member countries- the Kingdom of Saudi Arabia, Sultanate of Oman, State of Qatar, Kingdom of Bahrain, State of Kuwait and State of United Arab Emirates" (Naufal & Gence, 2012, pp.7-8). There were a total of 30.0 million migrants in GCC states in 2020 and it continuously increased from 1990 to 2019 due to a huge trend of migration from the rest of the world to GCC states. It is remarked that there are a total of 18.1 million South Asian migrants in Gulf countries which accounted for 60.4 per cent of the total stock of 30.01 million stocks of migrants in GCC states. In the context of India, India is the largest origin of migrants for GCC states because there are total stocks of 9.3 million stocks of Indian migrants in GCC states which account for 31.08 per cent of the total stock of migrants in GCC states (Table 1.1 and Figure 1.1).

Table 1.1. Trends of stock of south Asian migrants in GCC states

Origin countries	1990		2000		2010		2020	
South Asian countries	Number	Per cent of total	Number	Per cent of total	Number	Per cent of total	Number	Per cent of total
Afghanistan	169818	2.1	179601	1.8	290985	1.5	482513	1.6
Bangladesh	868071	10.6	1102772	11.0	2345627	11.8	3346430	11.1
India	1955742	23.9	2739058	27.2	6441256	32.3	9326699	31.08
Nepal	181494	2.2	191943	1.9	392998	2.0	800779	2.6
Pakistan	902311	11.0	1128309	11.2	2306422	11.6	3314910	11.04
Sri Lanka	302154	3.7	293588	2.9	517340	2.6	868821	2.8
Subtotal of South Asian in GCC states	4379590	53.6	5635271	56.0	12294628	61.7	18140152	60.4
Subtotal of rest of world in GCC states	3786785	46.4	4425097	44.0	7618208	38.3	11861362	39.6
Total	8166375	100.0	10060368	100.0	19912836	100.0	30001514	100.0

Source: Compiled and analyzed by author. Accessed from United Nation migrants stock by origin and destination, 1990-2019.

7

Figure 1.1. Trend wise analysis of stock of South Asian migrants in GCC states between 1990 and 2020

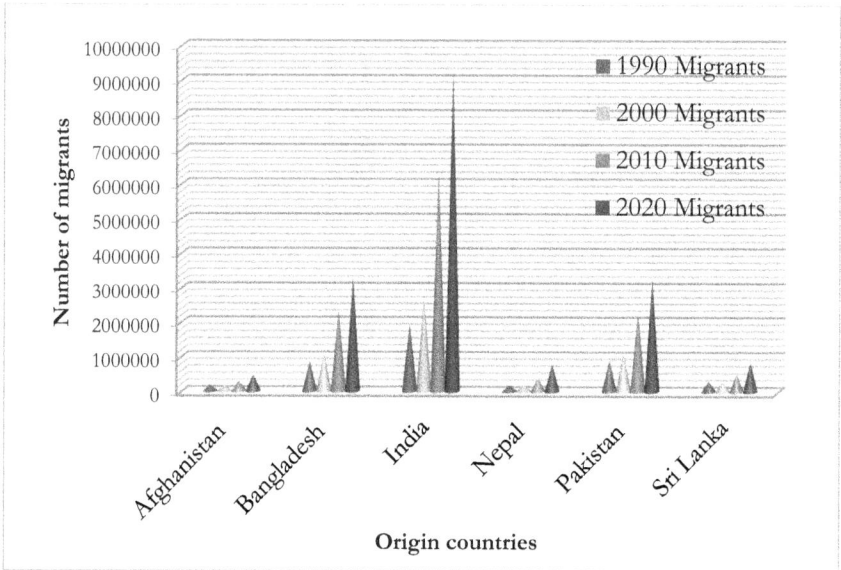

Source: Compiled and analyzed by author. Accessed from United Nation migrants stock by origin and destination, 1990-2020.

The proportion of Indian migrants is leading in GCC states where Indian migrants accounted for 58.0 per cent of the total stock of migrants in Oman followed by 43.0 per cent in Bahrain, 39.8 per cent in UAE, 37.0 per cent in Kuwait, 31.3 per cent in Kuwait and 18.6 per cent in Saudi Arabia. Nationalization policy of Saudi Arabia declined the trend of Indian migrants with the rest of the South Asian migrants in Saudi Arabia (Table 1.2 & Figure 1.2).

Table 1.2. Regional wise stock of migrants of India, Pakistan and Bangladesh in GCC states in 2020 (In per cent of total number of migrants)

Origin countries	Bahrain	Kuwait	Oman	Qatar	Saudi Arabia	UAE
India	43.0	37.0	58.0	31.3	18.6	39.8
Pakistan	10.6	10.9	10.5	10.6	11.0	11.4
Bangladesh	11.1	12.2	13.3	11.8	9.5	12.6
Combined total of above three	64.7	60.2	81.9	53.7	39.1	63.8
Total per cent of rest of world	35.3	39.8	18.1	46.3	60.9	36.2
Total numbers of migrants	741161	3034845	2286226	2229688	13122338	8587256

Source: Compiled and analyzed by author. Accessed from migrants stock data of United Nation, Department of Economic and Social Affairs, 2020.

8

According to Naufal & Ali (2010), GCC states are major remittances sending countries due to huge numbers of unskilled and semi-skilled migrant labourers, those working as temporary migrant labourers in the bottom segmentation of the labour market in Gulf countries. GCC states are major remittances-sending countries to India due to the huge stock of Indian migrants in GCC states. In 2021, India received $ 89375 million as remittances from across the globe, among them the proportion of GCC states was 58.0 per cent. Therefore, it can be analyzed that GCC states are major remittances sending countries for Indian remittances building (Table 1.3 & Figure 1.3).

Figure 1.2. Country wise analysis of proportion of migrants in GCC states in 2020

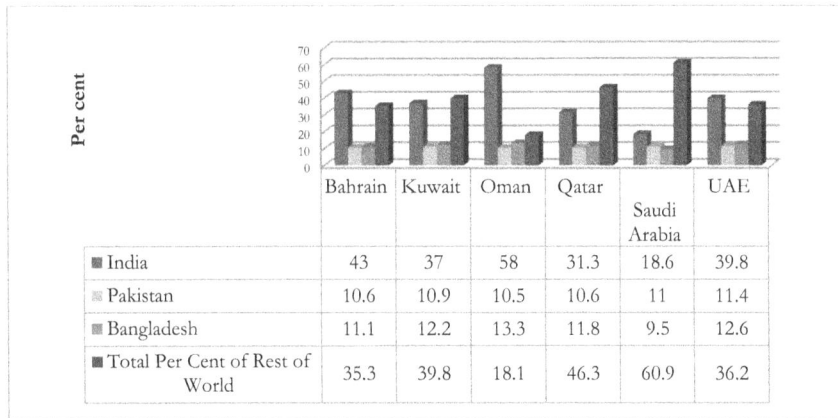

	Bahrain	Kuwait	Oman	Qatar	Saudi Arabia	UAE
■ India	43	37	58	31.3	18.6	39.8
▨ Pakistan	10.6	10.9	10.5	10.6	11	11.4
■ Bangladesh	11.1	12.2	13.3	11.8	9.5	12.6
■ Total Per Cent of Rest of World	35.3	39.8	18.1	46.3	60.9	36.2

Source: Compiled and analyzed by author. Accessed from migrants stock data of United Nation, Department of Economic and Social Affairs, 2020.

Table 1.3. Inflow of remittances in India in 2021

Sending countries	Remittances in million ($)	Per cent of total
Saudi Arabia	13052	14.6
Oman	6413	7.1
Bahrain	1833	2.0
UAE	19821	22.1
Kuwait	6356	7.1
Qatar	4432	4.9
Subtotal from GCC States	**51907**	**58.0**
Rest of world	37468	42.0
Total	89375	100.0

Source: Compiled and analyzed by author. Accessed from World Bank remittances matrix data 2021.Accessed from: www.worldbank.org.

Figure 1.3. Inflow of remittances in India in 2021

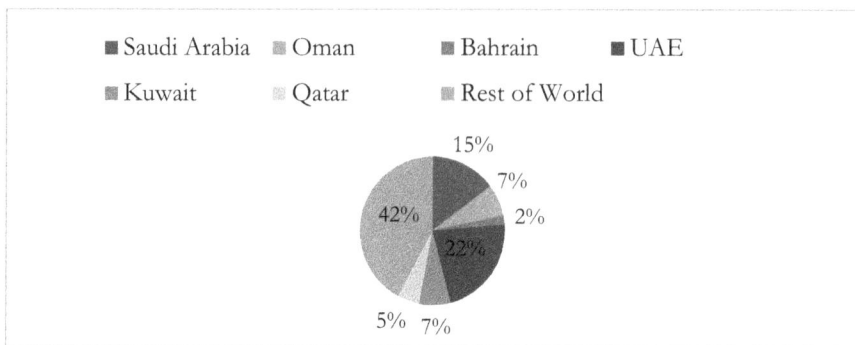

Source: Compiled and analyzed by author. Accessed from World Bank remittances matrix data 2021.Accessed from: www.worldbank.org.

1.2. Political-economic history of Gulf countries and labour migration

The role of the British Empire started with threats of "Gun Boat Diplomacy" between the British Empire and rulers of the Gulf region to sign a series of treaties for preventing piracy with British India's ships as well as ensuring a secure environment for the slave trade in the coastal region of Gulf. In these consequences, rulers of the Gulf region gave the rights to the British Empire to control the foreign affairs of the Gulf region with promises of providing British protection in the Gulf region. Britain signed its first Arabian treaty with the Sultan of Muscat (Oman) in 1798 for banning the French naval force in the Gulf region during the Napoleonic war (Holden, 1971, p.721). The role of the British Empire was focused on the search for a market for the economic benefit of their global capitalism. These consequences developed a socio-economic, geo-politic strategy British Empire and British India in the periphery of the Gulf region because the Gulf region was a "hotspot" between the British Empire and British India. The Gulf region was a secure line between the British Empire and British India in the context of strategic diplomatic communication because earlier mail was sent from British India to Britain by "East Indiamen ship" via the cape of Good Hope coast of South Africa but it was being later facilitated through Alexandria to Suez Canal railroad in 1858 as well as Suez Canal in 1869. In these consequences, the "British India Steam Navigation Company" opened its offices in the Gulf region and around the coastal region of British India. British Empire also improved the telegraphic communication of the imperial line which was established in 1864 in the Gulf and another submarine cable was linked between Bombay and the Suez Canal in 1869 (Peterson, 2009, pp. 277-280).

There is a long history of treaties between the British Empire and the Gulf region where the first anti-piracy "General Treaty" was signed in 1820 to establish a political residence in the lower Persian Gulf region. The other important treaty was known as "Maritime Truce" signed with the Sheikh of Abu Dhabi, Dubai, Ajman and the Qawasim of Sharjah, Ras Al- Khaimah and Lingah in 1835. Under the provision of the treaty, the British Empire was the role of protector, arbiter, mediator, and guarantor of settlement in the coastal region of the Gulf in the Arab region. In 1853, rulers of Persian Gulf regions signed a "Perpetual Maritime Truce" resulted in the British referring to the lower Persian Gulf region as "Trucial States". Britain eventually admitted the ruler of Bahrain to the Truce in 1861, Kuwait in 1899 and Qatar in 1916. After that, the British Empire signed other treaties with the British India office in Bombay. Later, "Exclusive Agreements" bounded the Gulf region and ensured the control of the British Empire in the Gulf region. The "Exclusive Agreement" was signed by the ruler of Bahrain in 1880 and 1892 followed by the rulers of the "Trucial States" (UAE) in 1888 and 1892, the ruler of Kuwait in 1899, the Saudi ruler of Najd and Hasa in 1915 and finally the ruler of Qatar in 1916. Hence, the international legal status of Gulf sheikhdoms transformed into "British-Protected States" states under the partial suzerainty of the British crown with the signing of "Exclusive Agreements" (Onley, 2009, pp.1-54.). The oil-based economy significantly improved the economic interest of the British Empire in eastern Arabia. Oil strongly influenced the policies of Britain in the Gulf. Therefore, Britain decided to stay in the Gulf after its withdrawal from India in 1947 (Onley, 2005, p.38). Later, Britain withdrew from Britain from 1967 to 1971 due to the changing dynamics of the political economy of the Middle East and the decline of British imperialism in India in 1947 was a major cause behind the loosing of British penetration in the Gulf region because the market of British India was strategically linked with British Empire in Gulf region (Naufal & Gence, 2012, p.15).

Before the discovery of oil in the Gulf countries, there was the existence of traditional occupations like pearling, agriculture of dates and construction of ships for fisheries in the Gulf countries. These occupations were the major source of labour migration from poor Arabian countries of Africa to Gulf countries. The discovery of oil changed the political economy of Gulf countries due to the discovery of oil fields in Bahrain in 1932 followed by Kuwait in 1934, Qatar in 1940, Abu Dhabi in 1958 (United Arab Emirates), and Qatar in 1960. The Role of the British petroleum company was so crucial in the discovery of oil in the Gulf countries due to better political and economic relations with Gulf countries and the British Empire (Onley, 2005, pp. 29-45). In Saudi Arabia, the first oil field was discovered in 1933 with the help of the Standard Oil Company of California (Waldron, 1999, pp.30-35). There was a significant role of the pearling industry in the economy of the Gulf countries because Gulf countries were the major exporting countries of pearling across the globe. Additionally, the economy of British India was cordially associated with the pearling-based industry of Gulf countries because Bombay was the largest market for the pearling industry of Gulf countries (Carter, 2005, pp. 139-209). The discovery of oil increased the role of the British Empire in the matters of oil-producing Gulf countries because oil was associated with the economy of global capitalism of the British Empire (Peterson, 2009, p. 284).

The phenomena of the discovery of oil established an economic and political strategic relationship between the British Empire and oil-producing Gulf countries because oil was the basic need for the functioning of the economy of the British Empire on the global level (Onley, 2009, pp. 1-44). The discovery of oil divided the economy of Gulf countries between poor and rich, and these consequences led to labour migration from non-oil producing poor Arabian countries namely – Yemen, Jordon, Egypt and Syria to oil-producing rich Arabian Gulf countries under "Arab-common labour market"[1]. The huge inflow of migration from poor Arabian countries to oil-producing countries created a hurdle for the political scenario of oil-producing Gulf countries because Arabian migrant labourers started demanding political rights in the oil-producing Gulf countries. Therefore, oil-producing Gulf countries shifted their demand for labourers toward South Asian countries because South Asian countries had surplus labourers, who could fill the demand for labourers and these South Asian labourers were hard-working labourers and kept muteness about the political matter of oil-producing Gulf countries (Choucri, 1983,pp. 16-27). The incident of the oil boom was a revolutionary incident in the economy of oil-producing Gulf countries because the incident of the Arab-Israel war increased the price of oil and these consequences generated huge revenues in the oil-producing Gulf countries. These consequences transformed the economy of Gulf countries into "rentier" states and gave a luxurious life to Arabians with rights of "no tax and no representation system" in the political economy of oil-

---

[1] Council of Arab Economic Unity (CEAU) approved an agreement on 3rd June 1957 for creation of Arab common labour market regarding with Arabian labourers could migrate within Arab region without visa for purpose of employment. Cited from: Farag, A. M. (1976). Manpower and employment in Arab countries Some critical issues. *Selected papers and reports of the ILO/ECWA Seminar on manpower and employment planning in Arab countries, Beirut, May 1975* (pp. 85-109). Geneva: International Labour Office.

producing Gulf countries. The consequences of a rentier-based economy created a dual labour market-based economy and led to labour migration from the labour surplus region to labour scarcity oil-producing Gulf countries (Winckler, 2010, p. 9-12). The model of the dual labour market theory is based on the *"Kafala"* (sponsorship) system because dual labour market theory increased the tendency of unskilled and semi-skilled labour migration from South Asian countries to oil-producing Gulf countries (Calton, 2010, pp. 34-36). The trend of labour migration from colonial India to oil-producing Gulf countries started due to the discovery of oil but the size of labour migration was not sufficient. The trend of unskilled and semi-skilled labour migration from India to Gulf countries increased due to the incident of the oil boom in the oil-producing Gulf countries in 1973 (Khadria, 2001, pp. 46-71).

1.3. History of labour migration from India to Gulf countries: An overview

There is long history of migration between India and Persian Gulf during the Indus civilization because Indian traders established settlement between seventeenth and eighteenth century in the region of Persian Gulf. It was also enhanced by British colonization in the Gulf region in the beginning of twentieth century (Jain & Oomen, 2016, p.3). There are different routes of migration to Gulf countries, skilled/professional migration from western countries and unskilled/semi-skilled labour migration from South Asia to Gulf countries. Third route of migration is based on intra-Arab regional labour migration associated with pearl-driving and oil companies (Seccombe & Lawless, 1986, p.549). Up to 1975, there were total 1.4 million migrants in Gulf countries including 63.7 per cent from Arab region followed by 23.4 per cent from Asian (148918 from India) and 12.9 per cent from other rest of world (Table1.4).

1.3.1. Determinants of labour migration from colonial India to the Gulf

Labour migration from colonial India to Gulf countries was led by the global power of imperialism of the British Indian government because the British Indian government established a strategic relationship with the Persian Gulf in 1757 (Gilbert,2002, pp.7-34). British Indian government occupied the port of Aden in 1839 as a coal depot because the port of Aden was a major strategic point between Europe and British India.

Table 1.4. Stock of migrant workers in Gulf countries till 1975 (In number and per cent)

Country	Arabian migrant labourers	India	Pakistan	Other Asian	Total Asian	Other	Total
		Asian migrant labourers					
Saudi-Arabia	699900 (90.6)	15000	15000	8000	38000 (4.9)	35000 (4.5)	773400 (100.0)
UAE	62000 (18.6)	61500	100000	2000	163500 (49.1)	106850 (32.3)	332350 (100.0)
Kuwait	14328 (69.1)	21475	11038	1103	33616 (16.0)	31105 (14.9)	208801 (100.0)
Qatar	14870 (27.6)	16000	16000	2000	34000 (63.2)	4846 (9.2)	53716 (100.0)
Bahrain	6200 (21.2)	8943	6680	981	16604 (56.9)	6424 (21.9)	29228 (100.0)
Oman	8800 (12.4)	26000	32500	200	58700 (83.0)	3200 (4.6)	70700 (100.0)
Total	935050 (63.7)	148918	181218	14284	344420 (23.4)	187925 (12.9)	1467395 (100.0)

Source: International migration and development in the Arab region. Published by International Labour Office Geneva, by Birks and Sinclair, 1980.

British Indian government exported convict[2] labour to the port of Aden because these convict Indian labourers were less expensive and more compliant and prolific in the working environment of the Gulf region (Ewald, 2000, pp. 69-91). A vast majority of the convict Indian labourers were Muslims, who were suitable for the social structure of the labour market in the Gulf region. These convict Indian labourers were invested as unskilled and semi-skilled labourers in the development projects of the Gulf region for developing Aden city during the British colonial period. These consequences were the major reason for convict labour migration from British India to the Gulf region before the discovery of oil in the 1930s in the Gulf region (Kumar, 2016, pp. 61-74).

After the discovery of oil in the Gulf region in the 1930s, these consequences led the unskilled and semi-skilled labour migration from British India to the Gulf region through a series of concession[3]labour agreements between the British Indian government and petroleum companies of the Gulf region. Under these provisions, petroleum companies only recruited unskilled and semi-skilled labourers through labour recruitment offices of British India in Bombay because British India had a surplus of labourers, who filled the

---

[2] The Convict labour system was based on forced migration of labourers under convict panel system of British Indian government in colonial India. Cited from: Arnold, D. (2015). Labouring for the Raj: Convict Work Regimes in Colonial India, 1836–1939. In *Global Convict Labour* (pp. 197-221). Brill

[3] The concessional labour agreement was a series of agreements between the British Indian government and oil companies of Gulf countries for the recruitment of labourers from British India. British Indian government first signed this agreement with Persia (Iran) in 1908 followed by Iraq in 1925, Bahrain Petroleum Company (BAPCO) in 1933, Kuwait Oil Company (KOC) in 1934, Anglo-Persian Oil Company (APOC) in 1935, Petroleum Concession Ltd (PCL) of Qatar and Petroleum Development Qatar (PDQ) in 1936. The Saudi–American Oil Companies (ARAMCO) recruited Indian labourers through agents of APOC but later ARAMCO opened a formal recruitment office in Bombay in 1944. Cited from: Seccombe, I. J., & Lawless, R. (1986). Foreign Workers Dependnece in the Gulf and the International Oil Companies 1910-50. *International Migration Review.Vol.20 No.3(Autumn)* , 548-574.

demand for labourers in petroleum companies of the Gulf region. Indian migrant labourers migrated to the Gulf region via Bombay because Bombay was the hub for labour migration from the rest of India. Additionally, migrant labourers migrated from British India to the Gulf region through their social network of migration. Anglo-Persian Oil Company (APOC) opened its first office in Bombay and recruited labourers from Burma Oil Company. Following this, Bahrain Oil Company opened its recruitment office in Bombay in 1936 followed by Kuwait Oil Company (KOC) in 1936. Saudi–American Company (ARAMCO) opened its office in Bombay in 1944 and the Qatar oil company opened its office in the same year in Bombay. Both Saudi Arabia and Qatar did not permit Hindus to work as labourers in oil companies due to religious reasons (Seccombe, 1983, pp. 3-20). The trend of labour migration from British India to oil petroleum companies of the Gulf region was led by wage differential because unskilled and semi-skilled migrant labourers got higher wages in the Gulf region compared to low wages in Bombay (Mumbai). Semi-skilled and unskilled migrant labourers got Rs. 71 to 475 per month in oil petroleum companies of the Gulf region compared to Rs. 45 to 140 per month wages in Bombay (Mumbai). There was a total of 2470 Indian migrant labourers worked for Anglo-Persian Oil Company (APOC) followed by 723 for Kuwait Oil Company (KOC), 602 for Saudi Arabia – American Company (ARAMCO), 553 for Bahrain petroleum company (BAPCO) and 194 for Qatar oil company (PDQ) till 1947 (Seccombe, 1986, pp.548-574). Labour migration from British India to the Gulf region was led and managed by the provision of the Indian Emigration Act 1922 followed by the abolition of indentured labour migration in 1917. The Indian Emigration Act of 1922 ensured the route of unskilled and semi-skilled labour migration from India to the Gulf region through the process of direct penetration of British India in exporting manpower from the labour-abundant zone of British India (Shirras, 1931, pp. 591-616).

1.3.2. Determinants of labour migration from post colonial India to the Gulf region

Surplus labourers in India

India had surplus labourers, who filled the huge demand for unskilled and semi-skilled labourers in the labour-intensive development projects of oil-producing Gulf countries. Therefore, these consequences led to the labour migration from India to the oil-producing Gulf countries due to the incident of the oil boom in the Gulf region in 1973 (Mckinley, 200, p. 18). The huge demand for labourers was an opportunity for India for exporting to manpower because India had a surplus of labourers according to the structure and demand of the labour market of the oil-producing Gulf region. Therefore, the Indian government involved itself in the recruitment process of their labourers in the labour markets of oil-producing Gulf countries in 1977 (Birks & Sinclair, 1980, p.108).

Accepted low wages by Indian migrant labourers

South Asian migrant labourers accepted low wage rates compared to Arabian migrant labourers, who demanded higher wage rates and luxurious working conditions. Indian migrant labourers accepted such kinds of risky jobs; those were denied by Arabian migrant labourers. These consequences were the major reasons for the huge demand for labour migration from post-colonial India to the oil-producing Gulf region (Choucri, 1986, pp. 252-273).

Political reasons in the Gulf countries

The initial phase of labour migration to the Gulf region was led by poor Arabian countries but Arabian migrant labourers were creating an environment of threats to the political security of oil-producing Gulf countries because these Arabian migrant labourers were demanding political rights in the Gulf countries. These consequences led to the ideology of leftist pan-Arab ideas in the Gulf countries. Therefore, oil-producing Gulf countries deported Arabian migrant labourers and these consequences created a gap in the labour market as well as increased the demand for unskilled and semi-skilled labourers in the labour market of oil-producing Gulf countries. Therefore, the paradigm of labour demand shifted toward South Asian countries because South Asian countries had surplus labourers, who could fill the demand for labourers as well as were not subject to radicalization for the political matter of the Gulf region (Kapiszewski, 2016, pp. 46-70).

Gulf war

The consequences of the Gulf War created a hurdle situation for oil-producing Gulf countries in 1991. The Kingdom of Saudi Arabia deported 1.5 million migrant labourers of Yemenis and Palestinians, who supported the invasion of Iraq on Kuwait. These consequences created a vacuum in the labour market of Saudi Arabia. Therefore, Saudi Arabia shifted the demand for unskilled and semi-skilled labourers toward South Asian countries. India supplied huge labourers according to the demand of Saudi Arabia during the

Gulf War of 1991. Therefore, the Gulf War was the turning point for the huge trend of labour migration from India to Gulf countries in the last decade of the twentieth century (Rahman, 2010, pp. 16-18).

Globalization

The consequences of globalization are leading factors in the integration between rich and poor countries because globalization works as a benefit for both poor and rich countries. Therefore, the phenomena of globalization are leading labour migration across the globe in the context of changing the paradigm of the labour markets in the periphery of globalization (Wolf, 2008, pp. 401-409). The trend of labour migration from India to the Gulf countries was led by revolutionary changes in the information technology and transportation system in the consequences of globalization in India (Rajan & Kumar, 2010, pp. 1-30).

1.3.3. An overview of history of labour migration from Kerala to the Gulf countries

Labour migration from Kerala to the oil-producing Gulf countries was caused by the discovery of oil in the Gulf region. The initial phase of labour migration from Kerala to the Gulf countries was led by Bombay in the colonial period because migrants worked as clerks, teachers and servants in Bombay. These labourers were recruited by the recruitment office of British oil companies in Bombay. Therefore, the process of international migration from Kerala to Gulf countries was led by internal migration in colonial India (Zachariah & Rajan, 2012, p. 2). In the colonial period, the tendency of labour migration was led by Kerala but there was social classification in the tendency of labour migration from Kerala to the Gulf countries in the colonial period. Skilled migrant labourers were from the Christian community, who worked as teachers in Bombay and clerks in British Oil Company while unskilled and semi-skilled labourers were Muslims, who worked as masons and manual labourers in the cities of India before migration to the Gulf countries (Kurien, 2002, p. 40).

The trend of labour migration from post-colonial India to Gulf countries was led by Kerala, Tamilnadu, Andhra Pradesh, Maharashtra, Goa and Punjab but more than fifty per cent of the labour migration was led by Kerala. In the initial phase of labour migration from post-colonial India, migrant labourers migrated from Bombay because there was the facility of passport office and emigration clearance office in Bombay. Labourers migrated through sea ports of Bombay until 1964 beginning air services to Gulf countries from Delhi, Calcutta and Madras. The vast majority of the migrant labourers migrated through the seaport of Bombay and the government of India opened a regional passport office in Kerala in 1974-75 to facilitate labour migration from Kerala (Nair, 1983, pp. 30-31). The trend of the initial phase of labour migration from Kerala to Gulf countries was based on the culture of internal migration from Kerala to Bombay, Delhi and Madras but the incident of the oil boom increased the direct labour migration from Kerala to Gulf countries. These consequences shifted the tendency of internal migration toward international migration to the Gulf countries in 1973-74 due to the beginning of labour-intensive projects in the oil-producing Gulf countries (Prakash, 1978, pp. 1107-1111). Recently, the trend of labour migration from Kerala to Gulf countries is being led by Muslims according to the Kerala Migration Survey (KMS) 2014.The matter of migration is associated with livelihood for the people of Kerala as well as giving an important role in the enhancement of the building capacity of the economy of Kerala (Zachariah & Rajan, 2016, pp. 66-71).

1.3.4. Recent phenomena of labour migration from north India to the Gulf countries

According to the Overseas, Employment Division, Ministry of External Affairs, Government of India (2015), the initial phase of labour migration from India to the Gulf countries was led by Kerala but recently both Uttar Pradesh and Bihar are leading states in unskilled and semi-skilled labour migration from India to the Gulf countries in the twenty-first century. According to Taukeer (2022), there is an inter-connection between colonial-based migration and post-colonial-based migration from Uttar Pradesh and Bihar because labourers migrate due to a similar set of economic and non-economic reasons based on the colonial experiences of migration in the twenty-first century. Heartlands of colonial indentured labour migration have emerged as major labour-sending regions in both Uttar Pradesh and Bihar in the recent twenty-first century. According to Azeez & Begum (2009), both Uttar Pradesh and Bihar are leading states in unskilled and semi-skilled labour migration compared to skilled labour migration from Kerala to the Gulf countries. It occurred due to the positive role of the vocational training institutions in Kerala, where labourers get training for jobs and get a certificate of skilled labourers. These consequences lead the skilled labour migration from Kerala to the Gulf countries under the emigration check not required passport (ECNR) category while there is an absence of such kinds of vocational training institutions in Uttar Pradesh and Bihar. Therefore, these consequences lead the unskilled and semi-skilled labour migration from Uttar Pradesh and Bihar under the emigration check required passport (ECR) category. According to Sasikumar & Thimothy (2015), the trend and pattern of unskilled and semi-skilled labour migration from Uttar Pradesh and Gulf countries are caused by wage differential between cities of India and the Gulf countries because migrant labourers get higher wage rates in the Gulf countries compared to low wages in cities of India. Additionally, unregistered private recruitment agencies and social network systems are playing a leading role in facilitating labour migration from Uttar Pradesh to the Gulf countries. According to Rajan et al. (2017), both Uttar Pradesh and Bihar are leading states in receiving remittances from unskilled and semi-skilled labourers from the Gulf countries. These consequences are the result of the huge supply of unskilled and semi-skilled labourers from Uttar Pradesh and Bihar to the Gulf countries.

1.4. Analysis of trend of labour migration from India to Gulf countries

Based on the above discussion, the trend and pattern of labour migration from India to the Gulf countries can be analyzed according to the following time framework analysis.

1948 to 1975

1976 to 1990

1991 to 2000

2001 to 2020

Regional trend and pattern of labour migration from India to the Gulf countries between 2011 and 2020

The analytical framework is based on the analysis of secondary data from various sources. The analytical framework of trends and patterns of labour migration between 1948 and 1990 is based on secondary data from published articles related to labour migration from India to the Gulf countries. The case of the trend and pattern of labour migration from 1991 to 2020 is based on the analysis of emigration clearance data of labour migration, Overseas Employment Division, Ministry of External Affairs, Government of India. Additionally, secondary data is accessed from www.indiastat.com regarding emigration clearance data for labour migration from India to the Gulf countries. Analyses of secondary data are explained by supporting published articles, chapters and reports as well as presented by the graphic presentation for a better interpretation of the analysis of secondary data.

1.4.1. Analysis of trend and pattern of labour migration from India to Gulf countries between 1948 and 1975

The trend of labour migration from India to the Gulf countries was not so sufficient from 1948 to 1970 because the total number of migrant labourers was 12277 in 1948 followed by 40000 in 1970 but the number of migrant labourers increased by 148918 in 1975 because of huge demand of unskilled and semi-skilled migrant labourers started lavish development projects in the Gulf due to incident of the oil boom in the Gulf in 1973 (Table 1.5).

Table 1.5. Stock of India migrant labourers in the Gulf region

Year	Total stock of Indian migrants
1948	12277
1970	40000
1975	148918

Source: Jain, 1982,p. 303; Birks & Sinclair, 1980,p .115; &Jain, 1989, p.156.

1.4.2. Analysis of trend and pattern of labour migration from India to Gulf countries between 1976 and 1990

The trend of labour migration from India to the Gulf region was enhanced in 1975 due to the huge demand for unskilled and semi-skilled migrant labourers in the job markets of oil-producing Gulf countries (Naidu, 1991, p. 349). According to Prakash (1998), the trend of labour migration from India to the oil-producing Gulf countries can be divided into the following phases between 1976 and 1990.

i. The initial phase of stable growth rate in migration between 1976 and 1979 (Table 1.6).
ii. The inclined phase of labour migration between 1980 and 1983 (Table 1.6).
iii. Declining phase in labour migration between 1984 and 1990 (Table1.6).

Table 1.6. Trends of labour migration from India to the Gulf region

Year	Total trend of migration	Year	Total trend of migration	Year	Total trend of migration
1976	42000	1981	276000	1986	113500
1977	22900	1982	239500	1987	125400
1978	69000	1983	225000	1988	170100
1979	171800	1984	206000	1989	126200
1980	236200	1985	163000	1990	141800

Source: Prakash, B.A, 1998, p.3210.

1.4.3. Analysis of trend and pattern of labour migration from India to Gulf countries between 1991 and 2000

The trend of labour migration from India to the Gulf region was enhanced by changing patterns of labour markets of Gulf countries due to economic and political reasons in Gulf countries and consequences of globalization also led to labour migration in the 1990s. The trend of labour migration from India to the Gulf countries is known as the revival phase between 1991 and 1995 due to the huge trend of labour migration (Prakash, 1998, p.3210). Oil-producing Gulf countries emerged as major destinations for unskilled and semi-skilled migrant labourers due to India's oriented demand for labourers in the Gulf countries (Khadria, 2006, p.2). Oil-producing Gulf countries opened their labour market for South Asian countries and these consequences led the labour migration from South Asian countries (Shah, 2006, pp. 1-20). Trends and patterns of labour migration from India to the Gulf countries are led by wage differential between India and the Gulf in the context of the culture of migration in the consequences of globalization of migration (Ali, 2007, pp.37-58).

Based on the above concise description, the trend and pattern of labour migration from India to the Gulf countries can be divided into the following two phases.

Inclined trends of labour migration between 1991 and 1995

The trend of labour migration from India to the Gulf countries was enhanced between 1991 and 1995 and the highest growth rate in labour migration was observed at 111.1 per cent in 1992 compared to 1991. The average number of migrant labourers was 360624 per annum between 1991 and 1995. These consequences were the result of the huge demand for labourers from India after the beginning of globalization in India with the changing political scenario of the Gulf countries due to the Gulf War of 1991. Therefore, there was a phase of the inclined trend of labour migration from India to the Gulf countries between 1991 and 1995 (Figures 1.4 & 1.5).

Declined trend of labour migration between 1996 and 2000

The trend of labour migration from India to the Gulf countries is known as a declining phase between 1996 and 2000 because the average number of migrant labourers was 285717 per annum between 1996 and 2000 compared to the average number of migrant labourers between 1991 and 1995. Trends of labour migration continuously declined between 1996 and 1999 but the trend of labour migration inclined in 2000 with a growth rate of 12.3 per cent compared to 1999 (Figures 1.4 & 1.5).

Figure 1.4. Trends of labour migration from India to the Gulf countries between 1991 and 2000

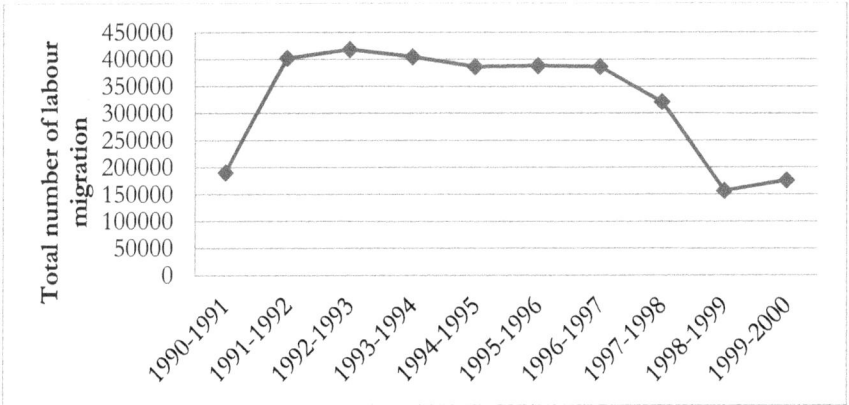

Source: Compiled and analyzed by author from emigration clearances data of labour migration from India to the Gulf Countries between 1991 and 2000. Accessed from data bank of www.indiastat.com .

Figure 1.5. Annual growth rate in labour migration from India to the Gulf countries between 1991 and 2000

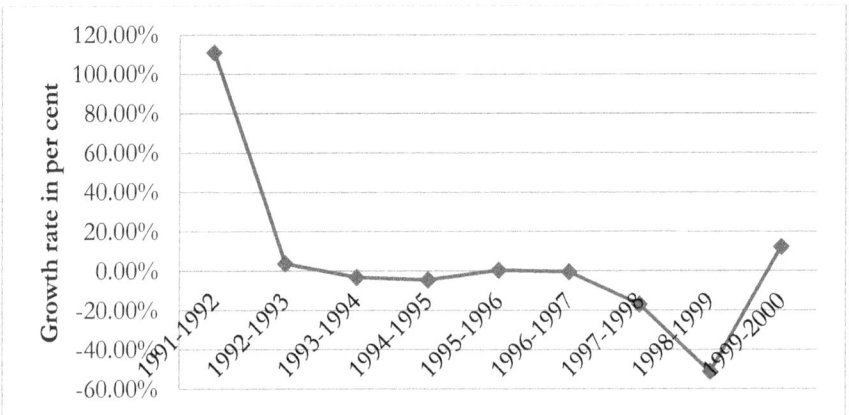

Source: Compiled and analyzed by author from emigration clearances data of labour migration from India to the Gulf countries between 1991 and 2000. Accessed from data bank of www.indiastat.com.

1.4.4. Trend and pattern of labour migration from India to the Gulf countries between 2001 and 2020

The trend and pattern of labour migration to the Gulf countries are based on the changing structure of the labour market because nationalization policies of the labour market are adversely influencing the trend of skilled labour migration from South Asia to the Gulf countries. The case of unskilled and semi-skilled labour migration leads to the huge tendency of labour migration from South Asia to the Gulf countries due to the demand for unskilled and semi-skilled labourers in the bottom segmentation of the labour market (Shah,2013, pp. 36-70). Therefore, policies of nationalization of the labour market are determining the structure of the labour migration from South Asian countries in the twenty-first century because Gulf countries are giving preference to local Arabians in the jobs market regarding managing the problem of unemployment among local Arabians (Baldwin,2011, p. 2).

In the case of labour migration from India to the Gulf countries, the policies of both Gulf countries and the policies of the government of India, are determining the trends of labour migration because the government of India are facilitating unskilled and semi-skilled labour migration from India to the Gulf countries. After all, these consequences are generating both employment and remittances in India (Rajan, 2010, p. 4). Trends and patterns of labour migration from India to the Gulf countries between 1990 and 2019 were led by globalization at the end of the twentieth century from the 1990s but it declined due to the global economic crisis in 2009 with nationalization policies of the labour market in the Gulf countries (Chandramalla, 2022, p. 32).

Inclined trend of labour migration between 2001 and 2008

It was the phase of the inclined trend of labour migration because an average of 496746 labourers migrated per annum between 2001 and 2008. Among the Gulf countries, Saudi Arabia and the United Arab Emirates were the major destinations for Indian migrant labourers. Out of the total labour migration from India to the Gulf countries, nearly 75.0 per cent of the labourers migrated to Saudi Arabia and the United Arab Emirates. The trend of share of Saudi Arabia declined from 33.0 per cent in 2001 to 28.0 per cent in 2008 while the trend of labour migration to the United Arab Emirates increased from 23.0 per cent in 2001 to 43.0 per cent in 2008. The highest growth rate in annual migration was observed as 44.0 per cent in 2003 compared to 2002 while the lowest growth rate was observed as 6.0 per cent in 2008 compared to 2007 (Figures 1.6,1. 7 & 1. 8).

Declined trend of labour migration in 2009

The trend of total number of migrant labourers declined from 885514 in 2008 to 592299 in 2009. The annual growth rate of migration was -27.6 per cent in 2009 compared to total labour migration from India to the Gulf countries in 2008. The trend of labour migration shifted from the United Arab Emirates to Saudi Arabia because nearly 47.5 per cent of the total migrant labourers migrated to Saudi Arabia in 2009. According to Narayan & Rajan (2012), the consequences of the global economic crisis declined the trend of labour migration from India to the United Arab Emirates because the economy of the United Arab Emirates was shocked by the global economic crisis of 2009 due to the global investment in Dubai but Saudi Arabia did not face the problem of economic crisis like the United Arab Emirates. These consequences shifted the trend of labour migration from India to Saudi Arabia due to the huge demand for Indian migrant labourers in Saudi Arabia (Figures 1.6, 1. 7 & 1. 8).

Re-inclined trend of labour migration between 2010 to 2014

It was the phase of the re-inclined trend of labour migration because an average of 729097 labourers migrated per annum between 2010 and 2014. Out of the total labour migration from India, nearly 76.0 per cent of the migrant labourers migrated to Saudi Arabia and the United Arab Emirates while the rest of the labourers migrated to Bahrain, Oman, Kuwait, and Qatar. Among the Gulf countries, Saudi Arabia was the favourite destination for Indian migrant labourers. The highest growth rate of migration was observed as 19.7 per cent in 2012 compared to a -1.0 per cent growth rate in 2011(Figures 1.6, 1. 7 & 1. 8).

Re –declined trend of labour migration from 2015 and onwards

It is observed that the trend of labour migration from India to the Gulf countries is continually declining, except the total number of migrant labourers with 353186 in 2019 compared to the total number of migrant labourers with 321721 in 2018. The highest growth rate was observed as 8.8 per cent in 2019 compared to 2018 while the lowest growth rate of migration was observed as – 289.0 per cent in 2020 compared to 2019 due to the pandemic of COVID-19 across the globe (Figures 1.6,1.7 & 1.8). According to Sasikumar (2021), the pandemic of COVID-19 largely affected the trend and pattern of labour migration from India to the Gulf countries because the consequences of the pandemic created reverse migration of migrant labourers in India.

Figure 1.6. Trends of labour migration from India to the Gulf countries between 2001 and 2020

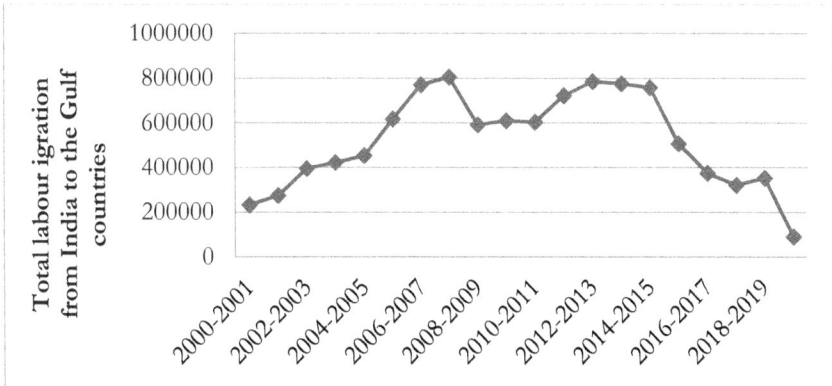

Source: Compiled and analyzed by author. Accessed from emigration clearances data of labour migration, Overseas Employment Division, Ministry of External Affairs, Government of India.

Figure 1.7. Annual growth rate in labour migration from India to the Gulf countries between 2001 and 2020

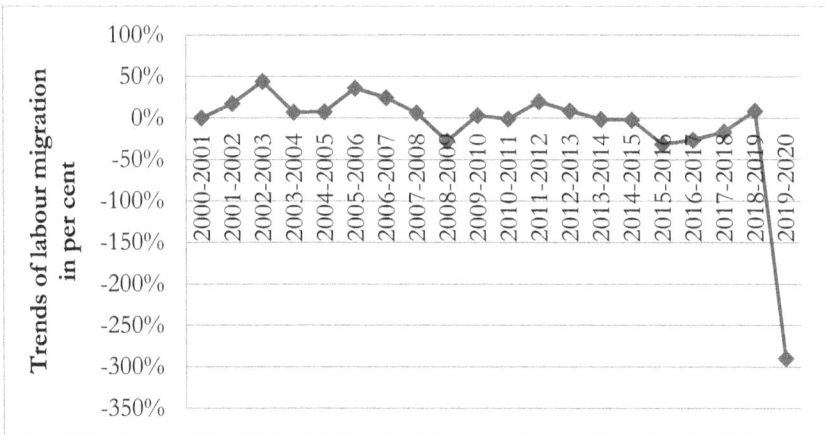

Source: Compiled and analyzed by author. Accessed from emigration clearances data of labour migration, Overseas Employment Division, Ministry of External Affairs, Government of India.

Figure 1.8. Destination wise trends of labour migration from India to the Gulf countries between 2001 and 2020

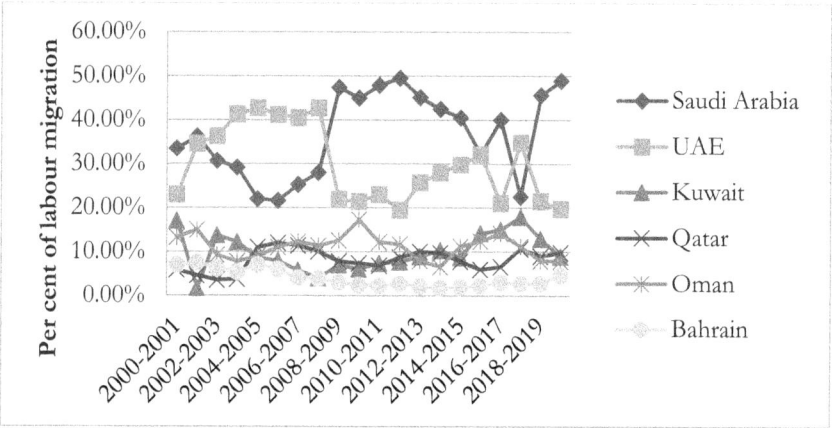

Source: Compiled and analyzed by author. Accessed from emigration clearances data of labour migration, Overseas Employment Division, Ministry of External Affairs, Government of India.

1.4.5. Regional trends of labour migration from India to the Gulf region

Both Uttar Pradesh and Bihar are leading states in labour migration from India to the Gulf countries. There are the following phenomena in the regional trend and pattern of labour migration from India to the Gulf countries.

1. Uttar Pradesh is the leading state in labour migration because Uttar Pradesh contributed the highest total labour migration from India to the Gulf countries between 2011 and 2020. Additionally, Bihar was also the leading state in labour migration to the Gulf countries after Uttar Pradesh. Both Uttar Pradesh and Bihar contributed 37.5 per cent to 47.0 per cent in total labour migration from India to the Gulf countries between 2011 and 2020. During the pandemic of COVID-19, both Uttar Pradesh and Bihar were the leading states in labour migration from India to the Gulf countries (Table 1.7).

2. Among the top 100 districts of India in labour migration to the Gulf countries in 2020, Siwan district of Bihar ranked first in labour migration from India to the Gulf countries followed by the Lucknow district of Uttar Pradesh ranked second, Murshidabad district of West Bengal ranked third, Kushinagar district of Uttar Pradesh ranked fourth and Kottayam district of Kerala ranked fifth in labour migration from India to the Gulf countries. Among the top five

districts, two districts were from Uttar Pradesh and one district was from Bihar (Table 1.8).

3. In Uttar Pradesh, Lucknow, Kushinagar, Deoria and Bijnor were the top international migration districts in labour migration from Uttar Pradesh to the Gulf countries between 2016 and 2020 (Table 1.9).

Table 1.7. Labour migration from Uttar Pradesh and Bihar to the Gulf countries

Year	Total emigration clearances from India	Total labour migration from Uttar Pradesh as per cent of total	Total labour migration from Bihar as per cent of total	Combined share of Uttar Pradesh and Bihar in per cent	Total labour migration from rest of India as per cent of total
2011	603159	25.8	11.7	37.5	62.5
2012	722139	26.1	11.4	37.5	62.5
2013	785291	27.3	12.0	39.3	60.7
2014	774846	29.2	12.5	41.7	58.3
2015	758684	30.8	14.0	44.8	55.2
2016	607296	28.0	15.0	43.0	57.0
2017	374560	24.0	18.0	42.0	58.0
2018	321721	26.0	18.0	44.0	56.0
2019	353126	32.0	15.0	47.0	53.0
2020	90602	31.0	15.0	46.0	54.0

Source: Compiled and analyzed by author. Accessed from emigration clearance data of labour migration between 2011 and 2020. Overseas Employment, Division Ministry of External Affairs, Government of India, accessed from www.mea.gov.in.

Table 1.8. Top Five districts of India labour migration from India to GCC states in 2020

All India ranked in labour migration	Top five districts among 100 districts in labour migration	Total labour migration to the Gulf countries
1	Siwan (Bihar)	2562
2	Lucknow (U.P)	2598
3	Murshidabad(W.B)	2242
4	Kushinagar (U.P.)	1883
5	Kottayam (Kerala)	1505

Source: Source: Compiled and analysed by author. Accessed from emigration clearance data of labour migration in 2020. Overseas Employment, Division Ministry of External Affairs, Government of India, accessed from www.mea.gov.in.

Table 1.9. Top three districts of Uttar Pradesh in labour migration to the Gulf countries

Year	Total numbers of labour migration from Uttar Pradesh Gulf	Labour migration from 1st rank district of Uttar Pradesh to Gulf in percent of total		Labour migration from 2nd rank district of Uttar Pradesh to Gulf in percent of total		Labour migration from 3rd rank district of Uttar Pradesh to Gulf in percent of total	
2016	141748	LUCKNOW	11.0	KUSHINAGAR	8.5	DEORIA	7.5
2017	88450	LUCKNOW	10.0	KUSHINAGAR	9.8	DEORIA	9.0
2018	82902	KUSHINAGAR	9.0	DEORIA	8.0	LUCKNOW	6.0
2019	112849	KUSHINAGAR	7.0	LUCKNOW	6.0	BIJNOR	5.5
2020	28249	LUCKNOW	9.0	BIJNOR	5.0	DEORIA	4.9

Source: Compiled and analyzed by author. Accessed from emigration clearance data of labour migration between 2016 and 2020. Overseas Employment, Division Ministry of External Affairs, Government of India, accessed from www.mea.gov.in.

1.5. Recent phenomena of shifting paradigm in internal to international labour migration from Uttar Pradesh and Bihar

The trend of labour migration from Uttar Pradesh to the Gulf countries is based on the pattern of internal labour migration because the pattern of internal migration is shifted toward Gulf migration due to wage differential between cities of India and Gulf countries (Majumder & Taukeer, 2019, pp. 162-174). Consequences of internal migration from rural north India to Mumbai led to the tendency of labour migration to Gulf countries in the context of the role of internal migration in international migration (Taukeer, 2023 & 2023). The social network system works as a pull factor in the process of labour migration from Uttar Pradesh to the Gulf countries because labourers migrate with the help of their kinship network in the Gulf countries (Taukeer, 2017, pp. 561-574).

In the case of labour migration from the Lucknow district of Uttar Pradesh to Gulf countries, it is found that the process of international migration is led by internal migration because migrant labourers migrate to Mumbai and Delhi for employment and gaining skills of occupation before migration to the Gulf countries (Taukeer, 2020, pp. 120-138). Unskilled and semi-skilled migrant labourers gain more wages in the Gulf countries compared to the low wages in Delhi and Mumbai. Consequences of wage differential lead the labour migration from Uttar Pradesh to the Gulf countries (Taukeer, 2021, p. 323). The impact of the Gulf migration developed a culture of migration from Uttar Pradesh to the Gulf countries because the social impact of Gulf migration is inspiring and motivating to youth for migration to the Gulf countries. Additionally, the culture of the Gulf migration is replacing the trend of internal migration from Uttar Pradesh to Mumbai and Delhi (Taukeer, 2022, pp. 292-305).

In the case of labour migration from Bihar to the Gulf countries, Siwan district is well known for the huge tendency of labour migration to the Gulf countries. Gulf migration generated huge remittances compared to internal migration in cities of India. These consequences lead to labour migration from Bihar to the Gulf countries (Rahman, 2001, p. 43). The inflow of international remittances led to the culture of international migration from Bihar as the consequence of a well-developed route of migration (Datta, 2016, pp. 85-93). Therefore, the recent trend of labour migration from India to the Gulf countries is being led by North Indian states like Uttar Pradesh and Bihar, and the tendency of the Gulf migration is a new phenomenon in the heartland of internal migration of Bihar and Uttar Pradesh (Sasikumar, 2019, pp.111-125). Both internal and international migration is being led by Bihar and the pattern of internal migration is also being replaced by international labour migration from Bihar to the Gulf countries (Srivastava, 2020, pp. 859-883).

1.6. Methodological framework

Based on the above concise analysis of selected pieces of review of literature, it can be summarized that there is a colonial reflection in the function of post-colonial Gulf migration in the context of internal and international migration. The major argument of this book is based on the analysis of explorative facts concerning the nexus of internal and international migration because it is found that selected existing kinds of literature do not give perfect information about the role of internal migration in the process of facilitating international labour migration from India to Gulf countries in the twenty-first century. Therefore, the book tries to give a new fact concerning the role of internal migration in international migration by its process, determinants and consequences of migration.

Study area

The study covers Uttar Pradesh as the root origin, Mumbai as the transit internal destination and the United Arab Emirates as an international destination where migrant labourers migrated from rural areas of Uttar Pradesh to Gulf countries namely –Saudi Arabia and the United Arab Emirates via internal migration to Mumbai within well developed cultural region of migration in the context of globalization of migration in rural North India.

Uttar Pradesh

Uttar Pradesh was selected purposively because Uttar Pradesh is the leading state inter-state rural-urban migration within India (Census, Government of India, 2011) and international migration to Gulf countries (Tables 1.7, 1.8 & 1.9). Sampling of the study coverage area was based on multi-stage sampling where Inayat Patti village was purposively selected in Prayagraj (Allahabad) district in Uttar Pradesh for the study of internal and international migration on M.Phil dissertation titled "Nature, Causes and Consequences of Migration to Gulf Countries: A Study of Inayat Patti Village in Allahabad District in Uttar Pradesh, India. A revised version of the submitted M.Phil dissertation was presented as a conference paper titled "Nature and Consequences of Migration to Gulf Countries: A Study of Inayat Patti Village of India" at The Migration Conference, organized by Transnational Press, London at Harokopio University, Athens, Greece, August 23-26, 2017. Apart from this, Lucknow district was also purposively selected to study a D.Phil thesis titled "Cross-Border Migration: An Analysis of Migration from India to Gulf Countries by Processes and Consequences". Lucknow district is well known for its international migration to Gulf countries because Lucknow was listed among the top 100 districts of labour migration from India to Gulf countries from 2016 to 2020 (Table 1.9). Therefore, the study is based on purposively selected Inayat Patti village in Prayagraj district, and rural-urban areas of Lucknow district in Uttar Pradesh for the study of internal and international migration.

Hence, multiple round field surveys were conducted in two phases in Inayat Patti village where the first round field survey was conducted from February 2015 to March 2015 and the second round field survey was conducted from October 2023 to November 2023 to justify the past phenomena of study in current phenomena. In Inayat Patti village, a total of 25 international migrant households were stratified randomly selected in the first round field survey and 75 international migrant households were also stratified randomly selected in the second round field through longitudinal study design. In the context of the data collection technique in Inayat Patti village, was applied ethnographic technique for the collection of qualitative data from 100 international return migrant labourers under the saturation stage of the information under qualitative study design. From the perspective of a socio-demographic profile, all the return migrant labourers were males due to the male-based society in Inayat Patti village. Out of the total international return migrant households, 97 per cent (n=97) of the international return migrant households were Muslims and the rest were Hindus. Qualitative data was collected by passive observation method, informal interviews, focus group interviews and in-depth interviews among international return migrant labourers, their family members and local migrant agents in Inayat Patti village. Collected qualitative data was analyzed by case studies, narratives and descriptions under the content analysis of qualitative study design for interpretation of the qualitative data according to the nature of the study.

In the case of Lucknow district, it was conducted multiple field surveys from November 2017 to March 2018 for the collection of empirical data. It was applied multi-stage sampling for a sampling of the study area, where ten migration-abundant villages and two urban wards were selected through stratified random sampling. At the third stage sampling, it was stratified randomly selected 180 international return migrant households including 150 international return migrant households in rural areas and 30 international return migrant households in urban areas. From the perspective of a collection of primary data, quantitative data was collected through a structured schedule using to situation recall method and cross-sectional study design. Collected quantitative data was analyzed by descriptive statistics and appropriate statistical test- paired sample t-test and chi-square for testing of hypotheses.

Mumbai: Transit destination

Mumbai was selected purposively for the study of socio-economic and cultural aspects of internal migration in international migration to Gulf countries. Therefore, a single-phase field survey was conducted in February 2019 among 180 stratified randomly selected North Indian migrant labourers. Both qualitative and quantitative data were collected through a structured questionnaire schedule. Collected qualitative data was analyzed by narrative, description and case studies while quantitative data was analyzed by descriptive statistics and appropriate statistical test-analysis of variance (ANOVA) model. Therefore, both qualitative and quantitative data give a broad aspect of working and living conditions of internal migrant labourers in Mumbai. Out of the total internal migrant labourers, there were 50 internal migrant labourers from Inayat Patti village because there was a well-developed culture of internal to international migration from Inayat Patti village to Gulf countries via Mumbai. Therefore, the Mumbai Mumbai-based field survey was focused on the study of internal to international migration in the context of internal migrant labourers of Inayat Patti village in Mumbai.

United Arab Emirates: International Destination

Dubai was selected purposively for the study of the working and living conditions of Indian migrant labourers in Dubai. Therefore, a single-phase field survey was conducted in December 2019 among 180 stratified randomly selected Indian migrant labourers in Dubai. Both, qualitative and quantitative data were collected where qualitative data was collected by in-depth interview, focus group interview and passive observation method with the help of an interview guide while quantitative data was collected through a structured questionnaire schedule. Collected qualitative data was analyzed by narrative, description and case studies while quantitative data was analyzed by descriptive statistics and appropriate statistical test-analysis of variance (ANOVA) model. Out of the total international migrant labourers, there were 10 international return migrant labourers from Inayat Patti village in Dubai; those migrated from Inayat Patti village to Dubai via internal migration to Mumbai.

Therefore, the study is relevant in the context of covering to broad holistic aspect of internal and international migration into a single framework under the agenda of sustainable development goals of migration. The entire study is based on a comprehensive framework of the study of migration in the perspective of cultural Islamic economy in the context of Gulf migration among Muslims in rural North India with its discrimination, contradictions and challenges from a global perspective. In these consequences, it can be realized that the study gives an understanding of the process, determinants and consequences of Gulf migration in the periphery of its realities and implication for the management of discrimination, contradiction and challenges of migration for ensuring the well-being of migrants and sustainable economic development under the agenda of United Nation.

1.7. Structure of the book

Structure of the book is structured into following seven chapters according to the nature of the objective:

The first chapter of this book presents an overview of the history of labour migration from India to Gulf countries in the context of retrospective to prospective manner with adopted methodological frameworks in chapters of the book.

The second chapter discusses the facts in the process and determines international labour migration from India to Gulf countries by the role of internal migration in leading international migration.

The third chapter presents the socio-economic and cultural impact of migration on migrant households and its role in the building and formation of diaspora philanthropy in north India. Apart, the chapter also explores the socio-economic impact of migration and migrants at their destinations in Mumbai and the United Arab Emirates.

The fourth chapter presents the nexus of migration and cultural paradigm through the lens of socio-economic and cultural transformation in the context of the reciprocal relation between migration and culture through the role of globalization in the cultural perspective of Gulf migration.

The fifth chapter analyzes the nexus of migration and ethnicity from the perspective of the study of confluence between the economic and cultural perspectives of migration in view of the re-designing of ethnicity and the well-being of migrants. The study also covers emerging challenges concerning the socio-economic, political and cultural identical matters among migrants, their family members, relatives and friends in the framework of the dynamic of globalization.

The sixth chapter analyzes the process, determinants and consequences of the culture of migration and its role in the process of cultural livelihood in the sense of migration and sustainability. The concept of a safe zone is a new phenomenon in the case of Gulf migration because depth penetration of the culture of migration from North India to cities of India and Gulf countries developed a safe zone whereby migrant labourers find themselves in the situation of expectation and guarantee of better to best position with the option of Gulf migration as a source of livelihood through their inter-generationally involvement in migration.

Finally, the seventh chapter presents the process of conceptualization of finding chapters in the framework of the agenda of sustainable development goals (SDGs) of the United Nations to give a new approach to the study of migration with the help of sustainable development goals and globalization.

CHAPTER 2

PROCESS AND DETERMINANTS OF MIGRATION

2.1. Phenomena of migration from Uttar Pradesh

According to Taukeer (2022), there are colonial phenomena in the process of labour migration from Uttar Pradesh to Gulf countries because recent phenomena of labour migration from India to Gulf countries are based on experiences of indentured labour migration. Both Uttar Pradesh and Bihar are leading states in labour migration from India to Gulf countries due to the huge demand for migrant labourers in Gulf countries (Overseas Employment Division, Government of India, 2015). According to Zachariah and Rajan (2012 & 2016), the tendency of labour migration from Uttar Pradesh and Bihar is being led by semi-skilled and unskilled labour migration to Gulf countries compared to skilled and professional migration from Kerala to Gulf countries. These consequences show that Uttar Pradesh receives India's largest remittances from Gulf countries because a huge trend of unskilled and semi-skilled labour migration ensures the huge inflow of remittances in Uttar Pradesh. A Study by Sasikumar and Thimothy (2015) shows that economic factors like wage differential between cities of India and Gulf countries and well-developed social network systems of migration work as pull factors in the process of facilitating Gulf migration. A study by Azeez and Begum (2009) shows that economic and non-economic phenomena lead to labour migration from Uttar Pradesh to Gulf countries. The study of Rahman (2001) also gives a realistic picture of the role of globalization in the process of Gulf migration in India.

A recent study by Majumder & Taukeer (2019) shows that the consequence of internal migration led to the process of international migration from Uttar Pradesh to Gulf countries due to wage differential between Mumbai and Gulf countries because migrant labourers worked in Mumbai before migration to the Gulf countries. Similar phenomena were found in the study of Taukeer (2021) because the study shows that migrant labourers gained more wages in Gulf countries compared to low wages in Delhi and Mumbai. These consequences worked as a pull factor in the process of migration from Uttar Pradesh to Gulf countries in the context of wage differentials. Therefore, the consequences of the culture of migration developed a safe zone in Uttar

Pradesh because the matter of migration is positively associated with Gulf migration. Therefore, the study of Taukeer (2023; 2023 & 2023) shows that the consequence of Gulf migration created a cultural region of migration from rural Uttar Pradesh to Gulf countries where the matter of Gulf migration worked as the source of livelihood for migrants. In the case of migration from a village of Uttar Pradesh namely- Inayat Patti, findings of the study of Taukeer (2017) & Majumder (2022) show that there is depth penetration of culture of migration from Inayat Patti village to Gulf countries but adverse impact of pandemic of COVID-19 largely influenced the migration as well as started re-verse migration from Mumbai and Gulf countries to Inayat Patti village in Uttar Pradesh.

2.2. Socio profile of return migrant labourers

It is found that the tendency of labour migration from Uttar Pradesh to Gulf countries was led by youth because the average age of return migrant labourers was 29.8 years. It shows that youths were involved in the process of Gulf migration due to the glamour of jobs in the Gulf countries. From the perspective of religion, nearly 96.0 per cent of the return migrant labourers were Muslims and the rest were Hindus. These consequences were the result of the depth penetration of the well–developed social network system of migration among Muslims compared to the lack of a social network system among Hindus. It is also observed that nearly 83.0 per cent of the return migrant labourers were from rural areas and the rest were from urban areas; therefore, there was significant explicit visibility of the rural-urban scenario of migration in the context of Gulf migration. In the context of the educational profile, 85.0 per cent of the return migrant labourers were educated from upper primary to intermediate, followed by 12.0 per cent of the return migrant labourers who had professional degrees, 2.0 per cent of the return migrant labourers had bachelor's degrees and the rest of return migrant labourers were illiterates. These consequences show that the entire process of the Gulf migration was led by less educated migrant labourers, those who found themselves in a secure position of livelihood in the context of Gulf migration. It is also observed that 52.0 per cent of return migrant labourers were unmarried and the rest of the return migrant labourers were married. These consequences were positively associated with the nexus of Gulf migration and the marriage market in rural North India where Gulf migrants used to take dowry due to dowry culture among Muslims (Table 2.1).

Table 2.1. Social profile of return migrant labourers

Age groups	Per cent of international return migrant labourers
20-30	64.0
31-40	36.0
Religious classification	**Per cent of international return migrant labourers**
Muslims	96.0
Hindus	4.0
Marital status	**Per cent of international return migrant labourers**
Unmarried	52.0
Married	48.0
Rural- urban location	**Per cent of international return migrant labourers**
Rural	83.0
Urban	17.0
Education profile	**Per cent of international return migrant labourers**
Illiterates	1.1
Upper Primary to high school	44.5
Intermediate education	41.1
Bachelor of education	1.7
Professional education	11.6
Total	**100.0 (n=180)**

Source: Field Survey, 2017-2018

2.3. Economic profile of return migrant labourers

Out of the total return migrant labourers, 88.0 per cent of return migrant labourers used to work as semi-skilled migrant labourers including drivers, tailors, welders, plumbers and electricians while the rest of the return migrant labourers used to work as skilled migrant labourers including managers and engineers (Table 2.2).

Table 2.2. Skill-wise classification of return migrant labourers

Skill of return migrant labourers	Numbers of international return migrant labourers	Per cent
Semi-skilled return migrant labourers	159	88.0
Skilled return migrant labourers	21	12.0
Total	180	100.0

Source: Field Survey, 2017-18

Training of skills of return migrant labourers

Out of the total return migrant labourers, nearly 88.0 per cent of return migrant labourers said that they got training in jobs through informal mode while the rest got training through formal mode (Table 2.3).

Table 2.3. Training mode of skills of migrant labourers

Training mode	Numbers of international migrant labourers	Per cent
Informal mode	159	88.0
Formal mode	21	12.0
Total	180	100.0

Source: Field Survey, 2017-18

2.4. Economic activity of return migrant labourers before involve in the process of migration

Out of the total return migrant labourers (n=180), nearly 75.0 per cent (n=135) of return migrant labourers were engaged in employment at root before being involved in the process of migration followed by nearly 13.7 per cent of the return migrant labourers reported that they were unemployed before migration while rest were involved in education before involved in internal and international migration. Among the employed migrant labourers, the average monthly income was INR 8370 per return migrant labourer in Uttar Pradesh (Table 2.4).

Table 2.4. Economic activity of return migrant labourers before involve in the process of migration

Indicators	Description
Economic activity of return migrant labourers	Out of the total return migrant labourers (n=180), nearly 75.0 per cent (n=135) were economically engaged in employment and rest were unemployed at root.
Employment status of economically engaged migrant labourers	Out of the total economically engaged migrant labourers(n=135), nearly 38.5 per cent of the return migrant labourers used to work as drivers followed by 34.1 per cent as tailors, 14.1 per cent as welders, 8.1 per cent as plumbers and 5.2 per cent as electricians at root.
Average monthly income of economically engaged migrant labourers in INR	Average monthly income was INR 8370 per economically engaged migrant labourers at root.

Source: Field Survey, 2017-18

2.5. Route of migration

Internal to international migration

It is found that the process of international migration from Uttar Pradesh to Gulf countries was led by internal migration where migrant labourers used to migrate to cities of India for employment. During that period, these migrant labourers gained skills of experiences of migration with skills of jobs according to the demand of the labour market in the Gulf countries. Therefore, the entire process of international migration from Uttar Pradesh to Gulf countries was led by dual-step migration where the internal destination worked as a transit destination between Uttar Pradesh and Gulf countries. In this study, it is found that 57.8 per cent of return migrant labourers said that they were involved in the process of internal migration before being involved in international migration (Table 2.5).

Direct international migration

It is also found that migrant labourers also migrated from Uttar Pradesh to Gulf countries without being involved in internal migration due to the well-developed social network system of migration from rural Uttar Pradesh to Gulf countries. In this study, nearly 42.2 per cent of the return migrant labourers directly migrated to Gulf countries without being involved in internal migration (Table 2.5).

Table 2.5. Routes of migration

Routes of migration	Numbers of international return migrant labourers	Per cent
Direct international migration	76	42.2
Internal to international migration	104	57.8
Total	180	100.0

Source: Field Survey, 2017-18

2.6. Process and determinants of labour migration from Uttar Pradesh to Gulf countries

2.6.1. Stages in process of migration

Stage I: In the first stage, *kafeel*[1] (sponsor) permitted authorized migrant agents to hire migrant labourers from India (Flow chart 2.1).

Stage II: In the second stage, authorized migrant agents gave full information to local migrant agents for hiring the migrant labourers from Inayat Patti village (Flow chart 2.1).

Stage III: In the third stage, migrant labourers used to take help from local migrant agents to complete the documentation process for migration to Gulf countries (Flow chart 2.1).

Stage IV: In the fourth stage, migrant labourers migrated to Gulf countries

---

[1] The *Kafala* system is based on a sponsorship system in regulating the labour market in oil-producing Gulf countries under *Kafeel* (sponsor) in the Middle East. Cited from: Colton, N. A. (2010). The International Political Economy of Gulf Migration. *Migration and the Gulf .Middle East Institute,* 34-36.

through the routes of internal to international and direct migration (Flow chart 2.1).

Box 2.1: Case Study[2]

"It is a case study of 34 years old migrant labourer, named Asif who was from Inayat Patti village in Prayagraj district, Uttar Pradesh. He said that he worked as a taxi driver in Mumbai from year 2010 to 2015 and he was also working as a taxi driver in Saudi Arabia due to the wage differential between Mumbai as well as the glamour of Arabian culture worked as a pull factor. He also said that there was a culture of "Bombai – Saudi" migration in Inayat Patti village where huge numbers of youth were migrating to Saudi via migration to Bombay because Mumbai-based migration opened to door of Gulf migration in Inayat Patti village. Migrant labourers of Inayat Patti village called Mumbai as Bombay due to their inter-generationally involvement in migration where these migrant labourers lived in their historical mentality of migration with a guarantee of better jobs in Mumbai and Gulf countries. Therefore, it can be analyzed that there was dual step migration by internal to international migration due to the globalization of culture of migration in the sense of historical consequences of migration in the process of migration from Inayat Patti to Gulf countries via internal migration to Mumbai."

These consequences can be analyzed in the framework of the reciprocal relationship between internal and international migration in the context of facilitating labour migration through the positive role of the migrant agents from rural Uttar Pradesh to Gulf countries via Mumbai.

Box 2.2: Case Study[3]

"It is interviewed a 45 years old migrant agent named Seth in Inayat Patti village, he said that the entire process of Gulf migration was based on the well-developed social network system of migration where a well-developed mechanism facilitated the labour migration from Inayat Patti village to Gulf countries in the consequence of the globalization of migration in Inayat Patti village. He also said that the culture of Gulf migration opened the door for migration-based industries in Inayat Patti and its surrounding villages".

2.6.2. Process and determinants of internal migration

It is found that a vast majority of the return migrant labourers said that they were involved in internal migration before migration to Gulf countries. These return migrant labourers migrated to Mumbai and Delhi for employment because these return migrant labourers got better jobs with higher wages and gained skills of jobs with experiences of migration for adjusting themselves in Gulf-based migration. It is observed that there was a crucial role of the social network system of migration in the process of facilitating labour migration from Uttar Pradesh to cities of India. Therefore, the consequence of the social network system of migration worked as a pull factor in the process of inter-state rural-urban migration in the context of leading factors

---

[2] Information is based on personal interviews of respondent in Inayat Patti village in October 2023.
[3] Information is based on personal interview of respondent in Inayat Patti village in October 2023.

in international migration. City-based internal migration was based on seasonal and temporary migration because migrant labourers used to work for one to three years in Mumbai before being involved in long-term international migration. These consequences can be analyzed in the framework of the role of internal migration in international migration because both economic and non-economic factors of short-term internal migration led to long-term international Gulf migration due to a well-developed route of migration from rural Uttar Pradesh to Gulf countries via Mumbai (Table 2.6).

Flow chart 2.1. Stages in process of migration

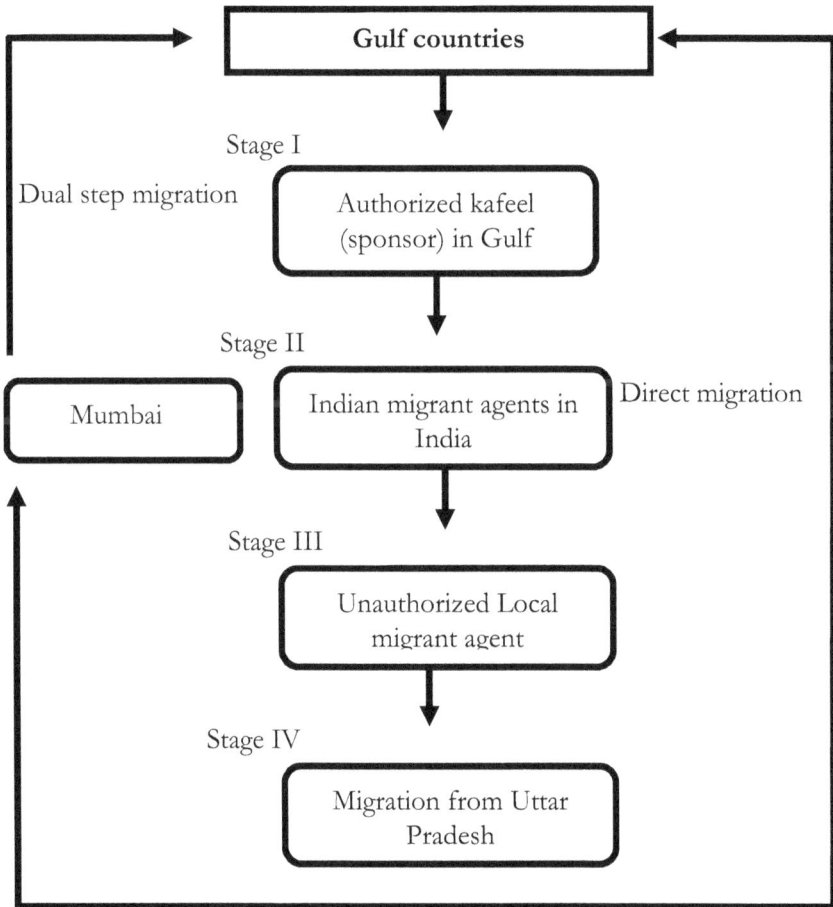

Source: Designed by the author on the basis of field -based information in Uttar Pradesh.

Table 2.6. Causes and process of internal migration

Reasons of migration	Per cent of international return migrant labourers
Higher wages at destinations	88.5
Problem of unemployment at root	11.5
Purpose of internal migration	**Per cent of international return migrant labourers**
Gained skills of occupation	77.0
Gained financial arrangement for gulf migration	16.3
Gained experiences of internal migration	6.7
Medium for social network in internal migration	**Per cent of international return migrant labourers**
Support of Family members	34.6
Support of relatives	47.1
Support of friends	6.7
Support of recruited companies/ contractors	11.6
Destinations of internal migration	**Per cent of international return migrant labourers**
Mumbai	65.4
Delhi	26.9
Bangalore	7.7
Tenure of internal migration in years	**Per cent of international return migrant labourers**
One year	71.0
Two years	27.0
Three years	2.0
Total	**100.0(n=104)**

Source: Field Survey, 2017-2018

It is found that return migrant labourers used to work as semi-skilled labourers including drivers, tailors, welders, plumbers, and electricians and the rest of the migrant labourers used to work as skilled/professionals including managers and engineers (Table 2.7).

The average per-month income was INR 25106 per return migrant labourer. As for remittances, the average per-month remittance was INR 18644 per return migrant labourer (Table 2.8).

2.6.3. Process and determinants of international Gulf migration

It is found that return migrant labourers migrated to Gulf countries namely-Saudi Arabia, the United Arab Emirates, Qatar and Kuwait due to availability of the better jobs with higher wages in the Gulf countries and causes of unemployment also led to the migration. These return migrant labourers used to work on contract bases for a minimum of two years to a maximum of five years in Gulf countries (Table 2.9).

Table 2.7. Occupational and skill wise classification of internal migrant labourers

Occupation	Per cent of international return migrant labourers
Drivers	37.5
Tailors	25.0
Welders	15.4
Plumbers	3.8
Electricians	6.7
Managers	9.6
Engineers	1.9
Skills of internal migrant labourers	Per cent of international return migrant labourers
Semi-skilled labourers	88.5
Skilled labourers	11.5
Total	**100.0 (n=104)**

Source: Field Survey, 2017-2018

Table 2.8. Per month income and remittances of internal migrant labourers

Income of international return migrant labourers in internal migration in INR	Per cent of international return migrant labourers
5000-15000	14.4
15001-25000	45.1
25001-40000	40.5
Total	100.0(n=104)
Remittances of international return migrant labourers in internal migration in INR	Per cent of international return migrant labourers
5000-15000	25.9
15001-25000	60.5
25001-35000	13.6
Total	100.0 (n=104)

Source: Field Survey, 2017-2018

It is found that the process of international migration from Uttar Pradesh to Gulf countries was based on the well-developed social network system of migration where informal channels like the support of family members, relatives and friends were so crucial compared to formal channels like recruitment agencies and companies in the process of facilitating labour migration. These consequences can be analyzed in the framework of the social network theory of migration with the institutional theory of migration where both formal and informal channels facilitate labour migration from rural Uttar Pradesh to Gulf countries (Table 2.10).

Table 2.9. Economic causes of international migration

Reasons of migration	Per cent of international return migrant labourers
Availability of the better jobs with higher wages in the Gulf countries	75.0
Problem of unemployment in India	25.0
Destinations in the Gulf	**Per cent of international return migrant labourers**
Kingdom of Saudi Arabia	76.0
United Arab Emirates	22.0
Qatar	0.6
Kuwait	1.4
Contract of migration in the Gulf in year	**Per cent of international return migrant labourers**
2.0	44.0
3.0	32.0
4.0	22.0
5.0	2.0
Total	**100.0 (n=180)**

Source: Field Survey, 2017-2018

Table 2.10. Social network system in Gulf migration

Source of information about jobs	Per cent of international return migrant labourers
Family members, friends and relatives	43.0
Migrant agents	46.0
Recruited companies	9.0
Contractors	2.0
Source of getting visa for migration	**Per cent of international return migrant labourers**
Family members, friends, and relatives	84.0
Recruited companies	13.0
Migrant agents	1.0
Contractors	2.0
Source for financial arrangement	**Per cent of international return migrant labourers**
Arranged from family support and relatives	88.0
Arranged from self saving	5.0
Given by contractors	1.0
Given by recruited companies	6.0
Total	**100.0 (n=180)**

Source: Field Survey, 2017-2018

The Average financial cost of the Gulf migration was INR 54555 per return migrant labourer because migrant labourers needed passports, visas, flight tickets and other necessary travel documents for Gulf migration (Table 2.11).

Table 2.11. Financial cost of Gulf migration

Financial cost of migration in INR	Per cent of international return migrant labourers
30000-50000	50.0
50001-70000	50.0
Total	100.0(n=180)

Source: Field Survey, 2017-2018

Hypothetical test of measurement of social network system of migration in international migration

Source of information about jobs in the Gulf countries

H_0: There is no association between sources of information about jobs and the migration of labourers to the Gulf countries.

H_1: There is an association between sources of information about jobs and the migration of labourers to the Gulf countries.

Here, we examined the association between the source of the job of information and migration to Gulf countries. Here, our independent variable is the source of information about jobs in the Gulf countries and the dependent variable is migrant labourers.

There are total sample size (n) is 180 (Table 2.12).

Table 2.12. Case processing summary

	Cases					
	Valid		Missing		Total	
	N	Percent	N	Percent	N	Percent
Source of information to jobs in Gulf countries * Migration of the migrant labourers in the Gulf countries	180	100.0%	0	0.0%	180	100.0%

Source: Field Survey, 2017-2018

Out of the total migrant labourers, 84 migrant labourers got information about the jobs from the help of migrant agents in the Gulf countries followed by 79 migrant labourers, who got information about the jobs from the help of their kinship network including family members, friends and relatives, who already worked in the Gulf while the rest 17 migrant labourers got information about jobs from the help of contractors and recruited companies in the Gulf countries (Table 2.13).

Table 2.13. Cross tabulation source of information about jobs in Gulf countries

Source of information about jobs	Destination countries				Total migrant labourers
	Saudi Arabia	United Arab Emirates	Kuwait	Qatar	
Family member	41	5	0	0	46
Friend	30	1	0	0	31
Agent	58	23	1	2	84
Contractor	1	0	0	0	1
Company	5	11	0	0	16
Relative	2	0	0	0	2
Total	137	40	1	2	180
Tests	**Value**	**Df**		**Asymp. Sig. (2-sided)**	
Pearson Chi-Square	36.160a	15		.002	
Likelihood ratio	36.808	15		001	
Linear-by-Linear association	15.683	1		.000	
N of valid cases	180				

Source: Field Survey 2017-2018
a. 17 cells (70.8%) have expected count less than 5. The minimum expected count is .01.

The value of Pearson Chi –Square is 36.16 and the associated significance value is .002 which is less than 0.05. Therefore, the null hypothesis is rejected and there is a significant association between the source of information about jobs in the Gulf countries and the migration of migrant labourers to the Gulf countries (Table 2.13).

Source of getting visa for work in the Gulf countries

H_0: There is no association between sources of getting visas for jobs and the migration of labourers to the Gulf countries.

H_1: There is an association between sources of getting visas for jobs and the migration of labourers to the Gulf countries.

Here, we examined the association between sources of getting the visa for jobs and migration to Gulf countries. Here, our independent variable is sources of getting visas for jobs in the Gulf countries and the dependent variable is migrant labourers. There are total sample size (n) is 180 (Table 2.14).

Cross tabulation between the source for the visa for migration to Gulf countries and migration to Gulf countries shows that out of the total 180 migrant labourers, 152 migrant labourers got visas from the help of kinship networks included to help of family members, friends and relatives who already worked in the Gulf countries while rest migrant labourers got visa from the help of migrant agents, recruited companies and contractors in the

Gulf countries (Table 2.15).

The value of Pearson Chi–Square is 51.755 and the associated significance value is .000 which is less than 0.05. Therefore, the null hypothesis is rejected and there is a significant association between the source of getting visas and migration to Gulf countries (Table 2.15).

Table 2.14. Case processing summary

	Cases					
	Valid		Missing		Total	
	N	Percent	N	Percent	N	Percent
Source of visa for jobs in Gulf countries * Migration to Gulf countries	180	100.0%	0	0.0%	180	100.0%

Source: Field Survey 2017-2018

Table 2.15. Cross tabulation source of visa for migration and migration to GCC countries

Source for visa for migration to Gulf countries		Gulf countries				Total
		Saudi Arabia	United Arab Emirates	Kuwait	Qatar	
	Family members	42	5	0	0	47
	Friends	22	1	0	0	23
	Agent	1	0	0	0	1
	Contractors	3	0	0	0	3
	Recruited Company	6	18	0	0	24
	Relatives	63	16	1	2	82
Total		137	40	1	2	180

Tests	Value	Df	Asymp. Sig. (2-sided)
Pearson Chi-Square	51.755[a]	15	.000
Likelihood ratio	47.261	15	.000
Linear-by-Linear association	10.064	1	.002
N of valid cases	180		

a.   16 cells (66.7%) have expected count less than 5. The minimum expected count is .01
Source: Field Survey 2017-2018

Source of financial arrangement for Gulf migration and migration to the Gulf countries

H₀: There is no association between sources of financial arrangement of the Gulf migration and the migration of labourers to the Gulf countries.

H₁: There is an association between sources of financial arrangement of the Gulf migration and the migration of labourers to the Gulf countries.

Here, we examined the association between sources of getting the visa for jobs and migration to Gulf countries. Here, our independent variable is the source of financial arrangement of the Gulf migration and the dependent variable is migrant labourers (Table 2.16).

Table 2.16. Case processing summary

	Cases					
	Valid		Missing		Total	
	N	Percent	N	Percent	N	Percent
Source for manage financial cost of travel of migration to Gulf countries * Migration to Gulf countries	180	100.0%	0	0.0%	180	100.0%

Source: Field Survey 2017-2018

The table shows that out of the total 180 migrant labourers, 156 migrant labourers got financial support from the help of family members followed by 14 migrant labourers got financial support from help recruited company, 8 migrant labourers managed financial support from self savings and the rest got financial support from relatives and contractors (Table 2.17). The value of Pearson Chi–Square is 30.098 and the associated significance value is .003 which is less than 0.05. Therefore, the Null hypothesis is rejected and there is a significant association between sources of managed financial cost for travel of migration and migration to Gulf countries (Table 2.17).

Table 2.17. Table: Cross tabulation between source of manage financial cost of travel for migration to Gulf countries

Source of financial cost of Migration		Gulf countries				Total
		Saudi Arabia	United Arab Emirates	Kuwait	Qatar	
	Family	124	29	1	2	156
	Borrowed from relatives	1	0	0	0	1
	Recruited company	3	11	0	0	14
	Contractor	1	0	0	0	1
	Self-Savings	8	0	0	0	8
Total		137	40	1	2	180
Tests		**Value**	**Df**	**Asymp. Sig. (2-sided)**		
Pearson Chi-Square		30.098[a]	12	.003		
Likelihood ratio		26.909	12	.008		
Linear-by-Linear association		1.662	1	.197		
N of valid cases		180				

Source: Field Survey 2017-2018
17 cells (70.8%) have expected count less than 5. The minimum expected count is .01.

Nearly 88.4 per cent of the return migrant labourers worked as semi-skilled labourers including drivers, tailors, welders, plumbers, and electricians and the rest of the return migrant labourers worked as skilled/professionals including managers and engineers. It was found that the average monthly income was INR 62666 per return migrant labourer and the average monthly remittance was INR 51416 per return migrant labourer (Table 2.18).

Table 2.18. Per month income and remittances of migrant labourers

Occupation of return migrant labourers	Per cent of international return migrant labourers
Drivers	33.9
Tailors	30.6
Welders	12.8
Plumbers	6.1
Electricians	5.0
Managers	7.2
Engineers	4.4
Skills of return migrant labourers	**Per cent of international return migrant labourers**
Semi-skilled labourers	88.4
Skilled labourers	11.6
Income of return migrant labourers in INR	**Per cent of international return migrant labourers**
25000-75000	79.4
75000-150000	20.6
Remittances of return migrant labourers in INR	**Per cent of international return migrant labourers**
20000-50000	67.0
50001-100000	31.0
100001-150000	2.0
Total	**100.0(n=180)**

Source: Field Survey, 2017-2018

2.6.4. Similarities, differences and connection between internal and international migration

It is observed that both internal and international migration were correlated to each other by similar economic and non-economic phenomena in the sense of the culture of migration from rural Uttar Pradesh to Gulf countries via Mumbai within the social and cultural region of migration. Both internal and international migration were caused by a similar set of reasons of migration where short-term internal migration led to long-term international migration based on cost and benefit analysis of input and output of migration by its process, determinates and consequences. Internal to international migration was caused by a well-developed social network system of migration with the matter of availability of better jobs with higher wages in international destinations compared to low wages in internal destinations. In these consequences, it is found that non-economic factors like the social network system of migration worked as pull factors in both internal and international migration within the social and cultural region of migration where a migrant labourer migrated with hopes of a better life in the safe zone[4] of migration because safe zone mechanism of migration gives a guarantee of better jobs compared to an expectation of better jobs in both internal and international destinations. Therefore, it can be conceptualized that migrant labourers considered both internal and international migration in similar conditions because these migrant labourers considered Gulf countries as second homes to Mumbai. Therefore, both internal and international migration were correlated to each other as well as led to each other by the functioning process of economic and non-economic phenomena of migration in the consequences of globalization of migration. Therefore, the consequence of globalization was positively associated with facilitating labour migration in the context of internal to international migration where internal migration paved the way for international migration in the aspect of the long-term impact of migration on migrant households in the form of culture of migration from Uttar Pradesh to Gulf countries via Mumbai.[5]

Both internal and international migration were assimilated each other in the perspective of economic and non-economic phenomena of migration but it was realized that the process of international labour migration from Uttar Pradesh to Gulf countries was more complex due to the difficult documentation process compared to the easy way of short term internal migration within India. Therefore, the mechanism of short-term internal migration was different compared to long-term international migration due to the huge return of migration in international migration. Both economic and non-economic parameters of migration were extended in long-term international migration because migrant labourers faced risks of long-term international migration compared to the possibility of little risks in internal migration. Both types of migration were caused by globalization but the boundary of international migration was so widespread compared to the narrow boundary of internal migration because migrant labourers passed socio-economic and psychological barriers in international migration compared to the least possibility of such kinds of barriers in internal

---

[4] The safe zone concept of migration is based on the historical consequence of migration in the context of the nexus of the social network system and globalization of migration in rural India. These consequences work as a safe zone of migration where migrant labourers consider migration as part of their cultural economy. Cited from: Taukeer, M. (2024). Ethnographic Analysis of "Safe Zone" Concept in Migration in Global Perspective. *Migration and Diversity*, 3(1), 71-87.

[5] Information is based on observation method and focus group interviews among return migrant labourers in Inayat Patti village from October 2023 to November 2023.

migration. Apart, wages also matter in both types of migration but it is found that the consequence of the comparison of wages between internal and international migration led to the mechanism of international migration by the significant role of internal migration in international migration. Therefore, both economic and non-economic causes were similar but these causes functioned differently by the nature of short-term internal migration and long-term international migration. These consequences showed that there was a reciprocal relationship between internal and international migration but the system of migration gives long-term consequences of migration in international migration whereby internal to international migration was being continuously shifted toward direct international migration without being involvement of migrant labourers in short-term internal migration due to well developed social network system of migration with the glamour of jobs in Gulf among migrant labourers in rural India. Therefore, both internal and international migration worked in similar sequences but differed in the process mechanism of migration from rural Uttar Pradesh to Gulf countries via Mumbai.[6]

Based on the above concise descriptions and discussion, both internal and international migration were connected by the response of migrant labourers because migrant labourers developed a mechanism of adjustment in long-term international migration while considering long-term international migration as short-term migration due to the well-developed safe zone mechanism of migration in Gulf countries. The consequence of the safe zone mechanism of migration transformed long-term international migration into short-term international migration where a migrant labourer invested experiences of internal migration in the process of adjusting themselves to long-term international migration in Gulf countries. In this study, it was a very important point of discussion that the initial phase of long-term international migration was considered as panic migration but matter of higher wages and gained experiences of internal migration gave a positive and motivational energy to migrant labourers in sustaining themselves in process of panic condition in long term international migration. Therefore, it can be realized that migrant labourers developed a mental image of migration where the boundaries of both internal and international migration worked in similar ways based on values, norms, attitudes, beliefs and myths concerning migration. It is observed that migrant labourers developed their mechanism for process and determinates of migration based on costs and benefits

---

[6] Information is based on observation method and focus group interviews among return migrant labourers in Inayat Patti village from October 2023 to November 2023.

analysis of the return of migration as the consequence of the globalization of migration. Therefore, it can be analyzed that connectivity between internal and international migrations can be realized as the implication of the system approach of migration through discussing both migrations on similar phenomena. Therefore, labour migration from rural Uttar Pradesh to Gulf countries was the transformation of the labour force from an agro-based economy to an urban-based economy as a consequence of the availability of higher wages in the urban-based economy in both internal and international migrations. Therefore, analysis of wage differential was a matter in the process of functioning of labour migration from rural Uttar Pradesh to Gulf countries via Mumbai.[7]

2.7. Case study about process and determinants of labour migration from Inayat Patti village in Uttar Pradesh

Migration from Inayat Patti in colonial India

There is a well-developed culture of migration from Inayat Patti village to Gulf countries due to its long historical consequence of migration in the form of Girmitiya[8] (indentured labourers) in British India as well as an emerged as a new form of Ghulam[9] (contract) labourers from Inayat Patti village to in Gulf countries in the twenty-first century. The history of migration started in the British era when underprivileged and marginalized villagers migrated to coal fields areas of coalourees[10] in undivided Bihar. These consequences were the result of the deep penetration of British imperialism in rural India because these migrant labourers were involved in the process of coal mining with the help of the British Indian government. Both upper-caste Muslims and lower-backwards castes Hindus migrated to undivided Bihar to sustain themselves through migration to coal mining of undivided Bihar. Apart from that, it was also found that there was an interconnection between internal and

---

[7] Information is based on observation method and focus group interviews among return migrant labourers in Inayat Patti village from October 2023 to November 2023.

[8] Girmitiya (indentured) labour migration was prominent in the Bhojpuri region of Uttar Pradesh and Bihar to European colonies during the British colonial period in British India. Cited from https://www.iias.asia/sites/default/files/2020-11/IIAS_NL30_12.pdf_Badri_Narayan

[9] Contract-based labour migration is prominent in rural Uttar Pradesh to oil-producing Gulf countries in the Middle East and these contract-based labourers are known as *Ghulam* (slave labour) among Arabians in Gulf countries. Cited from: Taukeer, M. (2020). Process and determinants of labour migration from selected rural areas of Uttar Pradesh to Gulf Countries. *Man and Development, 42* (4), 123-138.

[10] Coalourees region is a coal field area of Jharkhand in India and it is the heartland for In-labour migration from rural Uttar Pradesh and Bihar. Cited from: Majumder, B., & Taukeer, M. (2019). Dual-Step Migration from a Village in Uttar Pradesh: Causes, Process and Consequences . *Productivity* , *60* (2), 162-174.

international indentured migration[11] from Inayat Patti village to European colonies because migrant labourers migrated to Mauritius and the West Indies as indentured labourers via internal migration to Bengal. Villagers of Inayat Patti village shared untold stories of migration but they had enough information about the history of internal migration compared to international indentured migration in the British era because indentured labourers did never return to Inayat Patti village, therefore, these indentured labourers were invisible in the untold history of migration in Inayat Patti village. Therefore, villagers felt a lot of pain and emotion because of the long historical sequences of migration in the British era. These villagers shared their pain about the oral inter-generational historical consequences of migration through an oral historical library of the village where villagers developed oral library through passing oral history of migration through inter-generation transformation. These villagers showed their mythology concerning migration with facts of cause-effect analysis based on the narrative approach in the discourse of migration in the context of historical consequences of migration by religion and caste in the perspective of economic performance.[12]

These villagers had lots of narratives based discourse about freedom fighting of India against British India during the Mahatma Gandhi and Nehru era because these villagers said that there was a significant impact of the movement of Gandhi in Inayat Patti and its surrounding villages where migration was deeply rooted with livelihood practices of villagers through the movement of Gandhi. The consequence of Gandhi's movement was appreciated and criticized with untold stories and mythology about the role of Gandhi in the village in the perspective of migration because migrant labourers were deeply associated with the philosophy of Gandhi from root to destination and these consequences gave them a motivational energy in both root and destinations. Therefore, it can be analyzed that there was a crucial role in the untold stories of Gandhi among villagers because it is observed that villagers shared their untold stories about Gandhi, which are not documented in Gandhian pieces of literature. For example, upper-caste Muslims said that the Charkha (domestic spinning wheel used chiefly for cotton) movement of Gandhi was focused on backward Ansari caste Muslims. It can be analyzed in the framework of the matter of caste identity in the process of migration where upper caste Muslims and backward caste

---

[11] Indentured labour migration was being led by *Ghura Khan*, a British Guiana's sub-agent in rural North India during the British colonial period. In Allahabad, in the 1880s, recruiters received Rs. 5 for men and Rs. 8 for women. Cited from: Brij et al (2007). *The Encyclopedia of Indian Diaspora.*University of Hawaii, p.51.
[12] Information is based on focus group interviews among migrant labourers and villagers in Inayat Patti village from February 2015 to March 2015.

Hindus migrated to coal mines of undivided Bihar and Bengal while backwards Ansari caste Muslims were engaged in indigenous cotton industry in villages through Swadesi (national) Charkha movement of Gandhi. Therefore, the movement Gandhi played a crucial role in the function of migration from Inayat Patti village during the British era. These villagers were also attached to the Gandhi movement because British police officers humiliated poor villagers and these villagers called British police officers "*Goraa*" due to the white skin of Britishers. These consequences showed that Inayat Patti village was the centre of Gandhi's movement due to the exploitation by British police officers in Inayat Patti village. These consequences led to forced migration from Inayat Patti due to the destruction of the agriculture-based economy in rural India. These villagers used to sing a song about sharing the story of their harassment by British police officers in the following way according to the personal interview of 95 years old villager named Chotai Yadav in Inayat Patti village. "Bhaga, Bhaga, Gora Aayen" Bahut marhi, pithi (Run away due to the coming of British police officers in agricultural fields because British Indian police would beat innocent peasants). This poem shows the panic condition of the village in the context of migration in British India.[13]

In the case of *Dalits*[14], upper-caste Muslims and backwards Hindus said that there was a significant impact of Babasaheb Ambedkar in Inayat Patti village, who was the political leader of *Dalits* in Inayat Patti and its surrounding villages because villagers said that *Dalits* considered B .R. Ambedkar as God in coal fields in colouree region. Mostly *Dalits* of Inayat Patti village used to work in coal mines with upper caste Muslims whereby philosophies of Gandhi and Ambedkar were crucial and significant in the case of the nexus of matter of identity and migration from Inayat Patti village to coal mining of undivided Bihar and Bengal during British era. Therefore, the entire *Dalits'* discourse of migration was based on the philosophy of Ambedkar but the movement of Gandhi was so deeply rooted among *Dalits* compared to the least impact of Ambedkarism among *Dalits*, those considered Gandhi a safeguard for their rights and honour because Gandhi's movement was also significant in coal mines in the context of labourers' rights compared to the advocacy of *Dalits'* rights according to the ideology of Ambedkar.[15]

---

[13] Information is based on focus group interviews among migrant labourers and villagers in Inayat Patti village in February 2015.

[14] The Dalit community belongs to a marginalized group in the bottom segmentation of the social hierarchy system of India as well as listed as a scheduled caste (SC) in the Indian constitution. Cited from: Ghose, S. (2003). The Dalit in India. *Social Research: An International Quarterly, 70*(1), 83-109.

[15] Information is based on focus group interviews among villagers in Inayat Patti in October 2023.

Therefore, both Gandhi and Ambedkar are relevant for developing an understanding of the process, determinants and consequences of the history of migration in Inayat Patti village from the perspective of religion and caste.

During the partition of India in 1947, upper-caste Muslims showed their respect for Mohammed Ali Jinnah (leader of Muslim league and founder of Pakistan) with parallel Gandhi because both Gandhi and Jinnah were also associated with the mobility of Muslims in the context of migration. These Muslims had their own inter-generational untold stories about the role of Jinnah in Inayat Patti village because the emotion of Muslims was associated with Jinnah compared to Gandhi. Apart from that, these Muslims showed that their inherited forefathers were interested in migrating from Inayat Patti to Pakistan but they did not migrate from Inayat Patti to Pakistan due to emotional love with the dust of their village- Inayat Patti. Only Tai Jan-named women migrated to Lahore Pakistan in the 1950s and it is found that villagers said that they were unaware of Tai Jan because Tai Jan was an invisible woman for villagers of Inayat Patti village because there was not any postal address of Tai Jan in Lahore Pakistan.[16]

Before the independence of India, Baghel[17] Muslims were landlords in Inayat Patti and its surrounding villages and the Baghel dynasty played a crucial role in the process of facilitating labour migration because poor Muslims and Hindus used to work as bonded labourers in agro farmhouses of Baghel in British era and these consequences led to the forced migration from Inayat Patti and its surrounding villages to coal mining fields of undivided Bihar and West Bengal. The Baghel dynasty was close with the Congress Party in colonial India as well as supporting the movement of Gandhi for freedom fighting. These consequences can be analyzed as a function of the nexus of the landlord system and the role of Congress in spreading the ideology of Congress among underprivileged and marginalized Muslims and Hindus; those who were working as labourers as well as the backbone for the movement of Gandhi and congress.[18]

---

[16] Information is based on oral history based information among villagers in Inayat Patti in October 2023.
[17] Baghel community is known as Muslim Rajput in Inayat Patti and Its surrounding villages. Zamindar (landlord) Abdul Latif Khan was the landlord of Inayat Patti and its surrounding villages during last decade of colonial India and post colonial India until abolition of Zamindari (landlord) system in post colonial India.
[18] Information is based on personal interviews from the *Baghel* community in Inayat Patti village in February 2015.

Process and determinants of migration from Inayat Patti in post colonial India

It is observed that colonial experiences of migration shifted in the post-colonial phase of migration from Inayat Patti where the route of labour migration toward coal mining of undivided Bihar and West Bengal was so significant for livelihood practices for villagers from 1947 to the 1960s until the beginning of internal migration to Bombay (Mumbai) in the decade of 1960s. Therefore, Bombay-based migration was a turning point for poor people of the village due to availability of the better jobs with higher wages in Bombay as well as the glamour of jobs in Bombay also worked as a pull factor in the process of shifting direction of migration from the east India to west India. It was realized that Bombay-based migration was so significant for poor Muslims of Inayat Patti village because these poor Muslims found a well-developed route of migration toward Bombay in 1960. In the case of migration of *Dalits*, mostly *Dalits* belonged to *Chamar* caste and they were working as migrant labourers in coal mining fields in east India and backwards *Yadav* caste Hindus worked as agricultural labourers in agricultural farmhouses of rich Muslim families namely- Baghel dynasty, who was the landlord of Inayat Patti and its surrounding villages as well as belonged *Nawab* family of Allahabad district. These villagers said that Baghel were decision-makers in the socio-economic and cultural practices of the village as well as facilitated political mobility in the village because the Baghel family were so rich as well as they were known as Thakur due to the deep penetration of Thakur in the economy of Inayat Patti and its surrounding village. Villagers said that the Baghel family was aggressive and mostly *Dalits, Yadav* castes and poor Muslims used to work as bonded labourers in the agricultural fields of the Baghel dynasty. Therefore, the role of the Baghel family was so important in the process of forced migration of poor Muslims, because poor Muslims did not have sufficient sources of income at root, therefore, and they were involved in the process of migration toward coal mining and the cotton textile industry in Bombay. Villagers also accepted the order of the Baghel family for their voting in elections because mostly migrant labourers used to return to the village and vote according to the order of the Baghel family. These consequences can be analyzed as the role of the landlord system in the political mobility of migrant labourers in the rise of Indian democracy just after the independence of India. Therefore, there was a culture of internal migration in Inayat Patti village from 1947 to 1983 and the year 1984 was a turning point for Inayat Patti village when a Muslim migrated to the United Arab Emirates with the help of his relative, who already worked in Dubai. It was the beginning of post-colonial international migration as the consequence of a long historical sequence of migration from Inayat Patti village in colonial to post-colonial India. It was very difficult for poor Muslims to involve themselves in the process of international migration due to the difficult documentation process of migration with its high economic cost.[19]

It was also realized that the decade 1990s was crucial in the process of international migration from Inayat Patti to Gulf countries via Bombay (Mumbai) because these poor Muslims worked as semi-skilled and unskilled labourers in Bombay as well as earned for investment in the economic cost of Gulf migration. Therefore, the phenomena of internal migration led to international migration because internal to international migration opened the door to Saudi-based migration via Bombay (Mumbai) as well as giving new economic opportunities to migrant labourers. Therefore, the entire route of migration from Inayat Patti village to coal mining regions shifted toward Bombay (Mumbai) based migration due to the opening of Saudi-based migration. [20]

It was observed that the culture of international migration was improved in the twenty-first century as a consequence of the globalization of migration in Inayat Patti village due to a well-developed system of social network of migration from village to Saudi Arabia via Bombay (Mumbai). Mostly Muslim youth used the term "Bombay-Saudi" in the process of migration where Muslim youths existed in the cultural region of migration from Inayat Patti to Saudi Arabia via Mumbai in the twenty- first century.

During the COVID-19 era, villagers said that there was a negative impact of the pandemic of COVID-19 and the lockdown on the trend of internal and international migration because it started re-verse migration from Bombay and Saudi Arabia to the village as well as created a barrier in the process of internal and international migration from the village. The consequences of the pandemic of COVID -19 forced migrant labourers to reverse migration from Mumbai and Saudi Arabia to villages as well as created economic uncertainty before returning migrant labourers to villages.[21] Therefore, it can be realized that there is a well-developed history of labour migration from Inayat Patti from colonial India to post-colonial India in the consequence of

---

[19] Information is based on informal interviews among villagers in Inayat Patti from February 2015 to March 2015.

[20] Information is based on informal interviews among villagers in Inayat Patti from October 2023 to November 2023.

[21] Information is based on informal interviews among villagers in Inayat Patti village in October 2023.

its past to present with the future implication of migration in the development of the village.

CHAPTER 3

MIGRATION AND ECONOMIC PERSPECTIVE

3.1. Economic impact of migration

According to Naufal and Ali (2010), oil-producing Gulf countries are heartland for unskilled and semi-skilled Indian migrant labourers; those send huge remittances to their roots in India. According to Begum and Aziz (2009), there is a cordial nexus between remittances and economic impact in the context of Gulf migration due to the positive role of remittances in the socio-economic development of migrant households at the root level in India. Matter of inflow of remittances from Gulf countries to India was being functioned by the global financial-economic crisis because the study of Narayana & Rajan (2012) shows that the matter of remittances is positively associated with the economic performance of migrant households in India but global financial crisis 2009 adversely influenced the inflow of remittances in migrant families.

In the case of Uttar Pradesh, according to the study by Rajan et al. (2017), Uttar Pradesh is the leading state in receiving remittances from Gulf countries through the positive role of unskilled and semi-skilled migrant labourers, those works as long-term temporary contract migrant labourers in Gulf countries. According to Taukeer (2021), there is a significant impact of the skills of occupation on the structure of remittances of migrant labourers in both internal and international destinations and these consequences are positively associated with the investment of remittances in boosting the micro-based economy of migrant households in rural Uttar Pradesh. A similar study conducted by Taukeer (2022) shows that there is a cordial nexus between economic remittances and socio-economic changes in the context of socio-economic transformation in migrant households in rural Uttar Pradesh.

In the case of Inayat Patti village in Prayagraj district of Uttar Pradesh, the study of Taukeer (2017) shows that migrant households invested economic remittances in items of physical culture and these consequences led to the tendency of migration from Inayat Patti to Gulf countries via Mumbai. A similar study was also conducted by Majumder (2022), and the findings of

59

the study show that the impact of the pandemic of COVID-19 and the lockdown adversely influenced the trend of inflow of remittances in villages as well as created panic conditions in socio-economic conditions of migrant households.

In the case of Gujarat, a study conducted by Basu (2016) shows that there is a significant role of Gulf remittances in migrant households in the context of the function of international remittances through diaspora philanthropy in rural Gujarat. Similar phenomena were found in the study of Zachariah & Rajan (2016) in Kerala, where international Gulf remittances boosted the economy of migrant households in an abundant zone in Kerala. In the case of Bihar, the study of Rahman (2001) and Datta (2016) gave broad aspects about the impact of remittances on the micro economy of migrant households in Bihar because the economy of migrant households was based on the positive role of the remittances. In the case of study of Kaur (2021) there is a significant impact of the Gulf remittances on the economic performance of migrant households in the context of economic transformation in migrant households in Punjab, India.

Therefore, the matter of remittances boosted the economy of migrant households as a consequence of the long-term return of migration in India. These consequences developed a mechanism of the economic impact of migration in the process of economic transformation in migrant households at the root level in Uttar Pradesh. The consequence of depth penetration of the impact of Gulf migration leads to the phenomena of economic migration within well-developed social regions of migration in the context of demonstration impact of migration. Therefore, it is realized that both internal and international migration created a way of diaspora philanthropy due to the investment of remittances in the process of boosting the micro-based economy in migrant households with the economy of the village. These consequences created phenomena of positive and negative aspects about the impact of migration where the positive aspect of migration improved the economic development of migrant households but the negative aspect of the migration created an economic inequality between migrant and non-migrant households. In these consequences, the huge trend of labour migration from Inayat Patti village to Gulf countries created the phenomena of the neighbour effect of migration on non-migrant households because the impact of economic facts of migration inspired and motivated non-migrant households for migration to Gulf countries due to huge economic impact of migration on economic development of the village. Therefore, the economic impact of migration worked as a pull factor in the process of facilitating labour migration from Inayat Patti village to Gulf countries due to the depth penetration of the impact of international Gulf migration in the village. These consequences increased the economic behaviour of migrant labourers and their family members because they decided to migrate in the sense of economic rationalism where phenomena of cost and benefit analysis about migration ensured the well-developed economic route of migration from Inayat Patti village to Gulf countries via Mumbai in the context of globalization of migration. Therefore, flow chart 3.1 shows that the economic impact of migration developed economic inputs for economic transformation in the development of the village through the positive role of the investment of remittances in the economy of the village because the entire economic function of Inayat Patti village was moving around Gulf migration. These migrant labourers find themselves in the safe zone of migration because the impact of migration ensured the economic landscape in the village where the matter of remittances was the economic core in the process of facilitating a huge trend of labour migration from Inayat Patti village to Dubai via Mumbai due to well-developed pathways of migration in the context of dynamics of globalization of international migration in Inayat Patti village in current phenomena.

Flow chart 3.1. Economic impact of remittances in Inayat Patti village

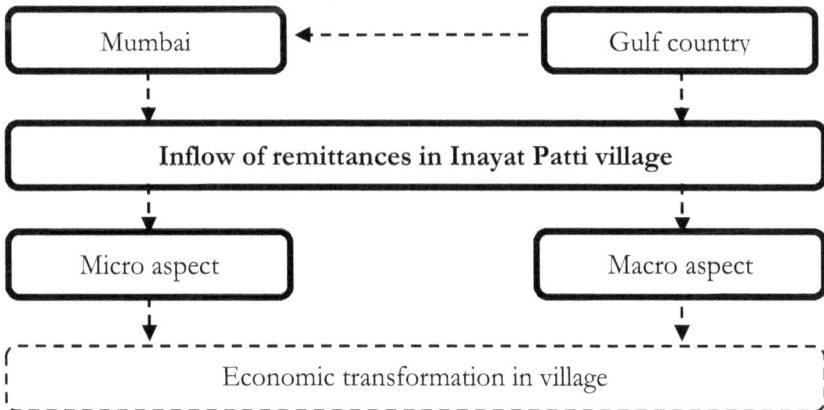

Source: Designed by Author, based on field survey, 2017-18

3.1.1. Economic impact of migration at root

Out of the total migrant households, nearly 95.0 per cent of migrant households had one internal migrant labourer and the rest of the migrant households had two internal migrant labourers (Table 3.1).

Table 3.1. Number of internal migrant labourers in migrant households

Number of internal migrant labourers	Number of migrant households	Per cent
One migrant labourer	171	95.0
Two migrant labourers	9	5.0
Total	180	100.0

Source: Field Survey, 2017-18

Out of the total migrant households, nearly 72.0 per cent of the migrant households had one international migrant labourer followed by 27.0 per cent of the migrant households had two international migrant labourers and the rest of the migrant households had three international migrant labourers (Table 3.2).

Table 3.2. Number of international migrant labourers in migrant households

Number of internal migrant labourers	Number of migrant households	Per cent
One migrant labourer	129	72.0
Two migrant labourers	49	27.0
Three migrant labourers	2	1.0
Total	180	100.0

Source: Field Survey, 2017-18

Out of the total international migrant households, a total of 94.0 per cent of the migrant households received INR 40000 to INR 120000 and the rest per cent of the migrant households received INR 120001 to INR 180000 per month. Average monthly remittances were INR 84805 per migrant household (Table 3.3).

Table 3.3. Inflow of remittances in migrant households

Per month remittances in INR	Number of migrant households	Per cent
40000-80000	109	61.0
80001-120000	60	33.0
120001-160000	9	5.0
160001-180000	2	1.0
Total	180	100.0

Source: Field Survey, 2017-18

Table shows that internal remittances were the major source of income for migrant households in pre-Gulf migration and international Gulf remittances were the major source of income for migrant households in post-Gulf migration. The average monthly income was INR 16280 in pre-Gulf migrations compared to INR 109600 in post-Gulf migration in migrant households (Table 3.4).

Table 3.4. Sources of income in migrant households in pre and post-Gulf migration

Sources of income	Pre-Gulf migration	Post –Gulf migration
	Per cent of total income	Per cent of total income
Gulf remittances	0.0	77.0
Internal remittances	88.5	18.0
Livestock	4.5	2.0
Agriculture	7.0	2.5
Total	100.0 (INR 16280)	100.0(INR 109600)

Source: Field Survey, 2017-2018

Table shows that the average monthly expenditure on consumption of food and non-food items was INR 15527 in migrant households in post–Gulf migration compared to INR 7148 in pre-Gulf migration (Table 3.5).

Table 3.5. Average monthly expenditure on consumption in migrant households

Food and non- food items expenditure	Pre-Gulf migration	Post-Gulf migration	Growth between pre and post - Gulf migration
	Per cent of total	Per cent of total	In per cent
Transport items	7.5	8.5	176.0
Entertainment items	5.0	5.0	145.0
Communication items	6.0	6.5	148.0
Health items	14.0	14.0	148.0
Education items	15.0	16.0	167.0
Food items	45.0	41.0	110.0
Other items	7.5	9.0	155.0
Total	100.0(INR 7148)	100.0(INR15527)	138.0

Source: Field Survey, 2017-2018

Note: Pre-Gulf migration shows the economic conditions of migrant households before their involvement in international Gulf migration and post-Gulf migration shows the economic conditions of migrant households after their involvement in international Gulf migration.

3.1.2. Hypothetical test of pattern of average monthly expenditure of migrant households in pre and post-Gulf migration

There are the following null and alternative hypotheses:

H_0: There is no difference between the average monthly expenditure between pre and post-Gulf migration in migrant households.

H_1: There is a difference between the average monthly expenditure between pre and post-Gulf migration in migrant households.

The table shows that the average monthly expenditure was INR 7148 in pre-Gulf migration compared to INR 15527 in post-Gulf migration in migrant households (Table 3.6).

Table 3.6. Paired samples statistics

		Mean of average monthly expenditure on consumption in INR	N	Std. Deviation	Std. Error Mean
Pair 1	Average monthly expenditure on consumption in pre-Gulf migration	7148.3333	180	2583.28263	192.54652
	Average monthly expenditure on consumption in post-Gulf migration	15527.7778	180	4235.30065	315.68067

Source: Field Survey, 2017-2018

The perspective of correlation measurement between the average monthly expenditure on consumption in pre-Gulf migration and the average monthly expenditure on consumption in post-Gulf migration shows a significant correlation (Table 3.7).

Table 3.7. Paired samples correlations

		N	Correlation	Sig.
Pair 1	Average monthly expenditure on consumption in pre-Gulf Migration and average monthly expenditure on consumption in post -Gulf migration	180	.760	.000

Source: Field Survey, 2017-2018

The table shows that the difference between the average monthly expenditure between pre-Gulf migration and post-Gulf migration was INR -8379.44 and the t –value is -39.770. The associated significance value is .000, which is less than 0.05. Therefore, we reject the null hypothesis and say that the economic condition of migrant households improved in post-Gulf migration compared to the economic conditions of migrant households in pre-Gulf migration in the perspective of improvement in average monthly expenditure on consumption in migrant households from pre-Gulf migration to post- Gulf migration (Table 3.8).

Table 3.8. Paired sample t-Test

		Paired Differences					t	Df	Sig. (2-tailed)
		Mean	Std. Deviation	Std. Error Mean	95% Confidence Interval of the Difference				
					Lower	Upper			
Pair 1	Average monthly expenditure on consumption in pre-Gulf migration – Average monthly expenditure on consumption in post-Gulf migration	8379.44444	2826.82081	210.69878	8795.21750	7963.67139	39.770	179	.000

Source: Field Survey, 2017-2018

3.1.3. Economic impact of migration in economy of villages in rural Uttar Pradesh: A case study

Economic impact of migration on migrant households

It is observed that Muslim migrant households received huge remittances from Gulf countries due to the depth penetration of Gulf migration in Inayat Patti village. It is also observed that Muslim migrant households received a huge amount of Riyal (currency of Saudi Arabia) in the form of zakat[1] (religious aid given by Arabians to poor Muslims) and returned migrant labourers expressed that they felt happiness in collecting zakat in Saudi Arabia because Arabians motivated them for helping to poor Muslims in India according to ideology of Islamic principles. In the case of Inayat Patti village, the economy of migrant households was based on remittances and zakat because they considered that Gulf migration was a matter of their bread and butter. Therefore, the consequences of a huge inflow of remittances created an economic transformation due to the investment of remittances in the process of boosting the micro economy of households because migrant households invested remittances and zakat in the development of physical culture like construction and re-construction of house, buying cars, jewellery, but these migrant households did not invest remittances in productive sources like education. These consequences were the result of the preference of migrant households for unproductive sources

---

[1] The *zakat* system is based on religious aid to poor Muslims as 2.5 per cent of total annual income according to Islamic principles. Cited from: Taukeer, M. (2022). Nexus of Social Remittances and Social Change: An Ethnographic Study of Impact of Gulf Migration on Linguistic Pattern of Migrants in Uttar Pradesh. In *India Migration Report 2021* (pp. 292-305). Routledge: India.

compared to the multiplier impact of productive sources like education because migrant households were interested in Islamic education in Madrasha (religious school) due to the deep impact of Gulf migration in Inayat Patti village. These consequences were helpful in the process of poverty removal through Gulf migration in Inayat Patti village because Muslim migrant households existed in the safe zone of Gulf migration with the aspect of an isolated household economy focused on remittances and zakat. Therefore, these consequences showed a demonstration impact of Gulf migration among migrant households in Inayat Patti village where Indian Muslim migrant households found themselves in the mental region of Arabian culture in the context of the role of Islamic ideology in the process of economic function of migrant households through investment of remittances and zakat. These consequences can be analyzed as the role of Gulf migration in improving the households' economy of migrant households according to the principles of Islamic ideology in democratic India in the twenty-first century. It may subject of discussion in the aspect of why and how the role of Islamic ideology in the economic function of migrant households in the perspective of positive sense and negative sense because the huge inflow of Gulf remittances created an economic inequality between migrant and non-migrant households where non- migrant Hindu households were engaged in the agro-based economy in Inayat Patti village but Muslims have excluded themselves in agriculture-based economy due to their cordial association with Islamic ideology based economic performance in democratic secular India. [2]

Box 3.1: Case Study[3]

"It is a case study of 32 years old boy named Gufram Siddique (Patte) in Dorhan hamlet in Inayat Patti village, he said that he received huge remittances and zakat from Saudi Arabia and Mumbai and invested part of zakat in the process of the economic performance of his households as well as helped poor Muslims according to the ideology of Islamic principles. These consequences showed that Muslim youths were frequently following the Islamic ideology in democratic secular India due to the depth penetration of Gulf migration in Inayat Patti village."

Therefore, the economic impact of Gulf migration created a form of Islamic economy in Inayat Patti village through the investment of *zakat* in the development of economic building of Inayat Patti and its surrounding villages in the context of globalization of Gulf migration. These consequences were positively associated with the role of Islamic laws in the

---

[2] Information is based on informal interviews and observation methods in Inayat Patti village from February 2015 to March 2018 and October 2023 to November 2023.
[3] Information is based on personal interview from respondent in Inayat Patti village in October 2023.

economy of migrant households but these migrant households did not have any ideas about the basic principles of Islam as well as the basic principles of the Indian economy because these Muslim migrant households preferred Islamic economy compared to democratic Indian economy.

Economic impact of daispora philanthropy in Inayat Patti village

It is observed that there was a significant impact of the Gulf migration in Inayat Patti and its surrounding villages namely- Mahrupur, Saidahan, Basgit, Utraon and Panch Purva. Inayat Patti village is located in the centre of these villages and works as the economic centre for its surrounding villages. It is observed that Inayat Patti village was known as Riyal *Gav* (Saudi village) and *Gav* (village) of Pardesiya (migrants) due to the depth penetration of economic migration from Inayat Patti to Saudi Arabia via short-term migration to Mumbai. These consequences developed the image of Inayat Patti village as a rich village among villagers because the entire economic function of Inayat Patti village was based on Gulf migration. It is observed that the consequence of Gulf migration improved the economy of the village because the impact of the Gulf migration developed the migration industry where youths of Inayat Patti and its surrounding villages worked as migrant agents and opened their offices in squares and markets of villages. These migrant agents were also operating online money transaction centres where family members of migrant households received sending remittances from Mumbai and Saudi Arabia. These consequences showed that the economic impact of Gulf migration created a multiplier impact in Inayat Patti due to its role in the creation of livelihood due to the investment of remittances in the development of the village. It is observed that there was a branch of the State Bank of India in the market of Inayat Patti village and the history of this bank is based on the beginning of migration from Inayat Patti to Saudi Arabia in the last decade of the 1980s. Therefore, the impact of Gulf migration boosted the economic function of Inayat Patti village due to the huge inflow of remittances and zakat.[4]

It is observed that villagers of Inayat Patti also received a huge part of zakat through informal mode as Hundi[5] but these villagers had no idea about the differences between formal and informal mode of inflow of

---

[4] Information is based on focus group interviews and passive observation methods in Inayat Patti village from October 2023 to November 2023.

[5] The *Hundi* system is prominent as an informal mode of inflow of remittances from Gulf countries to rural Uttar Pradesh. Cited from: Taukeer, M. (2020). Process and determinants of labour migration from selected rural areas of Uttar Pradesh to Gulf Countries. *Man and Development*, 123-138.

remittances and *zakat*. These consequences can be analyzed as depth penetration of the Islamic economy in the function of the Hundi system in the inflow of remittances and zakat from Saudi Arabia to Inayat Patti and its surrounding villages.[6]

Box 3.2: Case Study[7]

"It is a case study of 28 years old named Rakesh Maurya in Inayat Patti village; he worked as an operator of online money transactions in the village. He said that he had the license for the transaction of money where family members of Gulf migrants used to receive remittances. He accepted a visa card, master card and American Express card. He also accepted the unique identity AADHAR card of India because simple rural people used to withdraw remittances from the AADHAR card. Rakesh also said that his entire business was based on the gulf migration of Muslims in Inayat Patti village."

It is observed that local Muslim leaders used to help poor Muslims through zakat because these local Muslim leaders received huge zakat from their family members, those who worked in Saudi Arabia. These Muslim leaders gave zakat to poor Muslims for starting entrepreneurs according to the principles of Islamic ideology and Islamic economy. These consequences showed that Gulf migration paved the route of the Islamic economy in Inayat Patti and its surrounding villages. It is observed that these local Muslim leaders did not have any idea about the basic principles of the Indian economy because they did not consider the importance of the Indian economy in the development of the village. These consequences can be analyzed as the role of Gulf migration in economic transformation in the context of the multiplier impact of Gulf migration in Inayat Patti and its surrounding villages. Apart from this, the economy of local Madrasahs (religious schools) was based on the community help of the Muslim committee in Inayat Patti and its surrounding village because huge numbers of unregistered religious schools were based on mercy-based investment of zakat in Inayat Patti and its surrounding village. It is observed that there was a significant impact of the ideology of *Ahle–Sunnat–Wal–Jamaat*[8] ideology of Sufism of *Barelvi* school of Uttar Pradesh, among Muslims of Inayat Patti village. Muslims followed the principles of Maulana Ahamed Raza Khan, founder of *Barelvi* School as well as Islamic Sunni Muslim based thoughts of Al Azhar Univerity of Egypt. It is also observed that there was operating of Islamic school namely- Qadri public school in Inayat Patti

---

[6] Information is based on passive observation and focus group interviews among villagers in Inayat Patti in October 2023.

[7] Information is based on personal interview from respondent in Inayat Patti village in October 2023.

[8] Ahle–Sunnat–Wal–Jamaat is based on Sufism among Sunni Muslims in Uttar Pradesh. Cited from: Taukeer, M. (2023). Ethnographic Analysis of Nexus about Migration and Culture in Global Perspective. *Border Crossing, 13*(2), 115-131.

village based on Qadri Sufi sects of Sheikh Abdul Qadir Jilani, who was the founder of Qadri ideology in Bagdad, Iraq and South Asian countries. These consequences can be analyzed as the role of the economic impact of migration on the determination of the psychological economic behaviour of Muslim migrant labourers in Inayat Patti village, where Islamic-based education was prominent compared to modern Indian education due to the depth penetration of economic impact of migration. [9]

Box 3.3: Case Study[10]

"It is a case study of 45 years old local Muslim leader named Chotu Neta, he was known as neta (such type of political leader, who engaged in local politics), he said that he was engaged as a social activist and helped poor Muslims starting entrepreneurs through zakat according to the ideology of Islamic economy but he told that he did not have any idea about principles of Islamic ideology."

These consequences can be analyzed as the positive role of the *zakat* in the economic function of entrepreneurs in Inayat Patti and its surrounding villages according to Islamic ideology in the function of the local economy. It is also observed that there was a huge impact of economic mythology among Muslims in Inayat Patti village due to the impact of Gulf migration because Muslim women showed that they considered the impact of Gulf migration as the blessing of Bibi Fatima (daughter of the prophet Mohammed) and these Muslims women used to listen to myths about Bibi Fatima with logical interpretation about role of the message of Bibi Fatima in the function of Islamic economy.[11]

Box 3.4: Case Study[12]

"It is a case study of 56 years old woman in Inayat Patti village and she said that there was a crucial role of the story of Syeda Bibi and Das Bibi in Islamic economic function. She was famous for describing economic myths among local Muslim women as well as delivering mythology-based stories like- Syeda Bibi ki kahani and Das Bibi ki Kahani among Muslim women in Inayat Patti village. These consequences can be analyzed as the role of economic myths among women due to the impact of Gulf migration in Inayat Patti and its surrounding villages."

Women of the village said that these women used to operate their microfinance known as Bisi in Inayat Patti village. System of Bisi was a self-group committee of women, where members of self-group women contributed INR 100 to 500 per month in their account in Bisi. The entire economic function of Bisi was based on probability theory with an approach of equal chance and equal distribution for all member women of the self-help

---

[9] Information is based on the passive observation method in Inayat Patti village from October 2023 to November 2023.

[10] Information is based on personal interview from respondent in Inayat Patti village in November 2023.

[11] Information is based on focus group interviews among women in Inayat Patti village in October 2023.

[12] Information is based on personal interview from respondent in Inayat Patti village in November 2023.

group. Out of the total member women, a woman used to find INR 1500 to 3000 per month based on a rolling system. These consequences were helpful in the economic empowerment of women in Inayat Patti village but the consequence of Gulf migration and zakat-based economy ruined the microfinance-based system in the village because Muslim women were totally involved in the function of the zakat-based economy according to Islamic principles.[13]

It is observed that the economic impact of Gulf migration led to rural-urban migration. Most Muslim families migrated from Inayat Patti and its surrounding villages to Kareli town in Prayagraj (Allahabad) city because these Muslim youths were engaged in entrepreneurship through investment of zakat because the urban-based economy gave huge returns compared to low returns in the rural-based economy. It can be discussed as an investment of remittances in the form of the *Hawilaad*[14]- system where migrant labourers invest a huge part of *zakat* in the function of the informal economy under the unknown principles of Islamic investment. These Muslim youths followed the principles of Islamic ideology in Inayat Patti and Kareli towns as well as considered Inayat Patti and Kareli as a little Pakistan. These consequences can be analyzed as the role of Gulf migration and its return in the process of economic function through the investment of zakat according to the Islamic economy.[15]

Box 3.5: Case Study[16]

"It is a case study of 52 years old named Mirza Moid Beg, who lived in Kareli. He said that Muslim youths were robbing Riyal in Saudi Arabia and this was not any importance of modern education in their life. He considered Gulf migrants as Subuk (smart) heroes and Gulf wives as Burrak (female horse angel of Allah). He also said that Riyal was a matter, not education. These consequences showed that the economic impact of Gulf migration changed the economic values of people through the Islamic economy in democratic India. These consequences showed that Muslims lived in an imagined world with Islamic ideology in secular democratic India as well as followed economic Islamic mythology."

---

[13] Information is based on focus group interviews among women respondents in Inayat Patti village from October 2023 to November 2023.

[14] "The *Hawilaad* system is based on Somali traders. They collect hard currency from Somali migrants abroad and then use the money to purchase commodities that can be sold in Somalia. They returned periodically to Somalia, sold their goods, and then paid the equivalent in Somali currency to the migrants' families. Profit made on the sale of the goods effectively becomes the traders' commission. The system of transfer is very common among Somali communities across the world. In the aftermath of 9/11 attempts were monitor it or close it down, because of some evidence that funding for the attacks was channeled through Somalia. However, the system has proved hard to formalize and still appears to be widespread". Cited from: Koser, Khalid (2007). *International migration: A Very Short Introduction*. New York: Oxford University Press, pp.44.

[15] Information is based on informal focus group interviews among rural and urban respondents in Inayat Patti and Kareli town in Allahabad city in November 2023.

[16] Information is based on personal interview from respondent in Inayat Patti village in November 2023.

In the case of the negative impact of Gulf migration, it is realized that zakat based economy was creating a form of economic inequality between Muslims and Hindus in Inayat Patti village because Muslims were told that they could not help poor Hindus through zakat because there were provisions for helping to only poor Muslims through zakat according to Islamic economy. These consequences can be analyzed as a function of the isolated Islamic economy according to the zakat-based economy in Inayat Patti village where Hindus did not exist in zakat-based isolated economy in Inayat Patti village.[17]

During the period of the pandemic of COVID-19, Muslim returned migrant labourers said that the impact of COVID-19 started reverse migration from Gulf countries and Mumbai to Inayat Patti village because the vast majority of the Muslim returned migrant labourers lost their jobs at destinations. The consequences of the pandemic of COVID-19 created economic uncertainty among Muslims in the village as well as created an economic hurdle for the development of diaspora philanthropy in the village. Apart from this, villagers also said that COVID-19 adversely influenced the economic image of Inayat Patti and its surroundings as well as adversely influenced the Islamic-based economy of the village. Muslim migrant households helped poor Muslims through zakat during COVID-19 and lockdown. These consequences can be analyzed as the impact of the Islamic economy through diaspora philanthropy under the principles of Islam.[18]

3.2. Transit destination: Mumbai

Mumbai's urban agglomeration is the heartland of north Indian migrant labourers, who migrate to Mumbai for employment (Census, 2011). A study by Gavaskar (2010) shows that Mumbai is the hub for economic diversity in the context of the huge presence of North Indian migrant labourers in Mumbai. The study of Jha & Kumar (2016) gives a realistic picture of the vulnerable working conditions of North Indian migrant labourers in Mumbai because these North Indian migrant labourers work in the bottom segmentation of the labour market. A study by Kumar et al. (2012) shows that North Indian migrant labourers face the problem of accessing property rights in Mumbai due to their involvement in the bottom segmentation of the labour market. According to Mehra & Singh (2014), the huge presence of North Indian migrants created panic conditions for migrant labourers

---

[17] Information is based on the passive observation method among return migrant labourers and non-migrant respondents in Inayat Patti village in October 2023.
[18] Information is based on informal focus group interview among return migrant labourers in Inayat Patti village in October 2023.

because these North Indian migrant labourers were unable to access minimum conditions of labour rights in the working environment of Mumbai. A study by Mili (2011) & Singh (2007) realizes the role of north Indian migrant labourers in economic development in slum areas of Mumbai because slums are the cultural pattern of settlement and economic landscapes for north Indian migrant labourers.

In these contexts, the study of Taukeer (2022) shows that internal labour migration from Uttar Pradesh to Mumbai is based on emerging economic landscapes in Mumbai in the context of globalization of interstate rural-urban migration in rural Uttar Pradesh. These consequences are caused by wage differential between rural and urban-based economies as well as wage differential between Mumbai and Gulf countries led to the trend of labour migration from rural Uttar Pradesh to Gulf countries via Mumbai. A study by Taukeer (2023) shows that the process and determinants of labour migration from Uttar Pradesh and Bihar to Mumbai are caused by the purpose of labour migration to Gulf countries because Mumbai-based short-term internal migration led to the long-term international Gulf migration due to the availability of the better jobs with higher wages in Gulf countries compared to low wages in Mumbai.

Based on the above concise review of the process, determinants and consequences of internal migration in Mumbai, it is realized that there is a long history of labour migration from Uttar Pradesh and Bihar to Mumbai but conducted studies show that there is an inter-connection between internal and international migration where internal migration lead to the process of labour migration to Gulf countries in the consequence of the globalization of migration in recent phenomena. Study shows that matter of well-being of migrant labourers is an important phenomenon in the context role of economic catalysts in the working and living conditions of internal migrant labourers in Mumbai. Both qualitative and quantitative aspects of the study show that there is variation in the structure of per month income, remittances and expenditure of migrant labourers according to their skills of occupation in Mumbai and these consequences determine the economic impact of north Indian migrant labourers in informal economy of Mumbai. Therefore, it is observed that migrant labourers faced the problem of vulnerable working and living conditions as well as did not fulfill the basic requirement of the sustainability approach of Sustainable Development Goals (SDGs) 2030 for ensuring the well-being of migrants.

3.2.1 Profile of internal migrant labourers

Out of the total sample of migrant labourers (n=180), nearly 81 per cent (n=146) of the migrant labourers were from Uttar Pradesh and the rest 19.0 per cent (n=34) of migrant labourers were from Bihar. From the perspective of demographic classification, nearly 87.0 per cent (n=157) of the migrant labourers were in the age groups between 18 and 30 years while the rest 13.0 per cent (n=23) were between 31 and 40 years. From the perspective of religious classification, nearly 57.0 per cent (n=103) of migrant labourers were Muslims are rest were Hindus. These migrant labourers were educated from upper primary to intermediate because nearly 97.0 per cent (n=174) of migrant labourers were educated from upper primary to intermediate and the rest graduated.

3.2.2. Hypothetical test of variation of per month income, remittances and expenditure of migrant labourers

Occupation and per month income of migrant labourers

Null and alternative hypotheses are the following:

H_0= There is no difference in the mean monthly income of migrant labourers according to their skills of occupation.

H_1 = There is a difference in the mean monthly income of migrant labourers according to their skills of occupation.

There are differences in the mean monthly income of migrant labourers according to their skills of occupation in Mumbai. The average monthly income was INR 23611 per migrant labourer (Table 3.9).

Analysis of variance (ANOVA) table shows that the F value is 34.422 and its associated significance value (p-value) is .000, which is less than 0.05. Therefore, we reject the null hypothesis and say that there are differences in the mean monthly income of migrant labourers according to their skills of occupation (Table 3.10).

The means plot shows that there are differences in the mean monthly income of migrant labourers by their skills of occupation in Mumbai. Tailors got higher income followed by welders, drivers, plumbers, security guards, masons, street vendors, electricians and manual labourers (Figure 3.1).

Table 3.9. Description of per month income of migrant labourers by skill of occupations

Occupation of migrant labourers	N	Mean of per month income in INR	Std. Deviation	Std. Error	95% confidence interval for mean		Minimum	Maximum
					Lower Bound	Upper Bound		
Driver	20	26400	3939.00869	880.78912	24556.4872	28243.5128	20000.00	30000.00
Tailor	20	29500	2762.53126	617.72077	28207.0956	30792.9044	25000.00	35000.00
Welder	20	28000	4412.89975	986.75438	25934.6993	30065.3007	20000.00	35000.00
Plumber	20	26000	4436.68914	992.07385	23923.5656	28076.4344	20000.00	35000.00
Mason	20	22500	2564.94588	573.53933	21299.5684	23700.4316	20000.00	25000.00
Manual Labourer	20	15750	2291.28785	512.34754	14677.6443	16822.3557	12000.00	20000.00
Electrician	20	20600	2257.15237	504.71461	19543.6202	21656.3798	15000.00	25000.00
Security Guard	20	23000	3402.78524	760.88591	21407.4475	24592.5525	20000.00	30000.00
Street Vendor	20	20750	2446.80242	547.12165	19604.8612	21895.1388	15000.00	25000.00
Total	180	23611	5178.80175	386.00509	22849.4052	24372.8171	12000.00	35000.00

Source: Field Survey, 2019

Table 3.10. Analysis of variance (ANOVA)

	Sum of squares	Df	Mean square	F	Sig.
Between Groups	2961677777.778	8	370209722.222	34.422	.000
Within Groups	1839100000.000	171	10754970.760		
Total	4800777777.778	179			

Source: Field Survey, 2019

Figure 3.1. Means plot- occupation and per month income

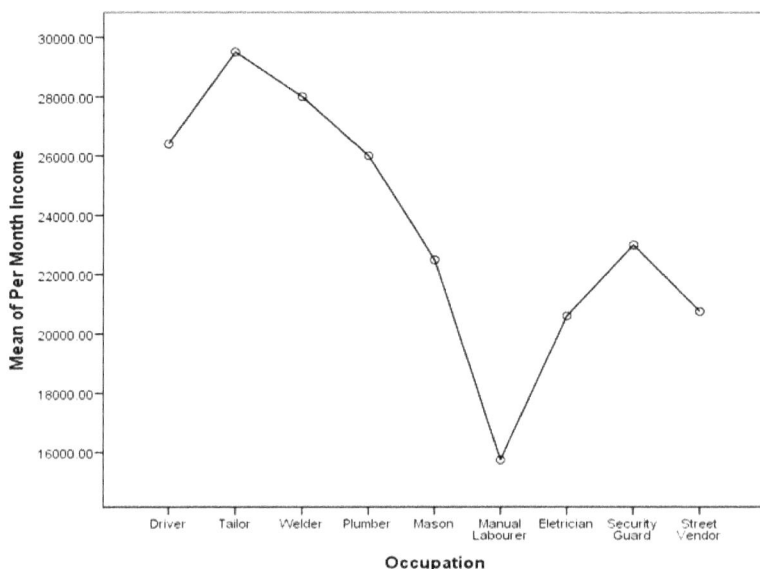

Source: Field survey, 2019

74

Occupation and per month remittances of migrant labourers

Null and alternative hypotheses are the following:

H_0= There is no difference in the mean monthly remittances of migrant labourers according to their skills of occupation.

H_1 = There is a difference in the mean monthly remittances of migrant labourers according to their skills of occupation.

There are differences in the mean monthly remittances of migrant labourers according to their skills of occupation in Mumbai. The average monthly remittance was INR 16988 per migrant labourer (Table 3.11).

Table 3.11. Description of per month remittances of migrant labourers by skill of occupations

Occupation of migrant labourers	N	Mean of per month remittances in INR	Std. Deviation	Std. Error	95% confidence interval for mean		Minimum	Maximum
					Lower Bound	Upper Bound		
Driver	20	16500	3103.47852	693.95889	15047.5273	17952.4727	10000.00	25000.00
Tailor	20	22250	3431.66371	767.34333	20643.9319	23856.0681	20000.00	30000.00
Welder	20	21000	3077.93506	688.24720	19559.4821	22440.5179	15000.00	25000.00
Plumber	20	19850	3468.27729	775.53038	18226.7963	21473.2037	15000.00	25000.00
Mason	20	16500	2350.81173	525.65748	15399.7862	17600.2138	15000.00	20000.00
Manual Labourer	20	10300	1525.22647	341.05101	9586.1720	11013.8280	8000.00	15000.00
Electricians	20	14000	2051.95670	458.83147	13039.6547	14960.3453	10000.00	15000.00
Security Guard	20	16500	2212.40522	494.70885	15464.5625	17535.4375	15000.00	20000.00
Street Vendor	20	16000	2051.95670	458.83147	15039.6547	16960.3453	15000.00	20000.00
Total	180	16988	4335.10922	323.11996	16351.2745	17626.5033	8000.00	30000.00

Source: Field Survey, 2019.

Analysis of variance (ANOVA) table shows that the F value is 37.685 and its associated significance value (p-value) is .000, which is less than 0.05. Therefore, we reject the null hypothesis and say that there are differences in the mean monthly remittances of migrant labourers according to their skills of occupation (Table 3.12).

Table 3.12. Analysis of variance (ANOVA)

	Sum of squares	Df	Mean square	F	Sig.
Between Groups	2146477777.778	8	268309722.222	37.685	.000
Within Groups	1217500000.000	171	7119883.041		
Total	3363977777.778	179			

Source: Field Survey, 2019.

Means plot shows that tailors sent the highest remittances followed by welders, plumbers, security guards, masons and drivers, street vendors, electricians and manual labourers (Figure 3.2).

Figure 3.2. Means plot- occupation and per month remittances

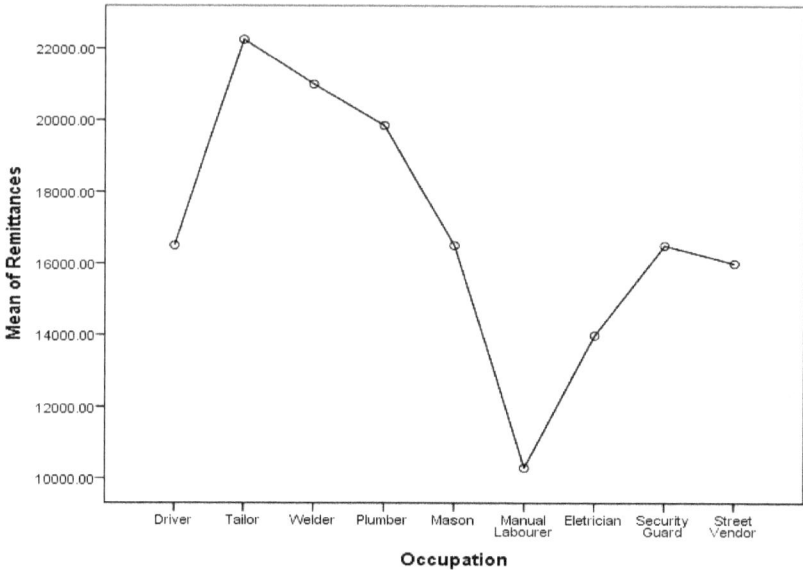

Source: Field survey, 2019

Occupation and per month expenditure of migrant labourers

Null and alternative hypotheses are the following:

H_0= There is no difference in the mean monthly expenditure of migrant labourers according to their skills of occupation.

H_1 = There is a difference in the mean monthly expenditure of migrant labourers according to their skills of occupation.

There are differences in the mean monthly expenditure of migrant labourers according to their skills of occupation in Mumbai. The average monthly expenditure was INR 5066 per migrant labourer (Table 3.13).

Analysis of variance (ANOVA) table shows that the F value is 25.519 and its associated significance value (p-value) is .000, which is less than 0.05. Therefore, we reject the null hypothesis and say that there are differences in the mean monthly expenditure of migrant labourers according to their skills of occupation (Table 3.14).

The means plot shows that the highest amount of expenditure was observed with INR 6675 in the case of security guards while it was in the range of INR 4850 to INR 4975 for drivers, tailors, welders, plumbers, electricians, masons, manual labourers and electricians (Figure 3.3).

Table 3.13. Description of per month expenditure of migrant labourers by skill of occupations

Occupation of migrant labourers	N	Mean of per month expenditure in INR	Std. Deviation	Std. Error	95% confidence interval for mean		Minimum	Maximum
					Lower bound	Upper Bound		
Driver	20	4750	500.00000	111.80340	4515.9928	4984.0072	3500.00	5000.00
Tailor	20	4775	343.16637	76.73433	4614.3932	4935.6068	4000.00	5000.00
Welder	20	4850	285.62029	63.86664	4716.3256	4983.6744	4000.00	5000.00
Plumber	20	4775	379.57733	84.87607	4597.3523	4952.6477	4000.00	5000.00
Mason	20	4875	319.33319	71.40507	4725.5475	5024.4525	4000.00	5000.00
Manual Labourer	20	4950	223.60680	50.00000	4845.3488	5054.6512	4000.00	5000.00
Electrician	20	4975	111.80340	25.00000	4922.6744	5027.3256	4500.00	5000.00
Security Guard	20	6675	1359.90518	304.08404	6038.5448	7311.4552	5000.00	8000.00
Street Vendor	20	4975	111.80340	25.00000	4922.6744	5027.3256	4500.00	5000.00
Total	180	5066	781.06073	58.21683	4951.7871	5181.5463	3500.00	8000.00

Source: Field Survey, 2019

3.14. Analysis of variance (ANOVA)

	Sum of Squares	Df	Mean Square	F	Sig.
Between Groups	59425000.000	8	7428125.000	25.519	.000
Within Groups	49775000.000	171	291081.871		
Total	109200000.000	179			

Source: Field Survey, 2019

Figure 3.3. Means plot- occupation and per month expenditure

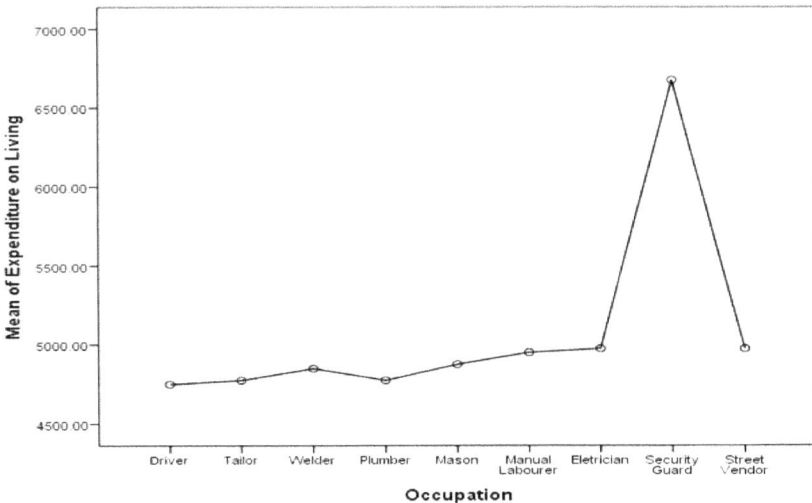

Source: Field survey, 2019

3.2.3. Economic aspects of Mumbai based migration

It is observed that the nature of migration from Uttar Pradesh and Bihar to Mumbai was based on seasonal and temporary migration from the perspective of the economic consequence of short-term internal migration. In this study, a vast majority of the seasonal and temporary migrant labourers migrated to Mumbai due to availability of the better jobs with higher wages compared to low wages in Uttar Pradesh and Bihar. Therefore, economic reason was the major cause behind the labour migration but it was also realized that a well-developed social network system of migration also worked as a pull factor in the process of seasonal and temporary migration from Uttar Pradesh and Bihar to Mumbai. In this study, it was also realized that both push and pull factors of migration were correlated with the function of migration but the pull factor of migration was the major trigger for labour migration from rural Uttar Pradesh and Bihar to Mumbai because migrant labourers decided about migration on the cost and benefit analysis about availability of the jobs with higher wages in Mumbai compared to low wages in Uttar Pradesh and Bihar. Therefore, it is found that the theory of new economics of labour migration led the entire process of migration from the geographical region of North India to Mumbai but it is also observed that migrant labourers migrated within the well-developed economic region of migration from rural Uttar Pradesh and Bihar to Mumbai through the well-developed route of migration.[19]

It is also observed that these North Indian migrant labourers were intergenerational involved in the process of internal migration based on their economic values about Mumbai-based migration because seasonally and temporary internal migrant labourers developed an economic landscape of migration in the consequences of globalization of migration. Therefore, Mumbai-based internal migration can be considered as economic migration based on the economic rationalism of migrant labourers about seasonal and temporary migration where the cycle of migration was based on the frequency of two spells (January to June & September to November) of migration in one year because mostly seasonal and temporary migrant labourers returned to root during heavy rainfall in Mumbai due to problem in adjustment in slums areas of Mumbai. In this study, it was a very important phenomenon that mostly migrant labourers were not interested in their engagement as agricultural labourers in rural Uttar Pradesh and Bihar due to

---

[19] Information is based on informal interviews and passive observation methods among migrant labourers in a sample area namely the Null bazaar area of Mumbai in February 2019.

low wages, as well as the glamour of Mumbai-based migration, was a major cause behind the process of exclusion of labourers from agriculture sector. Therefore, the nature of seasonal and temporary internal migration was the shifting of labourers from the primary sector of the agricultural economy to the tertiary sector service-based urban economy of Mumbai as the consequence of the globalization of the urban-based economy of India.[20]

In this study, it was also realized that there was an interconnection between internal and international migration because seasonal and temporary migrant labourers migrated to Mumbai with hopes of better jobs with higher wages in Dubai compared to low wages in Mumbai. Therefore, short-term internal migration facilitated the long-term international migration from rural Uttar Pradesh and Bihar to Dubai via Mumbai. Therefore, the matter of wage differential was a major cause behind the shifting of internal migrant labourers toward international migration in the context of globalization of migration in rural North India. In these perspectives, both internal and international migration were correlated to each other by similar economic causes like the matter of wage differential between root and destination led to the nature of economic migration.[21]

Therefore, the nature and function of short-term internal migration were based global urban economy from the perspective of response to low wages in the agriculture-based economy of rural Uttar Pradesh and Bihar. Therefore, the shifting of migrant labourers from an agriculture-based economy to an urban urban-based economy is the consequence of the huge return of urban-based economy compared to low return in an agriculture-based economy. From these perspectives, the economic image of internal migration was based on the transformation and shifting of labourers from an agro-based economy to an urban-based economy due to wage differential with well-developed economic regions of migration from Uttar Pradesh and Bihar to Mumbai. The consequence of economic migration was based on the globalization of the informal economy in the aspect of the positive role of labour intensive labour market where seasonal and temporary migrant labourers used to find a secure economic position in the urban-based economy of Mumbai.[22]

---

[20] Information is based on focus group interviews and passive observation among migrant labourers in a sample area namely Na Khuda Mohalla area of Mumbai in February 2019.
[21] Information is based on passive observation and informal interviews among migrant labourers in a sample area namely Na Khuda Mohalla area of Mumbai in February 2019.
[22] Information is based on focus group interviews among migrant labourers in a sample area namely Bhindi Bazar of Mumbai in February 2019.

Based on the above concise description and analysis, globalization worked as positive and negative aspects in the process of functioning migration from Uttar Pradesh and Bihar to Mumbai due to globalization of the informal economy with the transformation of migrant labourers from agro labourers to service-based labourers with the response of higher wages in economic migration of rural migrant labourers in Mumbai. Therefore, short-term internal migration was triggered by the role of individual economics of rural migrant labourers, who had their economic calculation concerning the inter-state rural-urban migration in the framework of globalization of migration. As a consequence, the matter of economic rationalism of migrant labourers was based on the cost and benefit analysis of investment of their labour power in the production of goods and services in the urban-based economy due to the huge return of investment in the informal economy of Mumbai. Therefore, seasonal and temporary migrant labourers migrated from an agro-based economy to an urban-based economy based on the logical interpretation of comparative analysis about the nature of jobs and wages between the rural-based economy of Uttar Pradesh and the urban-based economy of Mumbai in the context of globalization of the urban-based economy in India in the twenty-first century. Therefore, the nature of short-term internal migration was based on the heartland of the economic capital of India and its role in facilitating migration from rural India to urban India.

It is observed that unskilled and semi-skilled migrant labourers worked in the bottom segment of the informal labour market with the uncertainty of the labour market. These migrant labourers used to access minimum basic needs of lives in their life because there was not any proper mechanism of minimum wages for labourers in Mumbai due to a lack of social and economic needs for labourers. It is observed that there was a well-developed economic bond among migrant labourers as well as between North Indian migrant labourers and local *Marathis* of Mumbai. These consequences led to labour productivity with the investment of positive attitudes, values and norms concerning the working culture of Mumbai because the entire economic function of the informal economy was based on the investment of labour power of migrant labourers of Uttar Pradesh and Bihar. It is also observed that these migrant labourers were known as Bhaiya[23] and the term Bhaiya was associated with economic identity as hard and honest North Indian labourers in the economy of Mumbai. These consequences were helpful in the sense of increasing labour productivity in the informal economy in the consequences of the

---

[23] Bhaiya is the identity of North Indian migrant labourers in Mumbai. Cited from: Shrivastava, M. (2015). The 'Bhojpuriya'Mumbaikar: Straddling Two Worlds. *Contributions to Indian Sociology*, *49*(1), 77-101.

globalization of the nexus of migration and the informal economy.[24]

Migrant labourers of Uttar Pradesh and Bihar worked with uncertain conditions in the informal economy and these circumstances determined the vulnerable working and living conditions of migrant labourers in Mumbai because most migrant labourers of Uttar Pradesh and Bihar lived in the slums areas namely- *Dharavi* [25] in Mumbai due to huge presence of North Indian unskilled labourers in slums area. Therefore, it is observed that the living conditions of migrant labourers suffered from critical vulnerable conditions but migrant labourers developed their adjustment mechanism in the adjustment of life in Mumbai. These migrant labourers used to send monthly remittances to their households in Uttar Pradesh and Bihar as well as played an important role in the economic transformation in the development of Mumbai. These migrant labourers had their kholee (temporary unplanned tin-made single-storey houses and Mahalia kholee (double-storey houses) in slum areas of Mumbai but it is also observed that there was prominent chall (planned settlement pattern) settlement among migrant labourers in Mumbai.

Box 3.6: Case Study[26]

"It is a case study of 40 years old migrant labourer, named Ladle who was from Inayat Patti village, Prayagraj district in Uttar Pradesh, and worked as an entrepreneur in Mumbai. He said that he proudly considered himself a chedabhai. He also said that mostly migrant labourers of Inayat Patti village worked in an informal economy with the economic identity of chedabhai in Mumbai. These consequences can be analyzed in the framework of the role of economic function in the formation of the economic identity of migrant labourers in the informal economy of Mumbai."

These consequences can be analyzed in the framework of the settlement pattern of migrant labourers according to their economic capacity in the working environment of Mumbai. It was also observed that those migrant labourers lived in chall known as chedabhai (individual migrant labourers, who lived on rent in the room) and the identity of chedabhai was a new identity in the environment of Mumbai. These consequences showed that migrant labourers of Uttar Pradesh and Bihar were associated with the matter of identity in the context of investment of labour power in the function of the informal economy and its role in the building capacity of economic

---

[24] Information is based on focus group and informal interviews among migrant labourers in the sample areas namely the Masjid Bander area of Mumbai in February 2019.

[25]*Dharavi* is Asia's largest slum area in Mumbai as well as the heartland for seasonal and temporary migrant labourers of Uttar Pradesh and Bihar. Cited from: Dyson, P. (2012). Slum tourism: representing and interpreting 'reality'in Dharavi, Mumbai. *Tourism Geographies, 14*(2), 254-274.

[26] Information is based on personal interview with respondent in the Kolkata building in the sample area of Null Bazar of Mumbai in February 2019.

identities of migrant labourers in working and living culture of unskilled and semi-skilled migrant labourers.[27] vIt is also observed that there was a significant impact of women empowerment in the informal economy of Mumbai because wives of migrant labourers were also engaged in job markets and these consequences were helpful in the gender-based economic discourse and development practices in the informal economy in Mumbai. Wives of migrant labourers from Uttar Pradesh and Bihar used to operate community-based kitchens known as Bissee in the slum areas of Mumbai and migrant labourers used to take two times food per day to pay INR 3000 per month. These consequences led leading the role of women in developing adjustment mechanisms for male migrant labourers through the participation of women migrant labourers in the informal economy of Mumbai. [28]

Box 3.7: Case Study[29]

"It is a case study of 56 years old women migrant labourer named Chanda who belonged to Inayat Patti village and operated a community-based kitchen –Bissee in the slum areas of Mumbai. She said that the entire mechanism of Bissee was based on the positive role of women's participation in the informal economy of Mumbai. These consequences can be analyzed in the framework of feminism-based discussion concerning the role of women migrant labourers in the form of Nari Sakti (women's power) in the development of building capacity of the informal economy in Mumbai."

It is also observed that there was a huge presence of African Sudani women in Mumbai, those who came to Mumbai for business. These African women also played an important role in the development of the informal economy of roadside informal businesses in Mumbai. These consequences helped give a space to African women in the informal economy in Mumbai. These African women were known as Amma among the local Marathis people of Mumbai. It is observed that the identity of Amma emerged as a new economic identity for women in the informal economy of Mumbai in the sense of the positive role of African women as roadside entrepreneurs. These African women used to purchase commodities in Mumbai and sell in the local market of Sudan due to the globalization of the informal economy of Mumbai.[30]

Therefore, it can be analyzed that the informal economy was the heartland for migrant labourers of Uttar Pradesh and Bihar as well as gave an economic

---

[27] Information is based on focus group and passive observation method in the sample area of the *Dharavi* slum area of Mumbai in February 2019.

[28] Information is based on informal interview with respondent in the *Dharavi* sample area of Mumbai in February 2019.

[29] Information is based on a personal interview with a respondent named Chanda in Inayat Patti village, who operated *Bissi* in the *Dharavi* slum areas of Mumbai.

[30] Information is based on the passive observation method among African women at the roadside night market in Masjid Bander sample area of Mumbai in February 2019.

space to migrant labourers for developing their adjustment mechanism according to their working and living conditions in Mumbai.

3.3. International destination: Dubai

A study by Taukeer (2022) shows that the culture of Dubai is the hub for South Asian migrant labourers because these South Asian migrant labourers work in a diverse cultural environment in Dubai. A study by Zachariah et al. (2004) shows that Indian migrant labourers face the problem of vulnerable working conditions in the global working environment in Dubai. In these consequences, the study of Rahman (2010) gives a realistic picture of the issues of labour rights of Indian migrant labourers in Gulf countries because Indian migrant labourers face problems of harassment and exploitation in the working environment in Gulf countries. A study by Naufal & Ali (2010) shows that contract-based South Asian migrant labourers send huge remittances to India because they get higher wages and this consequence sustains them in the working environment of Gulf countries. A study by Nadjmabadi (2010) shows that result of assimilation and integration between Asian and Arab migrant labourers gives a global cultural working environment in Dubai. These consequences work as a pull factor in the migration process. In the case of Inayat Patti village, the study of Taukeer (2017 & 2023) shows that the economic impact of Dubai-based migration leads to economic migration from Inayat Patti to Dubai due to the expectation of better jobs with higher wages in Dubai compared to low wages in the rural-based economy in Inayat Patti village.

Based on the above concise description of the nature of migration in Gulf countries, it is realized that Dubai-based international migration is directly associated with the globalization of migration in rural Uttar Pradesh because the trend of internal migration continuously shifted toward international migration in the twenty-first century. Therefore, the findings of this chapter better advocate the consequence of international migration in the context of the economic function of migration. In the case of migration from Inayat Patti village to the United Arab Emirates, it is realized that the tendency of labour migration from Inayat Patti village to the United Arab Emirates is being led by internal migration to Mumbai in the consequence of the globalization of migration in the twenty-first century. Therefore, the findings of the chapter give a base for developing an understanding of the sustainability approach in the context of the nexus of migration and development from the perspective of well-being of migrant labourers in Dubai. Therefore, this chapter better emphasizes the mechanism of the well-being of migrant labourers in the context of the economic consequence of migration in Dubai.

3.3.1. Socio-economic profile of migrant labourers

Labour migration from South Asia to the United Arab Emirates was led by Muslim migrants as well as youth migrant labourers because the average age of the migrant labourer was 28.9 years. Among them, a vast majority of the migrant labourers were married and less educated. Therefore, they worked in the bottom segmentation of the labour market in the United Arab Emirates (Table 3.15).

Table 3.15. Socio-economic profile of migrant labourers

Indicators	Description
Age	Out of the total migrant labourers(n=180), nearly 97.0 per cent(n=175) of the migrant labourers were in the age groups between 22 and 33 years while the rest were in the age group between 34 and 39 years.
Religion	Out of the total migrant labourers (n=180), nearly 93.0 per cent (n=168) migrant labourers were Muslims and the rest were Hindus.
Marital Status	Out of the total migrant labourers (180), nearly 70.6 per cent (n=127) of migrant labourers were married and the rest migrant labourers were unmarried.
Education Status of Migrant Labourers	Out of the total migrant labourers (n=180), nearly 89.0 per cent (n=161) of the migrant labourers were educated from middle-level education to intermediate and the rest of the migrant labourers had a bachelor degree.

Source: Field Survey, 2019

3.3.2. Structure of income, remittances and expenditure of Indian migrant labourers in United Arab Emirates

Occupation and income of migrant labourers

Null and alternative hypotheses are the following:

H_0= There is no difference in the mean monthly income of migrant labourers according to their skills of occupation.

H_1 = There is a difference in the mean monthly income of migrant labourers according to their skills of occupation.

There are differences in the mean monthly income of migrant labourers according to their skills of occupation in the United Arab Emirates. The average per-month income was AED 2382 per migrant labourer (Table 3.16).

Table 3.16. Descriptive statistics of per month income of migrant labourers by skill of occupations

Occupation of migrant labourers	N	Mean of per month income of migrant labourers in Dirham (AED)	Std. Deviation	Std. Error	95% Confidence Interval for Mean		Minimum	Maximum
					Lower Bound	Upper Bound		
Manual Labourers	20	1907	105.47512	23.58495	1858.1361	1956.8639	1750.00	2000.00
Mason	20	2190	120.96106	27.04772	2133.3885	2246.6115	2000.00	2400.00
Carpenter	20	2155	135.62720	30.32716	2091.5245	2218.4755	1800.00	2400.00
Driver	20	2405	131.68943	29.44665	2343.3675	2466.6325	2200.00	2800.00
Welder	20	2290	116.52874	26.05662	2235.4629	2344.5371	2000.00	2400.00
Tailor	20	2340	94.03247	21.02630	2295.9914	2384.0086	2200.00	2400.00
Electrician	20	2870	159.27467	35.61490	2795.4572	2944.5428	2500.00	3000.00
Plumber	20	2915	134.84884	30.15312	2851.8888	2978.1112	2500.00	3000.00
Sweeper in Hotel/ Restaurants	20	2370	92.33805	20.64742	2326.7845	2413.2155	2200.00	2500.00
Total	180	2382.0	330.20541	24.61206	2333.9329	2431.0671	1750.00	3000.00

Source: Field Survey, 2019
Note: Average exchange rate of UAE Dirham (AED) was INR (India) 19.1681, 2019. Source: www.exchangerates.org.uk

Analysis of variance (ANOVA) table shows that the F value is 140.082 and its associated significance value (p-value) is .000, which is less than 0.05. Therefore, we reject the null hypothesis and say that there are differences in the mean monthly income of migrant labourers according to their skills of occupation (Table 3.17).

Table 3.17. Analysis of variance (ANOVA)

	Sum of Squares	Df	Mean Square	F	Sig.
Between Groups	16933500.000	8	2116687.500	140.082	.000
Within Groups	2583875.000	171	15110.380		
Total	19517375.000	179			

Source: Field Survey, 2019

The means plot also shows that there are variations and differences in the mean monthly income of migrant labourers according to their skills of occupation in the United Arab Emirates. Plumbers got higher per month income while manual labourers got the lowest per month income among groups of migrant labourers (Figure 3.4).

Figure 3.4. Means plot- occupation and per month income

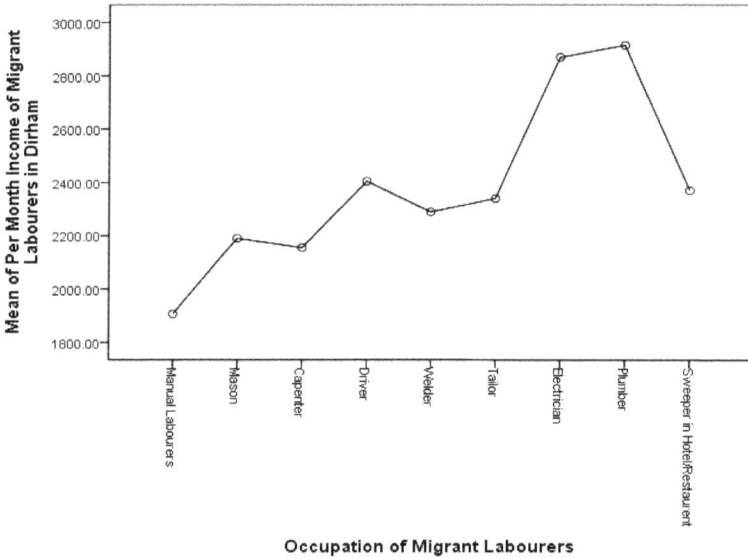

Occupation of Migrant Labourers

Source: Field survey, 2019

Occupation and remittances of migrant labourers

Null and alternative hypotheses are the following:

H_0= There is no difference in the mean monthly remittances of migrant labourers according to their skills of occupation.

H_1 = There is a difference in the mean monthly remittances of migrant labourers according to their skills of occupation.

There are differences in the mean monthly remittances of migrant labourers according to their skills of occupation in the United Arab Emirates. The average per-month remittance was Dirham (AED) 1741 per migrant labourer (Table 3.18).

Analysis of variance (ANOVA) table shows that the F value is 104.285 and its associated significance value (p-value) is .000, which is less than 0.05. Therefore, we reject the null hypothesis and say that there are differences in the mean monthly remittances of migrant labourers according to their skills of occupation (Table 3.19).

The means plot shows that there are differences in the mean monthly remittances of migrant labourers according to their skills of occupation. Here, the highest remittance was observed in the case of plumbers while manual labourers sent the lowest remittances among the group of migrant labourers (Figure 3.5).

Table 3.18. Descriptive statistics of per month remittances of migrant labourers by skill of occupations

Occupation of Migrant Labourers	N	mean of per month income in Dirham (AED)	Std. Deviation	Std. Error	95% Confidence Interval for Mean		Minimum	Maximum
					Lower Bound	Upper Bound		
Manual Labourers	20	1305	109.90426	24.57534	1253.5632	1356.4368	1200.00	1500.00
Mason	20	1550	68.82472	15.38968	1517.7890	1582.2110	1400.00	1600.00
Carpenter	20	1565	48.93605	10.94243	1542.0972	1587.9028	1500.00	1600.00
Driver	20	1790	71.81848	16.05910	1756.3879	1823.6121	1500.00	1900.00
Welder	20	1645	160.50906	35.89092	1569.8794	1720.1206	1400.00	1800.00
Tailor	20	1755	109.90426	24.57534	1703.5632	1806.4368	1500.00	1800.00
Electrician	20	2210	246.87521	55.20297	2094.4588	2325.5412	1800.00	2400.00
Plumber	20	2260	195.74419	43.76973	2168.3889	2351.6111	2000.00	2400.00
Sweeper in Hotel/Restaurant	20	1595	82.55779	18.46048	1556.3618	1633.6382	1500.00	1800.00
Total	180	1741	324.05858	24.15390	1694.0036	1789.3297	1200.00	2400.00

Source: Field Survey, 2019
Note: Average exchange rate of UAE Dirham (AED) was INR (India) 19.1681,2019. Source: www.exchangerates.org.uk

Table 3.19. Analysis of variances (ANOVA)

	Sum of Squares	Df	Mean Square	F	Sig.
Between Groups	15600000.000	8	1950000.000	104.285	.000
Within Groups	3197500.000	171	18698.830		
Total	18797500.000	179			

Source: Field Survey, 2019

Figure 3.5. Means plot- occupation and per month remittance

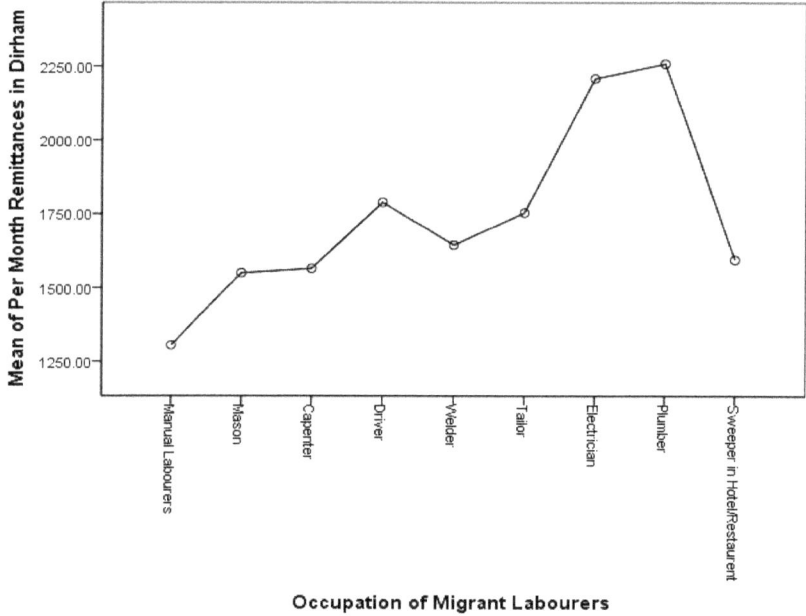

Occupation of Migrant Labourers

Source: Field survey, 2019

Occupation and expenditure of migrant labourers

Null and alternative hypotheses are the following:

H_0= There is no difference in the mean monthly expenditure of migrant labourers according to their skills of occupation.

H_1 = There is a difference in the mean monthly expenditure of migrant labourers according to their skills of occupation.

There are differences in the mean monthly expenditure of migrant labourers according to their skills of occupation in the United Arab Emirates. The average per-month expenditure was AED 633 Dirham per migrant labourer (Table 3.20).

Table 3.20. Descriptive statistics of per month expenditure of migrant labourers by skill of occupations

Occupational Classification of Migrant Labourers	N	Mean of per month expenditure in Dirham (AED)	Std. Deviation	Std. Error	95% Confidence Interval for Mean		Minimum	Maximum
					Lower Bound	Upper Bound		
Manual Labourers	20	605	51.04178	11.41329	581.1117	628.8883	500.00	800.00
Mason	20	615	81.27277	18.17314	576.9632	653.0368	400.00	800.00
Carpenter	20	585	48.93605	10.94243	562.0972	607.9028	400.00	600.00
Driver	20	640	68.05570	15.21772	608.1489	671.8511	600.00	800.00
Welder	20	645	51.04178	11.41329	621.1117	668.8883	600.00	700.00
Tailor	20	610	30.77935	6.88247	595.5948	624.4052	600.00	700.00
Electrician	20	695	75.91547	16.97521	659.4705	730.5295	600.00	800.00
Plumber	20	700	102.59784	22.94157	651.9827	748.0173	600.00	800.00
Sweeper in Hotel/Restaurants	20	605	22.36068	5.00000	594.5349	615.4651	600.00	700.00
Total	180	633	73.23338	5.45849	622.5621	644.1046	400.00	800.00

Source: Field Survey, 2019

Note: Average exchange rate of UAE Dirham (AED) was INR (India) 19.1681, in 2019. Source: www.exchangerates.org.uk

Analysis of variance (ANOVA) table shows that the F value is 8.150 and its associated significance value (p-value) is .000, which is less than 0.05. Therefore, we reject the null hypothesis and say that there are differences in the mean monthly expenditure of migrant labourers according to their skills of occupation (Table 3.21).

Table 3.21. Analysis of variance (ANOVA)

	Sum of Squares	Df	Mean Square	F	Sig.
Between Groups	265000.000	8	33125.000	8.150	.000
Within Groups	695000.000	171	4064.327		
Total	960000.000	179			

Source: Field Survey, 2019

The means plot shows that there are differences in the mean monthly expenditure of migrant labourers. Among the group of migrant labourers, plumbers expended highest on the consumption of food and non-food items while carpenters expended lowest on the consumption of food and non-food items (Figure 3.6).

Figure 3.6. Means plot- occupation and per month expenditure

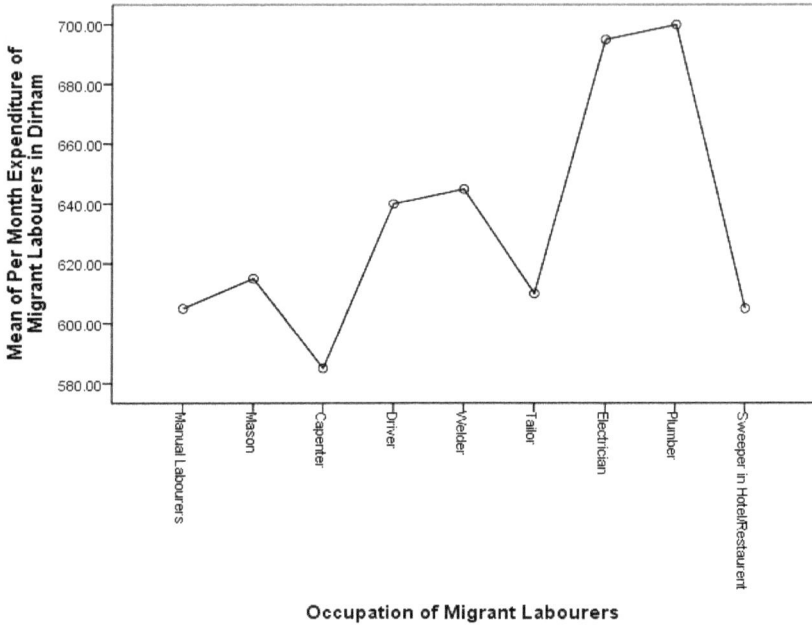

Occupation of Migrant Labourers

Source: Field survey, 2019

3.3.3. Nature of migration in Dubai

It is observed that the matter of migration from India to Gulf countries was based on the wage differential between India and the United Arab Emirates because migrant labourers got better jobs with higher wages compared to low wages in India. These consequences worked as a pull factor in the process of labour migration from India to Gulf countries in the context of globalization of migration in the twenty-first century. Both economic and non-economic phenomena like the well-developed social network system of migration were correlated with the process of migration from India to Gulf countries because the well-developed culture of migration was caused by the economic factors of migration in Dubai. It is realized that both push and pull factors worked in the process of facilitating labour migration from India to the United Arab Emirates but the expectation of availability of the better jobs with higher wages was more relevant compared to problems of unemployment and low wages in India because well developed social network system of migration forwarded the pull factor of migration from India to the United Arab Emirates. Therefore, it is found that the theory of new economics of labour migration was the major cause behind the migration from India to Gulf countries based on cost and benefit analysis about the availability of jobs and wages in the United Arab Emirates because labourers used to analyze both economic and non-economic benefit of international long term migration in the context of availability of jobs and wages in India. Therefore, the nature of migration from India to the United Arab Emirates was based on the individual economics of migrant labourers based on the social network system of migration within the well-developed economic region of migration from India to the United Arab Emirates. Therefore, migrant labourers found themselves in a better economic position in Dubai due to access to higher wages in Dubai compared to low wages in Mumbai. Therefore, the function of migration from India to the United Arab Emirates was being triggered by pull factors like higher wages in Dubai but there was the least impact of push factors like low wages in Mumbai as well and well-developed social network system of migration led to the entire economic migration.[31]

It was found that migration from rural Uttar Pradesh to the United Arab Emirates was based on internal to international migration because mostly migrant labourers worked in cities of India before migration to the United Arab Emirates. These consequences were directly associated with the role of the economic impact of internal migration in the process of facilitating labour migration from India to the global city of Dubai. Therefore, it is observed that Dubai's model of the economy was a heartland for labour migration from rural Uttar Pradesh and Bihar to Dubai via internal migration to Mumbai because migrant labourers migrated to Mumbai due to availability of the better jobs with higher wages compared to the low wages in the rural-based economy of Uttar Pradesh and Bihar but later then spending two to three years in Mumbai, these migrant labourers migrated to Dubai due to availability of the better jobs with higher wages in Dubai compared to low wages in Mumbai. Therefore, there was an interconnection between Mumbai-based internal migration and Dubai-based international migration in the process of dual step internal to international migration in the context of globalization of migration in rural Uttar Pradesh. The consequences of globalization of migration minimized the geographical and psychological distance between rural Uttar Pradesh and Dubai because migrant labourers found a well-developed social network system of migration with psychological bonding in Dubai. These consequences increased the role of social integration in labour productivity in the context of the positive role of

---

[31] Information is based on passive observation and informal interviews among migrant labourers in the sample area of Dubai in December 2019.

migration in the development of building capacity of the individual economic capacity of migrant labourers in the global city of Dubai.[32]

It is also observed that Indian migrant labourers played an important role in the development practices of Dubai because there was a huge presence of migrant labourers from Uttar Pradesh and Bihar, those were involved in the bottom segmentation of the labour market in Dubai as well as developed an economic identity of migrant labourers as "hard-working mute labourers" in the global working environment of Dubai. It was also found that Indian migrant labourers considered Dubai as Mumbai because these Indian migrant labourers found similar economic conditions in Dubai due to interconnection between Mumbai-based internal migration and Dubai-based international migration but only matter of wages were caused behind the differences between internal and international migration because migrant labourers gained higher wages in Dubai compared to low wages in Mumbai. Therefore, the shifting paradigm of internal to international migration was being led by global factors of migration like globalization of migration in rural Uttar Pradesh and Bihar due to well-developed economic region of migration from rural India to Dubai via internal migration to Mumbai.[33]

Box 3.8: Case Study[34]

"It is a case study of 24 years old migrant labourer, named Rakesh who was from the Fatehpur district of Uttar Pradesh, in India. He said that he worked in a marble factory in Jaipur city of India before migrating to Dubai. He also said that the experience of internal migration played giving important role in the process of adjusting to Dubai-based international migration. He gained higher wages in the marble factory of Dubai compared to India. These consequences showed that there was an interconnection between internal and international migration where internal migration led to the process of international migration in the context of globalization of migration."

Based on the above concise description, it can be analyzed that the matter of Dubai-based international migration was deeply associated with the phenomena of the global factor of migration due to the global image of Dubai. Therefore, the nature of international migration was based on internal migration where both economic and non-economic causes led to the process of migration from rural Uttar Pradesh and Bihar to Gulf countries within well-developed economic regions of migration. Migrant labourers used to make the economic decision of migration based on analysis of their economic capacity due to the depth penetration of globalization of migration on the

---

[32] Information is based on informal interviews among migrant labourers at parks in Dubai in December 2019.

[33] Information is based on a personal interview of a respondent at a park in Deira in Dubai in December 2019.

[34] Information is based on informal interviews among migrant labourers in a sample area of Dubai in December 2019.

ground level in rural Uttar Pradesh and Bihar. These consequences were the result of the desire of migrant labourers to engage them in the global city of Dubai because Dubai worked for them as a dream with the expectation of a better life. Therefore, Dubai worked as the economic culture for migrant labourers, who found the matter of migration a major source of bread and butter for their individual life with a strategy of survival for their family members at the root level in rural Uttar Pradesh and Bihar in the consequence of the globalization of migration in the twenty-first century. [35]

It is observed that there was the existence of a dual labour market system in the United Arab Emirates where unskilled and semi-skilled migrant labourers worked in the bottom segmentation of the labour market according to the dynamics of labour-intensive labour market. These consequences created an economic identity of migrant labourers as cheap and mute labourers because these migrant labourers accepted such kinds of jobs that were denied by Arabians due to poor working conditions in labour-intensive labour market. These Indian migrant labourers worked as contract labourers under their sponsor as well as accessed the social and economic rights of labourers according to the provisions of labour rights according to the rules, regulations and acts of labour laws of the United Arab Emirates. These Indian migrant labourers had sufficient information about the economic nature of the labour market of Dubai because they were more aware of the emerging phenomena of the dynamics of the job market in Dubai.

Box 3.9: Case Study[36]

"It is a case study of 48 years migrant labourer named Azaz Ahamed, who worked in Gulf countries and belonged to Inayat Patti village, He said that he worked as a manual labourer and Arabians called him Ghulam (slave labourer) but Azaz mutely tolerated pain of crisis of identity in Gulf country because his sponsor might cancel the visa. These consequences can be analyzed as the panic condition of unskilled migrant labourers in the bottom segmentation of the labour market in the Gulf country."

The economic consequence of the dual labour market system worked as a pull factor in the process of facilitating labour migration from India to labour labour-intensive labour market of Gulf countries under the dual labour market theory in Gulf countries. These consequences created a hurdle economic situation for unskilled and semi-skilled migrant labourers because these Indian migrant labourers have to face problems of economic challenges in the bottom segmentation of the labour market. After all, Arabians recognized these unskilled and semi-skilled Indian migrant labourers as slave

---

[35] Information is based on informal interviews among migrant labourers in a sample area of Dubai in December 2019.
[36] Information is based on personal interviews of respondent in Inayat Patti village in February 2015.

labourers.[37] It is also observed that these unskilled and semi-skilled Indian migrant labourers were happy with their working conditions. They got higher wages in Dubai as well as well-developed economic bonding between Indian migrant labourers and Arabians because both completed necessity of each other. There was a proper mechanism of management of income for migrant labourers in the United Arab Emirates because these Indian migrant labourers got training about managing income in the Tawjeeh centre in the United Arab Emirates. Therefore, these Indian migrant labourers used to manage their income into three parts including to sixty per cent of income was sent as remittances in India followed by twenty per cent used to spend on expenditure on food and non-food items and the rest part of the income deposited in a savings account in United Arab Emirates. These consequences can be analyzed as the role of economic management of income for unskilled and semi-skilled migrant labourers; those are the backbone for the economy of India with the economy of the United Arab Emirates.[38]

Box 3.10: Case Study[39]

"It is a case study of 28 years old migrant labourer, named Saddam Ahamed, who was from Inayat Patti village and worked as an AC technician in Dubai. He said that there were favourable economic conditions for Indian migrant labourers in the United Arab Emirates due to the global economic image of India among Arabians in the United Arab Emirates. Therefore, Indian migrant labourers liked to working environment of the United Arab Emirates due to availability of the better jobs with higher wages in Dubai compared to low wages in Mumbai. These consequences can be analyzed as the role of Dubai's model of economy in the process of facilitating labour migration from India to Gulf countries."

It is also observed that these consequences determined the working and living conditions of Indian migrant labourers in the global economic working conditions of the United Arab Emirates and these consequences were helpful in the development of building capacity of the Indian economic diaspora in the global economic culture of Dubai. It was also observed that these unskilled and semi-skilled Indian migrant labourers lived in labour apartments where they used to access better facilities of electricity, air conditioning rooms, bathrooms, washrooms and kitchens. These consequences minimized the psycho–panic conditions of long-term migration as well as providing them an economic space for adjusting to the

---

[37] Information is based on the passive observation method among migrant labourers in the sample area of Dubai in December 2019.

[38] Information is based on passive observation and informal interviews among migrant labourers in labour apartments in Dubai in December 2019.

[39] Information is based on a personal interview of a respondent at a restaurant in Dubai in December 2019.

global economic culture of Dubai.[40]

Therefore, it can be finalized that Indian migrant labourers played an important role in the economic function and development of Dubai through depth penetration of globalization of migration with the well-developed route of migration from rural Uttar Pradesh and Bihar to Dubai via internal migration to Mumbai. These consequences were directly associated with the culture of migration in the context of the safe zone of migration within the economic region of migration from rural India to Dubai in the context of globalization.

---

[40] Information is based on the passive observation method among migrant labourers in a sample area of Dubai in December 2019.

CHAPTER 4

MIGRATION AND CULTURAL PARADIGM

4.1. Nexus of migration and culture

According to Taukeer (2022), there is a reciprocal relationship between migration and culture because culture leads to migration as well as migration creates cultural phenomena in the context of the nexus of social remittances and social changes in migrant households. These consequences are positively associated with cultural transformation among migrants in the context of the positive role of social remittances like values, norms, and cultural beliefs. These perspectives developed a mechanism concerning the social and cultural benefits of migration. In the case of Uttar Pradesh, the study of Taukeer (2021) shows that both internal and international remittances ensured the socio-economic and cultural benefit of migration in the consequences of globalization of culture of migration from rural Uttar Pradesh to Gulf countries via Mumbai. A study by Taukeer (2020) shows that cultural benefit of migration is positively associated with the phenomena of internal to international migration where the culture of internal migration leads to the culture of international migration due to the long-term benefit of migration in the sense of diaspora philanthropy in Uttar Pradesh.

In the case of Uttar Pradesh, the study of Taukeer (2023) shows that cordial nexus between culture and migration developed a cultural region of migration in rural Uttar Pradesh as well as created a neighbour effect of migration on non-migrant households because non-migrant households were being continuously involved in process of Gulf migration due to well-developed culture of migration in rural Uttar Pradesh. In the case of Inayat Patti village, according to Taukeer (2017), there is a significant impact of the Gulf remittances on the socio-economic development of the village and consequences of socio-economic development ensured the cultural transformation in migrant households due to the confluent of north Indian culture and Arabian culture in the village. The consequence of assimilation and integration between north Indian and Arabian cultures developed a mixed cultural landscape in Inayat Patti village in Prayagraj district, Uttar Pradesh, India. A study by Majumder & Taukeer (2019) shows that impact of Gulf remittances created a demonstration impact of migration and these consequences developed a culture of migration from Inayat Patti to Saudi Arabia via short-term internal migration in Mumbai. Hence, the phenomena of the culture of short-term internal migration caused the culture of long-term international migration. A study by Majumder (2022) shows that impact of the pandemic of COVID-19 started a reverse migration from Saudi Arabia and Mumbai to Inayat Patti. These consequences developed cultural values about the nexus of migration and the pandemic of COVID-19 because migrant labourers had lots of mythology, values, beliefs and norms concerning the Gulf migration in the context of the pandemic of COVID-19.

Based on the above concise analyses of selected review of literature, the present section of the paragraph emphasizes the broad aspect of process, determinants and consequences of the nexus of migration and culture from root to destinations in the context of globalization of migration. Therefore, it is realized that there is a cordial nexus between migration and culture because migration creates cultural phenomena and cultural phenomena lead to the process of migration due to the depth penetration of globalization on ground level. In these consequences, this paragraph gives a realistic picture of the role of cultural values, beliefs, norms, attitudes and myths in the formation of building capacity of migration from rural India to Gulf countries in the twenty-first century.

4.1.1. Migration creates culture and culture leads migration

It is observed that there is a cordial nexus between migration and culture because there is a reciprocal relationship with each other. In this study, it is found that the phenomena of migration were deeply associated with the function of globalization of cultural values of migrants regarding its role in the formation of migration building from rural Uttar Pradesh to Gulf countries via Mumbai. The process of migration from rural Uttar Pradesh to Gulf countries was based on the positive role of the social network system of migration within well-developed cultural regions of migration where a migrant labourer decided based on his/her cost and benefit analysis about the economic decision of migration in the context of dynamics of wishes and abilities of migration. Both wishes and abilities of migrant labourers played important roles in the development of building capacity of cultural migration because it is well known that matter of migration was associated with the aspect of livelihood through their positive role in the cultural migration where these migrant labourers willingly intergenerational involved in the process of migration and taken migration as the key of bread and butter. In this study, it is also realized that the entire function of migration was based on the aspect of cultural values for migrant labourers because these migrant labourers had their own stories, beliefs, values and norms about migration and these consequences developed a mental cultural region among migrant labourers and these consequences determined the psychological behaviour of the migrant labourers as well as socio-economic and cultural transformation in rural Uttar Pradesh, Mumbai and United Arab Emirates. These consequences paved the route of migration through well-developed cultural route of migration from rural Uttar Pradesh to Gulf countries via internal migration to Mumbai.[1]

At the root level in Inayat Patti village, it was found that there was well developed cultural route of migration from rural Uttar Pradesh to Gulf countries via Mumbai where the culture of internal migration was positively associated with the culture of international migration to Gulf countries because both types of migration were correlated to each other by similar cultural phenomena of migration in the context of globalization of migration in rural India. It was found that there was a long historical sequence of migration in Inayat Patti village where both internal and international migration were caused by a similar set of cultural values of migration because migrant labourers migrated from the village to Gulf countries via internal migration to Mumbai. These consequences developed a culture of dual-step[2] migration in the context of a similar index of cultural migration. Apart, these consequences developed a cultural route of migration within the well-developed cultural region of migration because these migrant labourers used to take the matter of migration as an aspect of cultural status due to availability of the better jobs with higher wages in Gulf countries compared to low wages in the rural-based economy in the village. It was also found that both economic and non-economic phenomena were positively associated with the culture of migration but non-economic phenomena like the culture of migration led to the entire process of migration through the well-developed route of migration where migrant labourers found socio-economic and cultural support in the entire routes of migration. These consequences were helpful in the process of facilitating labour migration through the role of culture of migration. In the context of the impact of COVID-19, it is observed that the impact of the pandemic COVID-19 changed the

---

[1] Information is based on informal interviews and passive observation methods among migrants through conducting field surveys from India to Gulf countries from February 2015 to December 2019.

[2] Dual-step migration is a function of internal to international migration where internal migration leads to international migration. Cited from: Majumder, B., & Taukeer, M. (2019). Dual-Step Migration from a Village in Uttar Pradesh: Causes, Processes and Consequences. *Productivity*, *60*(2), 162-174.

perception of return migrant labourers toward migration because these return migrant labourers considered the pandemic COVID-19 as a barrier to migration and livelihood practice.[3]

Box 4.1: Case Study[4]

"It is a case study of 38 year old named Abrar in Inayat Patti village; he said that he migrated to Saudi Arabia via internal migration to Mumbai due to a well-developed route of the culture of migration from the village to Saudi Arabia via Mumbai. He also said that the consequence of the culture of migration paved the route of migration because the matter of Gulf migration was being taken as key to livelihood in the village as well as led to cultural forms of diaspora philanthropy in the village. These consequences can be analyzed as the role of cultural aspects in the process of internal to international migration from Inayat Patti village to Saudi Arabia via internal migration to Mumbai."

In Mumbai, it is realized that there was well developed cultural heartland for migrant labourers of rural Uttar Pradesh and Bihar because these migrant labourers used to take Mumbai as the heartland for their livelihood because these migrant labourers willingly involved in the process of migration with hopes of better life of their family members at root. Therefore, Mumbai-based internal migration was caused by a well-developed route of cultural migration in the context of the globalization of culture of migration in rural Uttar Pradesh and Bihar.

Box 4.2: Case Study[5]

"It is a case study of 54 years old migrant labourer named Zakir Ahamed, who migrated from the neighbouring village of Inayat Patti namely Basgit village in Prayagraj district, Uttar Pradesh. He also said that the matter of Mumbai-based migration was associated with him as a cultural practice of livelihood because he used to take the culture of Mumbai-based migration as the key of livelihood and did not think of another source of income instead of migration. Therefore, it can be analyzed that the matter of culture of internal migration was deeply rooted in the cultural livelihood practices of migrant labourers in Mumbai."

It is observed that there was a huge cultural impact of migration on the livelihood practices of migrant labourers because migrant labourers developed a cultural region of north India in Mumbai and these consequences worked as a pull factor within well developed cultural region of migration from rural Uttar Pradesh and Bihar to Mumbai. It was also found that there were huge numbers of such kinds of migrant labourers, those who worked in Mumbai to gain skills of experiences regarding hopes of migration to Saudi Arabia and the United Arab Emirates with cultural experiences of Mumbai-based internal migration. These consequences were helpful in the ensuring

---

[3] Information is based on passive observation and informal interview methods among return migrant labourers in Inayat Patti village in February 2015.

[4] Information is based on personal interviews from return migrant labourer in Inayat Patti village in March 2015.

[5] Information is based on personal interview from migrant labourer in the Null Bazar area of Mumbai in February 2019.

role of migration in the development of cultural diaspora as well as the role of cultural values in the process of migration from rural Uttar Pradesh and Bihar to Mumbai. These consequences developed a cultural region of migration where short-term internal migration was assimilated into long-term international migration in the form of cultural migration.[6]

In the case of Dubai, it was realized that there was a well-developed cultural diaspora of North Indian migrant labourers, those who worked as contract labourers in the bottom segmentation of labour in the labour market. It is observed that there was a huge presence of migrant labourers from Uttar Pradesh and Bihar in Dubai and these consequences were the result of well-developed cultural migration from rural Uttar Pradesh and Bihar. The form and nature of Dubai-based international migration were deeply associated with the culture of Mumbai-based migration because most migrant labourers expressed that there was a crucial role of the culture of internal migration in the process of their adjustment in the long-term international migration in Dubai.

Box 4.3: Case Study[7]

He also said that there was a well-developed cultural region of migration from Inayat Patti to Dubai via Mumbai because the youth of Inayat Patti never thought about other sources of livelihood instead of migration. Apart from that, the matter of migration was deeply rooted in a form of culture of migration where the wishes and abilities of youth were moving around migration. These consequences can be analyzed in the form of culture of migration by the positive role of the cultural impact of Gulf migration on the wishes and abilities of youth due to the depth penetration of globalization of migration in Inayat Patti village and the consequence of globalization of migration led the cultural migration from village to Dubai."

Therefore, the culture of both internal and international migration was caused by the role of the cultural impact of migration on the living practices of migrant labourers and their family members and these consequences ensured the route of migration within the well-developed cultural region of migration according to the dynamic of wishes and abilities of migrants. Therefore, it was found that the confluent of wishes and abilities determined the cultural boundary of migration from rural Uttar Pradesh and Bihar to Gulf countries where migrant labourers found socio-economic and cultural support for adjusting in the process of long-term cultural migration in Dubai. Therefore, the cultural boundary of migration was determined by values, norms, attitudes, and beliefs about the long journey of the historical consequence of migration in the form of cultural migration led by the

---

[6] Information is based on focus group interviews and passive observation methods among migrant labourers in Nakhuda Mohalla of Mumbai in February 2019.
[7] Information is based on personal interviews from migrant labourer at Karachi Darbar restaurant in Abu Dhabi in December 2019.

globalization of the nexus of migration and culture.[8]

4.2. Formation and consequence of cultural region of migration from root to destinations

4.2.1. Culture of migration: A phenomena

According to Sirkeci (2003), the culture of migration works as a pull factor in the process of labour migration because the consequences of the globalization of migration pave the way for the culture of migration from root to destination in the context of a long journey of the result of migration. Findings of the study of Cohen & Sirkeci (2011) give similar facts concerning the role of cultural facts in the process of facilitating labour migration within well-developed cultural regions of migration because the wishes and abilities of migrants create cultural values of migration as well as facilitate labour migration from origin to destination. The findings of Rahman (2001) show that the culture of labour migration from rural India to Gulf countries is based on the nexus of globalization and migration where depth penetration of globalization leads the way of cultural facts of migration and these consequences ensured the route of culture of migration from rural India to Gulf countries. Apart, the study also shows that there is a cordial nexus between migration and culture because migration creates culture and culture leads migration in the context of the positive role of the cultural globalization of migration in rural India. In these consequences, there is the important role of the cultural region of migration in the context of internal to international migration because findings of the study of Taukeer (2023) show that there is a cordial nexus between the culture of internal and culture of international migration where internal migration from rural India to Mumbai leads the culture of long term international migration to Gulf countries within well-developed culture region of migration. Therefore, the culture of migration work within the well-developed region of migration based on the positive role of the cultural values, beliefs, norms, and attitudes of migrant labourers, is concerning around the international migration from rural India to Gulf countries via internal migration to Mumbai. Likewise, the study of Taukeer (2023) gives a realistic picture of the phenomena of cultural migration in the context of *culturalization* of the economy of migration due to the depth penetration of globalization of migration where the consequence of the globalization of migration reduces the geographical distance between root and destinations as well as paved the route of migration within well developed

---

[8] Information is based on informal interviews of migrant labourers in parks of Dubai in December 2019.

cultural region of migration from rural India to Gulf countries.

4.2.2. Formation of cultural region of migration in Inayat Patti village

It is observed that there was an important role of cultural values in the process of facilitating labour migration from rural Uttar Pradesh to Mumbai and Dubai because migrant labourers used to decide migration based on their wishes and abilities where both wishes and abilities determine the cultural consequence of migration in the context of cost and benefit analysis of migration by role of cultural phenomena of migration. In the case of migration from Inayat Patti village to Saudi Arabia via Mumbai, it is found that there was a long historical sequence of migration within the well-developed cultural route of migration from the village to Saudi Arabia via Mumbai in the consequence of globalization of migration. The consequence of the globalization of migration was deeply associated with cultural practices of livelihood of migrant labourers because a migrant labourer used to be willingly involved in the process of migration. After all, the matter of migration was associated with the socio-economic development of migrant households. Therefore, migrant labourers found migration as a source of livelihood with the support of their kinship network from rural areas to Mumbai and Gulf countries. These consequences motivated migrant labourers to migrate to Saudi Arabia via a culture of internal migration to Mumbai. It is observed that there was the culture of "Bombay-Saudi" migration in Inayat Patti village because both cultural practices of migration were deeply associated with the mobility of youths in the village regarding lead cultural migration in the context of dual step migration where the culture of Mumbai based internal migration led to a culture of Saudi based international migration. It is also observed that migrant labourers used to take both internal and international migration under similar cultural indexes because similar cultural beliefs and norms paved the pathways of migration from Inayat Patti to Saudi Arabia via internal migration to Mumbai. Therefore, both the culture of internal migration and the culture of international migration were assimilated and correlated with each other by the function of the positive role of the globalization of migration in the economy of the village. These consequences developed a cultural landscape of migration due to socio-economic transformation in the village in the context of migration where the micro economy of the village was based on the positive role of the culture of migration among youths. These consequences paved the mechanism of migration as a tool of measurement of cultural phenomena with the aspect of nexus of economy and sociology of migration as a consequence of the culture of migration within the geographical region of migration.[9]

Box 4.4: Case Study[10]

"It is case a study of 34 years return migrant labourer named Ranu in Inayat Patti village, he said that he used to take both internal and international migration as a source of cultural practices of livelihood because he did never think about another source of livelihood instead of migration because matter of migration was deeply associated with bread and butter for him. These consequences can be *analyzed in the form of a nexus of migration and livelihood in the context of the culture of migration from Inayat Patti to Saudi Arabia via internal migration to Mumbai."*

Based on the above concise, analysis of the formation of the culture of migration in Inayat Patti village to Saudi Arabia via internal migration to Mumbai is based on the well-developed route of migration in the context of dynamics of globalization because consequences of globalization minimized the geographical distance between Inayat Patti and Saudi Arabia as well as created a cultural route of migration where migrant labourers migrated with their cultural belief about migration in the sense of livelihood practices of cultural migration. Therefore, the culture of migration worked as a pull factor in the process of migration from Inayat Patti village to Saudi Arabia via a culture of internal migration to Mumbai. In the context of the impact of COVID-19, it was observed that the culture of migration was adversely affected by the consequence of the pandemic of COVID-19 in Inayat Patti village.[11]

4.2.3. Consequences of culture of migration and globalization in Inayat Patti village

The consequence of the culture of migration improved the socio-economic and cultural image of the village due to the positive role of the culture of migration in development through diaspora philanthropy in the cultural development of the village. It is observed that the consequence of the culture of migration was based on the positive role of the innovative approach of migration through the investment of wishes and abilities of migrant labourers in the formation of the cultural building of migration from Inayat Patti to Saudi Arabia via internal migration to Mumbai. Therefore, the consequence of the culture of migration created a socio-economic transformation in the

---

[9] Information is based on passive observation and informal interviews among return migrant labourers in Inayat Patti village in March 2015.

[10] Information is based on personal interviews from return migrant labourer in Inayat Patti village in March 2015.

[11] Information is based on passive observation and informal interviews among return migrant labourers in Inayat Patti village in October 2023.

village and consequences of socio-economic transformation emerged in the form of cultural transformation in the development of the village because migrant labourers used to find matter of migration as key to livelihood in the context of globalization of migration due to its long historical sequences of migration. In the case of historical sequences of migration, it is observed that colonial experiences of migration led to phenomena of post-colonial facts of migration in the consequences of the long journey of migration in the consequence of the globalization of migration in the twenty-first century.[12]

It was also realized that economic and non–economic facts of migration were correlated and assimilated to each other because the matter of wages was determined by the wishes and abilities of migrant labourers because migrant labourers used to find the matter of migration as a tool for safeguarding to cultural livelihood. Apart, well developed social network system of migration developed the building capacity of the cultural region of migration from Inayat Patti to Saudi Arabia via the culture of internal migration to Mumbai and the consequences of the social network system of migration motivated and inspired migrant labourers for their involvement in process of migration. Therefore, a well-developed social network system of migration worked as a pull factor in the process of ensuring the cultural route of migration as the consequence of the globalization of migration in the form of cultural migration.[13]

It is also observed that there was a well-developed social network system of migration among Muslims compared to less development of the social network system of migration among Hindus because Hindus considered Gulf migration as a source of livelihood for Muslims and Hindus recognized Gulf migration as a Muslim-based migration. These consequences can be analyzed as the role of culture of migration created a cultural inequality between Hindus and Muslims where there were different routes of migration among Hindus and Muslims because Hindu migrant labourers migrated to Surat and Ahmadabad city of Gujarat as well as these Hindus hesitated to involve in the process of "Bombay- Saudi" migration due to depth rooted of cultural prejudice about Gulf migration among Hindus in Inayat Patti village. These consequences can be analyzed in the form of the role of cultural values in the formation of building capacity of migration in Inayat Patti village and its impact on the development of the village in the context of globalization of

---

[12] Information is based on passive observation and informal interviews among return migrant labourers in Inayat Patti village in November 2023.
[13] Information is based on passive observation and informal interviews among return migrant labourers in Inayat Patti village in October 2023.

migration in the village.[14]

Box 4.5: Case Study[15]

"It is a case study of a 35 years old return migrant labourer named Guddu Yadav in Inayat Patti village, He said that he was not interested in Saudi-based migration due to the lack of a social network system of migration in Saudi Arabia but he expressed that he applied for a passport with help of Muslim migrant agent of the village and decided for migration to Saudi Arabia due to poor economic conditions of his family. Therefore, the economic crisis of his family pushed him to migrate to Saudi Arabia with hopes of a better individual life with his family. These consequences can be analyzed as the role of push and pull factors of migration from Inayat Patti to Saudi Arabia in the twenty-first century."

4.3. Nexus of social remittances and cultural changes: A concise debate

According to Gentry & Mittelstaedt (2010), there is a cordial nexus between social remittances and social changes because these consequences created a form of cultural transformation in socio-economic development in migrant-origin countries. Apart, the study also shows that the mode of social remittances transfers itself within the well-developed cultural region of migration from origin to destination country through the help of the positive role of the social network system of migration. These consequences developed the migration-based community in the context of response of social action and re-action in the aspect of inflow of social remittances and its impact in designing of socio-economic and cultural behavior of migrants and their family members. A study by Levit & Nievas (2011) gives similar phenomena in the context of the role of social remittances in the process of formation of the cultural building of development through the positive role of migration because the inflow of social remittances plays an important role in the process of shaping and re-shaping the cultural values, belief, norms, attitudes and myths in the function of migration and development among migration based community on ground level in the context of globalization. The finding of the study of Suksomboon (2008) also gives facts about the nexus of social remittances and cultural changes in the context of measurement of the impact of globalization on the cultural livelihood practices of migrants. The study also shows that the nexus of social remittances and cultural changes plays an important role in the formation of a cultural region of migration where migrant labourers move within the cultural region of migration with their cultural values about migration in the context of inflow of social remittances. The study of Zachariah et al. (2014)

---

[14] Information is based on focus group interviews and passive observation methods among return migrant labourers in Inayat Patti village in November 2023.

[15] Information is based on personal interview from return migrant labourer in Inayat Patti village in November 2023.

is also based on the impact of social remittances and cultural changes in Kerala because it is well-known that there is a long history of migration from Kerala to Gulf countries due to well-developed social network system of migration with the positive role of the organizations of states in the process of facilitating labour migration from Kerala to Gulf countries. These consequences ensure the huge inflow of both economic and social remittances and utilization patterns of both economic and social remittances created socio-economic and cultural transformation among migration-based communities in Kerala. Therefore, the study of Zachariah & Rajan (2018) shows that the consequence of socio-economic and cultural transformation leads the migration from Kerala to Gulf countries due to a well-developed social network system of migration within the cultural region of migration from Kerala to Gulf countries in the twenty-first century. A study by Zachariah & Rajan (2022) shows that the culture of migration from Kerala to Gulf countries is based on the dynamics of the process, determinants and consequences of the inflow of cultural remittances and its role in the formation of building capacity of cultural migration due to depth penetration of role of international migration in the economic behaviour of migrant labourers in rural Kerala. In the context of labour migration from north India to Gulf countries via internal migration to Mumbai, the finding of a study by Taukeer (2023) shows that there are well-developed mechanisms of exchange of social remittances from rural India to Dubai as well as Dubai to India, and these consequences developed a form of cultural region of migration from rural Uttar Pradesh, India to Dubai via culture of internal migration to Mumbai. Therefore, the result of cultural transformation developed a safe zone of migration in the context of depth penetration of cultural migration on the ground level in rural Uttar Pradesh and these consequences ensured the inflow of economic remittances in the response of result of action and re-action of cultural remittances and cultural behaviour of migrant labourers from rural Uttar Pradesh to Gulf countries via Mumbai.

Based on the above concise analysis of the nexus of social remittances and cultural change in the context of the nexus of migration and development, it is realized that migration creates culture and culture leads migration in the context of the function of the cultural region of migration from rural Uttar Pradesh to Gulf countries in the context of the positive role of the globalization in the function of migration. Therefore, the section of this paragraph emphasizes the process, determinants and consequences of the nexus of migration and culture in rural Uttar Pradesh as the root followed by Mumbai as the transit destination and the United Arab Emirates as the international destination. Therefore, the exchange of social remittances from destinations to root with root to destination created a cultural region of migration through the positive role of the social network system of migration. These consequences played an important role in the formation of a cultural diaspora of migrants in both Mumbai and the United Arab Emirates with a positive role of the diaspora philanthropy in Inayat Patti village in Prayagraj district, Uttar Pradesh. Apart, it is also observed that the consequence of migration and culture developed a migration-based community in rural Uttar Pradesh where both internal and international migration is being taken as the major source of income due to a huge inflow of remittances. The result of the consequence of huge inflow of remittances played an important role in shaping and reshaping cultural values, beliefs, norms, attitudes and myths about migration among migrant labourers and their family members in rural Uttar Pradesh. It is also realized that the function of migration was working within well developed cultural region of migration where migrant labourers and their family members never think about other sources of income instead of migration due to the inherited cultural pattern of migration from rural Uttar Pradesh to Gulf countries via Mumbai.

4.3.1. Nexus of social remittances and cultural changes at root level: Inayat Patti village

It is observed that there was a cordial nexus between social remittances and cultural changes in the development practices of Inayat Patti village because there was a well-developed culture of migration from Inayat Patti to the United Arab Emirates via culture of internal migration to Mumbai. These consequences developed a cultural region of migration due to the huge inflow of economic remittances and its impact on the designing of cultural behaviour of migrant labourers and their family members in Inayat Patti village because the matter of migration was based on the practices of cultural livelihood of migrant labourers in the village. It was observed that migrant labourers used to return with the cultural values of Mumbai and the United Arab Emirates and these consequences were being reflected in the socio-economic and cultural behaviour of migrant labourers and their family members at the root level in the village. Migrant labourers and their family members followed the cultural norms of Mumbai and Dubai with their native traditional culture of the village. It is observed that there was a significant impact on the Arabic culture in Inayat Patti village and these consequences developed a mixed cultural landscape in Inayat Patti village. Return migrant labourers used to frequently use the Arabic language with their native

Bhojpuri[16] language and these consequences were the direct result of the impact of Gulf migration on the indigenous traditional culture of the village because the cultural geography of the village was being functioned by the impact of Mumbai based Marathi culture and Dubai based Arabic culture in the context of the consequence of globalization of migration on ground level. These consequences developed a new form of cultural practices where social remittances designed the hybrid cultural practices in the village due to the positive role of the Mumbai and Dubai-based migration.[17]

The consequence of hybrid culture gave space to Mumbai-based Marathi and Dubai-based Arabic culture, developed a new pattern of dialect system among villagers in Inayat Patti village because return migrant labourers recognized themselves as Arabic migrants with Bombaiya migrant labourers due to their involvement in Mumbai and Dubai based migration. These return migrant labourers used to speak the local popular Marathi language with their native Bhojpuri language as well as used to listen to Arabic songs in the village. These consequences developed Arabic and Mumbai-based culture in the village and these consequences played an important role in the formation of a migration-based community through the positive role of both internal and international migration in the development of the village. These return migrant labourers shared their emotions and feelings about Mumbai and Dubai-based migration among youth and these consequences were working as a pull factor in the process of facilitating labour migration from Inayat Patti village to Dubai via a culture of internal migration to Mumbai. It is also observed that there was a crucial role in the Arabic folk song about Prophet Mohammed because return migrant labourers were shown the depth of belief about Prophet Mohammed with Arabic song. [18] They used to sing Arabic song like: "*Habibi, al Habibi, marhaba ya Mustafa, Marahaba habibi, al habibi , ya Mustafa*" (These return migrant labourers gave thanks to the prophet Mohammed due to their swift earnings in Gulf countries).[19]

These consequences can be analyzed as role of the migration in the cultural

---

[16] Bhojpuri language is a geographical dialect of eastern Uttar Pradesh and Bihar, India. Both states were leading states in labour migration of indentured labour migration in colonial India. Cited from: Ojha, A. K., & Zeman, D. (2020, May). Universal Dependency tree banks for low-resource Indian languages: The case of Bhojpuri. In *Proceedings of the WILDRE5–5th workshop on Indian language data: resources and evaluation* (pp. 33-38).

[17] Information is based on informal interviews and passive observation methods among return migrant labourers in Inayat Patti village in October 2023.

[18] Information is based on informal focus group interviews among return migrant labourers in Inayat Patti village in October 2023.

[19] Information is based on informal interviews among return migrant labourers in Inayat Patti village in November 2023.

development of a village through the inflow of social remittances in the village in the context of the function of globalization of migration in the village. It is also found that indigenous traditional folk cultures of villages like – Birha, Kajri, Ahla, Udal, Nach, and Nautanki[20] were being neglected by the depth culture of migration among youth and Muslim youth were not interested in traditional folk culture due to the impact of "Islamic ideology" on ground level in Inayat Patti. These consequences can be analyzed as the role of Islamic ideology in the process of removal of traditional Bhojpuri culture in villages as the consequence of globalization of migration.[21]

It is observed that there was a crucial role of social media in the process of inflow of remittances from Mumbai and Dubai to the village because mostly Muslim youth used to receive cultural values of Arabic countries through communication with their friends, family members, and those who worked in Gulf countries. These consequences were the result of the digital transformation of social remittances from Mumbai and Dubai to the village and its role of diaspora philanthropy in socio-economic and cultural transformation in the village.[22]

Box 4.6: Case Study[23]

"It is a case study of 55 years old woman named Chanda, *who operated* Bissee *(community-based kitchen) in* Mumbai *and presently works as a Gulf wife in a village, She said that her husband and son worked in Saudi Arabia and she also visited Saudi Arabia for purpose of* Umrah *(religious pilgrimage) in* Makkah *and* Madinah. *She also said that the inflow of economic and social remittances gave space to the voice of women in households because women of migrant households lived a luxurious life in the village but these women were not allowed to work as migrant labourers in Saudi Arabia the story of* Chanda *was an example of women empowerment because* Chanda *gave an important role in the building capacity of diaspora philanthropy in the village through the inflow of social remittances from Mumbai and Gulf countries. She also said that her son was* Hafiz –e – Quran *(orator of the Quran) and worked as* an Imam *(Islamic scholar) in a mosque in Saudi Arabia."*

It was also observed that the youth of the village were more interested in Mumbai and Dubai-based migration due to their desire for jobs in global cities in Mumbai and Dubai but it is observed that there was not any role of women in Gulf migration because patriarchal based Islamic tradition did not allow to women in participation in Gulf migration. These consequences

---

[20] Birha, Kajri, Nautanki, Ahla,Udal and Nach are famous folk cultures of eastern Uttar Pradesh and Bihar. Cited from: SINGH, N. (2016). My Life My Story: Narratives. *Social and Cultural Dimensions of Indian Indentured Labour and Its Diaspora: Past and Present*, 51.

[21] Information is based on informal interviews and passive observation methods among return migrant labourers in Inayat Patti village in February 2015.

[22] Information is based on the passive observation method among return migrant labourers in Inayat Patti village in November 2023.

[23] Information is based on personal interviews from woman return migrant in Inayat Patti village in March 2015.

showed that the cultural impact of Gulf migration created a gender-based inequality in the village as well as giving a base for developing feminism discourse around the Gulf migration.[24]

These consequences can be analyzed in the form of the impact of Gulf migration on the cultural behaviour of Muslim youth because Muslim youth felt proud of Arabic culture as well as did not consider the importance of modern education in their life. After all, Arabic migration was an associated cultural symbol of a sheikh (citizen) of Arab. Therefore, the cultural impact of Gulf migration was continuously removing the Hindi culture of north India as well as improving the phenomena of Islamic ideology in Inayat Patti and its surrounding villages. These consequences also created a form of environment of fear among local Hindus because it is observed that local Muslim youth used to organize and arrange religious programs like eid – milad e- nabi (birthday of Prophet Mohammed) with an approach of Islamic agenda and told that they belonged to Ahle-e-sunnat-wal- Jamaat [25] group of sufism of Barelvi school of Uttar Pradesh as well as hated the Islamic ideology of Darul Uloom Deoband [26] ideology but these Muslims youth had no idea about basic principles of Ummat-e- Rasool (peace message of Prophet Mohammed) because these Muslims were uneducated due to depth impact of Arabic migration. It is also observed that there was a significant impact of the Islamic ideology of Al Azhar University of Egypt in the village but these Muslim youths were not aware of Indian universities because these Muslim youth denied the impact of modern education in their life due to Arabic migration. These consequences have created a line of silent tension between *Ahle –e-* Sunni wal-Jamat and Deoband Jamat in Inayat Patti and its surrounding villages as well as creating an environment of uncertainty among local poor Hindus, who were engaged in the rural-based economy and did not affected by the impact of Arabic culture because these Hindus were not involved in Gulf migration due Islamic based image of Gulf migration.[27]

In the context of the impact of COVID-19, it was observed that the impact

---

[24] Information is based on the passive observation method among return migrant labourers in Inayat Patti village in October 2023

[25] Ahle-e-sunnat-wal- Jamaat is the Sunni ideology of Muslims in north India. Cited from: Taukeer, M. (2023). Ethnographic Analysis of Nexus about Migration and Culture in Global Perspective. *Border Crossing, 13*(2), 115-131.

[26] Darul Uloom Deoband is ideology of Deoband School of traditional Islam in India. Cited from: Taukeer, M. (2022). Nexus of Social Remittances and Social Change: An Ethnographic Study of Impact of Gulf Migration on Linguistic Pattern of Migrants in Uttar Pradesh. In *India Migration Report 2021* (pp. 292-305). Routledge India.

[27] Information is based on informal interviews and passive observation methods among return migrant labourers from February 2015 to March 2015.

of the pandemic COVID-19 changed the cultural behaviour of migrant labourers because these return migrant labourers found themselves in the panic condition of migration due to the adverse impact of the pandemic of COVID-19 in Inayat Patti village.[28]

Box 4.7: Case Study[29]

"It is a case study of 34-year-old return migrant labourer named Sheru, who was returned from Mumbai during the pandemic of COVID-19. He said that the impact of the pandemic of COVID-19 created a cultural phobia about COVID-19 without knowing to actual facts of COVID-19 in the village. These consequences can be analyzed as the role of COVID-phobia in the formation of cultural phobia among migrants in Inayat Patti village."

These consequences can be analyzed as the cultural impact of Gulf migration on the psychological and cultural behaviour of migrants in the consequence of Gulf migration in Inayat Patti village as well as developed a cultural region of migration among Muslim youth due to the deep impact of Islamic ideology among youth. These consequences can be analyzed as the role of a huge inflow of social remittances in the context of response of cultural action and re-action in the Hindi belt region of rural Uttar Pradesh, where Islamic ideology was so prominent due to the impact of Arabic culture in Inayat Patti and its surrounding villages in the modern twenty-first century of India. These aspects gave a discourse about the nexus of social remittances and cultural changes in rural Uttar Pradesh due to the culture of migration to Gulf countries via Mumbai.

4.3.2. Nexus of social remittances and cultural changes: Mumbai

It is observed that there was a significant impact of Bhojpuri culture among migrant labourers of Uttar Pradesh and Bihar due to the huge presence of migrant labourers in Uttar Pradesh and Bihar in Mumbai. These migrant labourers were symbols of the culture of Uttar Pradesh and Bihar as well as developed a form of Bhojpuri region in Mumbai. These migrant labourers used to migrate with the traditions, norms and culture of Uttar Pradesh and Bihar and these consequences were helpful in the process of observing occurring cultural phenomena in Mumbai-based culture as well as developing an outline of Bhojpuri culture in Mumbai. Therefore, it is realized that these migrant labourers did not migrate to Mumbai for the fulfillment of economic purposes but also searched for social and cultural space in Marathi-based

---

[28] Information is based on personal interviews from return migrant labourer in Inayat Patti village in October 2023.
[29] Information is based on personal interviews from return migrant labourer in Inayat Patti village in October 2023

culture in Mumbai. Therefore, a huge inflow of labour migration from Uttar Pradesh and Bihar paved the route of inflow of social and cultural values of Uttar Pradesh and Bihar to Mumbai and migrant labourers were important tools in the process of formation of building capacity of social and cultural remittances in Mumbai in the context of globalization in the twenty-first century. The consequence of globalization played an important role in the process of ensuring the way of inflow of social and cultural remittances from Uttar Pradesh and Bihar to Mumbai because the entire function of labour migration from Uttar Pradesh and Bihar to Mumbai because Mumbai opened the door for labour migration to Gulf countries due to positive role of the culture of internal migration to Mumbai in the twenty-first century.[30]

Box 4.8: Case Study[31]

"It is a case study of 24 years migrant labourer named – Rakesh, who was from Uttar Pradesh; He said that he considered Mumbai as the heartland of livelihood for him because his entire cultural function was based on Mumbai-based migration. He also said that the matter of migration was associated with their cultural livelihood practices as well as the door for migration to Gulf countries. These consequences can be analyzed role of Mumbai in the process of labour migration within a well-developed cultural route of migration from rural Uttar Pradesh to Mumbai."

In the context of the cultural impact of the huge presence of migrant labourers of Uttar Pradesh and Bihar, it is realized that there was a deep assimilation and integration between Bhojpuri and local Marathi cultures and these consequences developed a form of hybrid culture in Mumbai. It is observed that the consequence of hybrid culture was the result of the cultural impact of the Bhojpuri culture in Mumbai as well as gave a cultural space to migrant labourers regarding their adjustment to the culture of Mumbai. These consequences developed a cultural route of migration from rural Uttar Pradesh and Bihar to Mumbai as well as developed a mini Bhojpuri region in Mumbai. It is observed that migrant labourers gave important role in cultural development through participation in their traditional cultural practices like- the chat[32] festival in Mumbai according to the cultural norms of Bihar and also in Ganpati[33] festival according to the cultural norms of Mumbai. Therefore, the result of assimilation and integration between Bhojpuri and

---

[30] Information is based on informal focus group interviews among migrant labourers in the Null Bazar area of Mumbai in February 2019.

[31] Information is based on personal interviews of respondent in the Null Bazar area of Mumbai in February 2019.

[32] The *chat* traditional famous festival of the Bhojpuri region of eastern Uttar Pradesh and Bihar. Cited from: Taukeer, M. (2023). An Analysis of the Living and Working Conditions of Migrant Labourers in Mumbai. *Productivity*, *64*(1), 95-108

[33] The *Ganpati* festival is celebrated for lord *Ganesha* according to Hindu-Marathi culture in Mumbai. *Ibid*.pp.95-108.

Marathi cultures developed a new form of cultural practices by languages and dialectic patterns because migrant labourers of Uttar Pradesh and Bihar used to speak both Bhojpuri and Marathi languages. It is also observed that there was a trend of Bhojpuri movies, songs and folk among migrant labourers and these aspects gave them a feeling of their roots in the culture of Bollywood in Mumbai. Therefore, migrant labourers of Uttar Pradesh and Bihar developed a cultural diaspora in Mumbai through their positive role in the socio-economic and cultural function of Mumbai. These consequences can be analyzed as the impact of cultural migration in the developed Bhojpuri diaspora in Mumbai due to developed social–cultural and psychological bonding among migrant labourers because these migrant labourers were working as cultural agents of Bhojpuri culture in Mumbai as well as developed a building capacity of Bhojpuri world in Mumbai.[34]

Box 4.9: Case Study[35]

"It is a case study of 54 years migrant labourer named Abid Ahamed, who was from Prayagraj district; He said that he was the second generation of his family, who worked as Panwala in Mumbai. He also said that he considered himself as Bombiya due to the depth of penetration of Mumbai-based culture in his life because the matter of Mumbai was associated with his livelihood practices."

It is observed that a huge trend of labour migration from Uttar Pradesh and Bihar to Mumbai created socio-cultural challenges in Mumbai because these migrant labourers faced the problem of cultural inequality due to the variation of occupation of skills in Mumbai. It is observed that permanent migrant labourers of Uttar Pradesh and Bihar adopted the culture of Mumbai and kept social and cultural distance from their traditional Bhojpuri culture, these consequences created a hurdle situation for sustaining Bhojpuri culture in Mumbai. In the case of temporary migrant labourers, it was found that there was cultural inequality between permanent and temporary migrant labourers due to economic differences because permanent migrant labourers lived a luxurious life in Mumbai compared to the poor working and living conditions of temporary migrant labourers, those worked in bottom segmentation of labour market in Mumbai. Therefore, variation of economic function determined the cultural inequality between temporary and permanent migrant labourers as well as between Marathis and North Indian migrant labourers because local people of Mumbai considered a huge inflow of Bhojpuri migrant labourers in the insurgency of their cultural world. It is

---

[34] Information is based on informal interviews and passive observation methods among migrant labourers in the Na Khuda Mohalla of Mumbai in February 2019.
[35] Information is based on personal interviews from migrant labourer in Null Bazar area of Mumbai in February 2019.

observed that it was difficult to frame a line between Bhojpuri and Marathi culture among migrant labourers due to the depth of assimilation and integration between Bhojpuri and Marathi culture. These consequences emerged as a form of hybrid cultural practices where migrant labourers tried to adjust to two different cultures to develop their adjustment mechanism in the global culture of Mumbai. Therefore, the function of hybrid culture played giving important role in the development of a mixed cultural landscape where Bhojpuri culture was being continuously neglected by Marathi culture because migrant labourers of Uttar Pradesh and Bihar adopted the Mumbai-based culture because they considered Mumbai-based culture as their world where there was not any place for Bhojpuri culture.[36]

> **Box 4.10: Case Study[37]**
>
> "It is a case study of a 55-year-old migrant named Mojib Siddique, who was from Inayat Patti village; he said that he migrated to Mumbai 30 years ago at age 25 years. He lived with his family in his apartment. He expressed that he felt happiness and pride regarding considering himself a Mumbiya but he also sad due fading of Bhojpuri culture among his children. These consequences showed that permanent migrant labourers adopted the local Marathi culture as well as keeping a geographical and cultural distance from Bhojpuri culture."

4.3.3. Nexus of social remittances and cultural changes: United Arab Emirates

It is observed that there was a significant impact of the Bhojpuri diaspora in the United Arab Emirates due to a huge trend of labour migration from Uttar Pradesh and Bihar to the United Arab Emirates. It is observed that these migrant labourers migrated with their traditional cultural values, norms, beliefs and attitudes and these consequences were reflected in their cultural practices in the Arabic environment of Dubai. It is observed that the visibility of the Bhojpuri culture was a new phenomenon in the Arabic environment because the trend of labour migration from Uttar Pradesh and Bihar was being led by phenomena concerning migration. It was also observed that these migrant labourers migrated with cultural values of the Bhojpuri region with Mumbai-based culture because mostly migrant labourers used to work in Mumbai before migration to Gulf countries. Therefore, there was an interconnection between the culture of internal and international migration because there was the deepest confluent of Arabic culture, Marathi culture and Bhojpuri culture in Dubai. It was found that these migrant labourers led

---

[36] Information is based on informal interviews and passive observation methods among migrant labourers in Bhindi Bazar area of Mumbai in February 2019.
[37] Information is based on personal interviews from migrant labourer at Kolkata building of Mumbai in February 2019.

their cultural roots in Dubai with Bhojpuri language, dialects, movies, songs and folk. These consequences showed that the huge presence of Bhojpuri migrant labourers was working as the mode of inflow of cultural remittances from rural Uttar Pradesh and Bihar to Dubai via internal migration to Mumbai. These migrant labourers used to work as contract labourers for two to three years and they led to their traditional Bhojpuri culture in the living practices in Dubai because the role of traditional Bhojpuri culture was so crucial in their strategy of adjustment in the Arabic culture of Dubai. These consequences showed that Bhojpuri migrant labourers were a major factor in the process of facilitating the inflow of cultural values from rural Uttar Pradesh and Bihar to Dubai with a confluent of Mumbai-based culture, Bhojpuri culture and Arabic culture in Dubai.[38]

Box 4.11: Case Study[39]

"It is a case study of 35 years old named Asif, who was from Uttar Pradesh; He said that he was habited in Bhojpuri culture with Mumbai-based culture in the environment of Arabic culture in Dubai. He also said that these consequences developed a form of hybrid culture in Dubai due to a huge trend of migration from rural Uttar Pradesh and Bihar to Dubai via a culture of internal migration to Mumbai. These consequences can be analyzed as the role of Bhojpuri culture in Arabic culture because Bhojpuri culture minimized the pain of the long journey of migration among Bhojpuri migrant labourers."

It is also observed that migrant labourers developed their world in the Arabic environment in Dubai through the development of cultural Bhojpuri diaspora in Dubai because these migrant labourers felt proud of their traditional Bhojpuri culture including Bhojpuri cuisines like Litti and Chokha, Bhojpuri actors like- *Manoj Tiwari, Ravi Kishan, Khesari* and *Nirahua* as well as folk singer namely *Maithili Thakur* was so famous among Bhojpuri migrant labourers in Arabic environment of Dubai. These consequences showed that Dubai was the heartland for the confluent of various cultural streams where Bhojpuri culture found a little bit of space in the global cultural space of Dubai. It is also realized that there was a crucial role of the movies of Bollywood with Bhojpuri movies among Bhojpuri migrant labourers and these consequences developed a form of Hindi diaspora in the culture of the Arabic environment of Dubai in the context of depth penetration of globalization of culture of Hindi belt region of Uttar Pradesh and Bihar in Dubai.[40]

---

[38] Information is based on informal interviews and passive observation methods among migrant labourers in Dubai in December 2019.

[39] Information is based on personal interviews from migrant labourer in Dubai in December 2019.

[40] Information is based on informal interviews and passive observation methods among migrant labourers in Dubai in December 2019.

> **Box 4.12: Case Study**[41]
> "It is a case study of 44 years migrant labourer named Khabeer, who was from a border village of the Indo-Nepal border of Bihar, India. He said that he felt proud himself considered as Bhojpuri migrant in Dubai. He also told that Bhojpuri migrant labourers developed a hybrid culture due to the confluent of Arabic and Bhojpuri culture in Dubai due to well-developed social and cultural bonding between Bhojpuri migrants and Arabians. It is observed that he was looking toward the blue sky in Dubai and these consequences showed that there was a dream of hope in his eyes for the survival of their left-behind family members in rural Bihar."

These consequences created a challenge for Bhojpuri migrant labourers to survive in Dubai because these Bhojpuri migrant labourers were facing the problem of cultural inequality between unskilled, semi-skilled Bhojpuri migrant labourers and skilled/professional migrants due to economic differences but these Bhojpuri migrant labourers, especially Muslim Bhojpuri migrant labourers found themselves in tradition form of Islamic culture in friendly way because these Muslim migrant labourers followed the traditional Islamic tradition of Arab in the context of modernization of Islamic culture in development practices of United Arab Emirates. These consequences gave a lesson to them for exploring the basic principles of Islam according to Arabic culture compared to the existence of different types of Islamic sects among Indian Muslims in India. Therefore, these consequences emerged as a form of both challenges and opportunities for Bhojpuri migrant labourers regarding exploring their space in the "confluent" culture of Dubai.[42]

> **Box 4.13: Case Study**[43]
> "It is a case study based on participant observation among Muslims during prayer in a Mosque in Dubai; it was found that Muslim migrants of different parts of the world prayed together in the mosque without any discrimination and contradictions in the democratic principles of the United Arab Emirates. These consequences showed that Namaz (Islamic prayer) was playing an important role in the communal harmony among followers of different sects of Muslims in Dubai."

These consequences were helpful in the process of developing an understanding of Bhojpuri migrant labourers by socio-economic and cultural phenomena in the context of globalization of cultural migration in Dubai.

4.4. Migration and Social Identity: Problem and Challenges

A study by La Barbera (2014) shows that there is a cordial nexus between migration and identity because the consequences of migration create

---

[41] Information is based on personal interviews from migrant labourer at a labour apartment in Dubai in December 2019.

[42] Information is based on informal interviews and passive observation methods among migrant labourers in Dubai in December 2019.

[43] Information is based on personal interviews from migrant labourers in Dubai in December 2019.

socioeconomic and cultural transformation among migrants and the result of these consequences gave a base for developing an understanding of facts about the matter of identity of migrants as being taken by problem and challenges. Likewise, the study of Bhugra (2004) also gives realistic-based phenomena concerning the debate about the emerging concept of the nexus of migration and crisis of cultural identity in the context of globalization of migration across the globe. The study also shows that the phenomena of migration create culture and culture leads to migration and consequences of the nexus between migration and culture create a crisis of identity for migrants because the dynamics of migration generate a transformation in the components of culture according to the wishes and abilities of migrant labourers, those take a matter of migration as source of cultural practices of livelihood in the context of depth penetration of globalization on ground level across the globe. The study of Jones & Krzyzanowski (2008) gives similar phenomena concerning the role of matter of migration in the formation of building capacity of the cultural identity of migrants because the nexus of socio and economic transformation transformed the individual psychological behaviour of migrants and consequences of individual psychological behaviour is based cost and benefit analysis cultural benefit of migration in the process of the economic function of migrants. Therefore, the result of the cultural benefit of migration creates a matter of cultural identity due to assimilation and integration between cultural values of origin and destinations in the context of the dynamics of globalization of migration.

A study by Taukeer (2017) shows that migrant labourers of Inayat Patti village faced the problem of cultural identity in both Mumbai and Gulf countries and these consequences isolated them in the culture of Mumbai and the United Arab Emirates. Apart, the study also shows that the impact of Gulf migration created a cultural inequality between Hindus and Muslims in Inayat Patti village because Muslim migrants lived with an identity of economic prosperity compared to the poor economic identity of non-migrants Hindus in the village. Likewise, a similar study by Majumder & Taukeer (2019) shows that the culture of internal and international migration from Inayat Patti improved the economic identity of Muslims but also created problems and challenges for the economic and cultural identity of non-migrant Hindus because Hindus are not affected by Muslim based Gulf migration due to its influence of Islamic ideology in Inayat Patti village due to Gulf migration. The findings of a study by Majumder (2022) show that the impact of the pandemic of COVID-19 created an economic crisis for returned migrant labourers in Inayat Patti village, who returned from Mumbai and Gulf countries. The identity of these returned migrant labourers was being considered as corona meant labourers and labourers meant corona in both root and destinations and these consequences created hurdle panic conditions for the survival of migrant labourers at root in Inayat Patti village in Uttar Pradesh.

In the case of the matter of cultural identity of internal migrant labourers in Mumbai, the study of Bhagat (2011) shows that temporary migrant labourers faced the problem of identity of cultural crisis in the global culture of Mumbai because these migrant labourers did not have access social rights in Mumbai. The study of Jha & Kumar (2016) also gives a base for understanding about facts of working and living conditions of temporary migrant labourers in Mumbai because these migrant labourers faced the problem of crisis of economic identity due to a lack of social rights in Mumbai. A study by Kumar et al. (2012) shows that temporary migrant labourers from Uttar Pradesh and Bihar did not have social and economic benefits in Mumbai and these consequences created a panic condition for migrant labourers as well as created a crisis of economic identity in Mumbai. Likewise, a similar study was given by Taukeer (2023) in this study it was found that migrant labourers of Uttar Pradesh faced the problem of a crisis of cultural identity in Mumbai and the United Arab Emirates due to their involvement in the bottom segmentation of labour market in both Mumbai and United Arab Emirates.

In the case of migration from India to Gulf countries, it is well known that there is a crucial role of the matter of cultural identity in the matter of migration. A study by Rahman (2010) shows that Indian migrant labourers face the problem of identity of cultural crisis among Arabians because a vast majority of the Indian migrant labourers work in the bottom segmentation of the labour market in Gulf countries and these consequences created a hurdle situation for Indian migrant labourers, those belong to the cultural diversity of India and work in the different cultural perspective in Arabic environment in Gulf countries. Likewise study by Taukeer (2022) shows that South Asian migrant labourers developed a cultural diaspora in the Arabic environment of the United Arab Emirates by the positive role and function of South Asian cultural practices among migrants. The study also shows that the process of assimilation and integration between diversified South Asian and Arabian cultures re-shaped the cultural identity of South Asian migrant labourers but these contexts created phenomena of crisis of identity for South Asian migrant labourers because South Asian migrant labourers are treated as Ghulam (slave labour) and Kafeer (non-Muslims) due to their involvement in bottom segmentation of labour market. These consequences showed that the process of assimilation and integration between South Asian culture and Arabian culture re-designed the shape of the cultural identity of migrant labourers as well as created both problems and challenges for migrants. Study of Taukeer (2022) gives a similar study about the forced undocumented migration of South Asian migrant labourers from Saudi Arabia to Greece via Iran and Turkey, findings of the study show that Kafeel (sponsor) used to retain the passport as well as hold the salaries of unskilled migrant labourers, and these consequences created a hurdle situation for the identity of migrant labourers because these migrant labourers did not have any option return to the root, therefore, they involved in forced undocumented migration from the middle east to Europe due to problem of cultural crisis of identity. These consequences played an important role in reshaping the cultural identity of migrant labourers in the Middle East and forced them to look forward beyond the Middle East. Similar phenomena were given in the findings of the study of Taukeer (2022) which showed that migrant labourers suffered from an identity of cultural crisis in Saudi Arabia due to their involvement in the bottom segmentation of the labour market and these consequences gave them an inferior economic identity in labour intensive market-based system in Saudi Arabia. The result of these consequences created economic hurdles for unskilled migrant labourers as well as created a crisis in the matter of identity for migrant labourers. A study by Naweed (2023) shows that there is a gender-based crisis in the matter of migration and cultural debate in Kuwait because the masculinity-based labour market system is not favourable for women in Kuwait. These consequences created a gender-based inequality as well as led to a gender-based crisis for women migrant labourers in Kuwait. In these consequences, it can be analyzed that these perspectives give a base for developing facts about the role of gender-based dimension in the study of the cultural identity of women in male based labour-intensive labour market in Kuwait. A study by Rahman (2023) shows that the impact of the pandemic of COVID-19 created a hurdle situation for migrant labourers because the pandemic of COVID-19 created panic conditions for migrant labourers and these consequences isolated the migrant labourers in Gulf countries as well as forced them to reverse migration from Gulf countries to India. These perspectives also created a hurdle economic situation for returned migrant labourers at their roots in India.

Based on the above concise description of the debate of the problem and challenges of the social identity of migrants, it is realized that there is a cordial nexus between migration and identity because migration creates identity and the matter of identity leads the migration. In the context of labour migration from rural Uttar Pradesh to Gulf countries via internal migration to Mumbai, it is found that migrant labourers faced the problem of crisis of cultural inequality in both Mumbai and the United Arab Emirates but these consequences also gave phenomena of panic conditions for both migrant and non-migrants at root level in Inayat Patti village because impact of both internal and international migration created an economic inequality in the form of cultural inequality in Inayat Patti village. These consequences showed that the cultural impact of both internal and international migration created a migration-based community who moved within the cultural region of migration from Inayat Patti village to Gulf countries via Mumbai but isolated the non-migrant Hindus due to the cultural impact of Muslim-based Gulf migration in Inayat Patti village. Therefore, these consequences gave a separate cultural identity to both Muslims, who migrated to Mumbai and Gulf countries due to the image of upper caste identity because these Muslims hesitated to involve themselves in the rural-based economy in the village due to upper caste identity as well as higher wages at destinations worked as pull factor in the process of labour migration of Muslims while backward caste Hindus denied Gulf migration due to its impact of Islamic based migration with occurring crisis in Middle East.

Therefore, a section of this paragraph advocates the debate about migration and the social identity of migrant labourers from root to destinations in the context of the study of the globalization of migration and its impact on the cultural behaviour of migrant labourers. Therefore, the findings of the study compiled the findings of empirical-based surveys from root to destination with the parallel review of the literature for better justification of the study. Therefore, the entire analysis of the study is based on the nexus of migration and culture in the context of globalization of cultural factors of migration in Inayat Patti village where both cultures of internal and international migration play an important role in the process of re-shaping and re-designing of cultural identity of migrant labourers in Inayat Patti village, Mumbai and United Arab. These consequences developed a cultural region of migration with diversity, contradictions and discriminations concerning around the opportunity and challenges of the nexus of migration and the social identity of migrant labourers. This paragraph also emphasizes the role of globalization of migration in the cultural economic development of villages where well-developed routes of migration ensured the cultural migration to Gulf countries via internal migration to Mumbai. These consequences determined the cultural behaviour of migrant labourers from root to destinations and gave a base for developing an understanding of the phenomena of migration in the context of culture. Therefore, root-to-destinations analysis emphasized the broad aspect of the nexus of migration and culture in rural Uttar Pradesh.

4.4.1. Problem and challenges of nexus of social identity and migration in Inayat Patti village

It is observed that the impact of Muslim-based Gulf migration created an isolated social and cultural identity of Muslims in Inayat Patti village and Muslims found themselves in the mental region of Saudi Arabia in the Hindi belt region of Uttar Pradesh. These consequences re-designed the identity of Muslims as Arabian *sheikhs* and these Muslims used to feel proud of the identity of *sheikh* compared to considering themselves as Indian Muslims because these Muslims return migrant labourers did not have any ideas about basic principles of Indian democracy. These Muslim return migrant labourers said that it was the blessing of Prophet Mohammed in Inayat Patti village because the entire function of migration was based on Islamic principles given by Prophet Mohammed. These consequences showed that the impact of Gulf migration created the identity of fundamentalist Muslims in Inayat Patti village. These consequences created challenges for Hindus in Inayat Patti village; those told that they used to feel suffocation in Inayat Patti village because there was economic inequality between migrations-based Muslims and non-migrant-based Hindus. Therefore, these consequences created a hurdle situation for a matter of identical issues in Inayat Patti village as the question before secular India because it is observed that Muslims were showing their aggression in Julus e- Mohammed [44] (road show ceremony on the occasion of the birthday of Prophet Mohammed) during the celebration of the birth ceremony of Prophet Mohammed. These Muslim return migrant labourers were considered pure Muslims due to the impact of Gulf migration as well as created an environment of Arabian culture in the environment of Hindi culture in the village. These consequences can be analyzed as a nexus of Gulf migration and social identity in Inayat Patti and its surrounding villages. These Muslims were confused about the meaning of the identity of Indians because they said that they considered themselves Muslim before the identity of Indians due to their economic engagement in Islamic-based culture in Saudi Arabia.[45]

Economic consequences of Gulf migration gave the identity of the village as Saudi Gav (village) where non-migrant Hindus were pushed down to the bottom segmentation of the economic hierarchy due to the huge inflow of

---

[44] *Julus-e-Mohammed* is celebrated by followers of *Ahle-sunnat-wal-Jamat* of Barelvi School of Sufism in Uttar Pradesh. Cited from: Taukeer, M. (2022). Nexus of Social Remittances and Social Change: An Ethnographic Study of Impact of Gulf Migration on Linguistic Pattern of Migrants in Uttar Pradesh. In *India Migration Report 2021* (pp. 292-305). Routledge India.

[45] Information is based on informal focus group interviews and passive observation methods return migrant labourers in Inayat Patti village in October 2023.

Gulf remittances and zakat in Muslim households compared to low-income in non-migrant Hindus. These consequences created Amir (rich) Muslims for migration-based Muslims and Garib (poor) Hindus for non-migrant Hindus in Inayat Patti and its surrounding villages. Economic inequality created a separated identity for both Muslims and Hindus where non-poor Hindus lived with the philosophy of Santosam Param Sukham (philosophy of economic satisfaction in their economic development according to Hindu philosophy) because these non-migrant Hindus were engaged in agriculture-based economy and inter-state migration in Surat and did not consider importance of social impact of Gulf migration due its Islamic based identity while rich Muslims were living in demonstration physical culture with feeling of Islamic identity due to Gulf migration in Saudi Arabia.[46]

It was also observed that Muslim youth were uneducated as well as so aggressive about their belief in Prophet Mohammed because these Muslim youths excluded themselves from modern education where they had good information about the ideology of Islam but did not have any ideas about the social implications of Gulf migration in society. These Muslim youths were showing their social identity as Dabang (powerful) in localities of Inayat Patti village because these Muslim youths said that they could purchase police power due to the huge inflow of *Riyal* in the village and also told that they invited police to party in village and gifted to police. These consequences created a problem for social existence for non-migrant poor Hindus in Inayat Patti village. These consequences can be analyzed as the dark impact of Gulf migration among Muslims of Inayat Patti village because Muslims willingly denied the impact of modern education because they frequently adopted the Islamic-based identity and these consequences led to the formation and re-shaping of the social identity of Muslim youth as Bhai (Brother) among non-migrant Hindus. The identity of Bhai was taken as the identity of power in Inayat Patti and its surrounding village because uneducated Muslim youth felt proud of the social identity of Bhai in the village.[47]

It is observed that these Muslim youths were dressed in white paint and shirts with white shoes, a classical dress of roadside political leaders in Uttar Pradesh. These consequences were considered question-like jokes before the world's largest Indian democracy. It is also observed that Vinod Yadav introduced himself as Gram Pradhan (head of the local body government of

---

[46] Information is based on informal interviews among return migrant labourers in Inayat Patti village in November 2023.
[47] Information is based on focus group interviews and passive observation methods among return migrant labourers and non-migrants Hindus in Inayat Patti village from February 2015 to March 2015.

the village), and he was so friendly with local Muslim Chutbahiya netas (roadsides political leaders) in Inayat Patti village because Pradhan used to decide according to the order of local Muslim leaders, those were uneducated due to Gulf migration as well as lived luxurious life. It is also observed that local roadsides Muslim political leaders of Inayat Patti village were showing their political image with the social impact of Gulf migration because these roadsides Muslim political leaders had enough money to spend on local politics of Inayat Patti village. On these roadsides, Muslim political leaders were improving their social identities with their participation in local politics without knowledge of the basic principles of the Indian political system.[48]

Box 4.14: Case Study[49]

"It is a case study of 56 years old named Akbar Kha who was known as Akbar Neta in Inayat Patti village. He worked as a taxi driver in Mumbai as well as participated in local politics of Inayat Patti village. He was also punished as a lifetime prisoner in a murder case and got bail from the court. He felt proud of the identity of Neta without basic knowledge of the leadership quality of Indian democracy. These consequences can be analyzed as the role of migration and migrant labourers in local politics of Uttar Pradesh in the periphery of Muslim politics."

These consequences can be analyzed as the role of culture of internal and international migration among Muslims in Inayat Patti village, who migrated to Mumbai with the dream of migrating to Saudi Arabia as well as improving their social and cultural identity as Dabang (powerful) in Mumbai and Inayat Patti village while Yadav caste Hindus called Muslim as Bhai due to participation of Muslims in Saudi and Mumbai based migration. Muslim hamlets were more developed due to luxurious houses compared to the cottages of the *Yadav* caste Hindus of the village. Apart, from these poor Yadav caste Hindus called Muslim hamlets Turkan due to the aggressive identity of Muslims their Islamic identities in the periphery of Gulf migration in Inayat Patti village. These consequences created a problem in the way of social harmony where Muslim youths promoted Islamic ideology in the village as well as created challenges for social democracy in Inayat Patti village.[50]

---

[48] Information is based on passive observation methods among villagers, *Pradhan* and return migrant labourers in Inayat Patti village November 2023.

[49] Information is based on informal personal interviews from return migrant labourer in Inayat Patti village in October 2023.

[50] Information is based on informal interviews and passive observation methods among return migrant labourer in Inayat Patti village in November 2023.

4.4.2. Problem and challenges of nexus of social identity and migration in Mumbai

It is observed that there was a huge presence of Muslim and Hindu migrants of Inayat Patti and its surrounding villages in Mumbai and these migrant labourers lived their separate social identities where Muslims were involved in the self business and Hindu migrant labourers used to work as unskilled labourers in the unorganized sector of Mumbai. These consequences led to a huge inflow of remittances from Mumbai to Muslim migrant households in Inayat Patti village compared to the least inflow of remittances from Mumbai to Hindu migrant households in Inayat Patti village. Therefore, differences in the inflow of remittances created a separate social identity for migrants of Inayat Patti village in Mumbai because Muslim youths migrated to Mumbai with hopes of migrating to Saudi Arabia due to well developed social network system of migration due to the lack of such kinds of the social network system of migration among Hindus of Inayat Patti village.[51]

It is observed that Muslims of Inayat Patti village worked as permanent migrants and lived in chall in a planned settlement system in Mumbai while Hindu migrants lived in temporary kholee in an unplanned settlement system in the slums area of Mumbai. These consequences created a social identity as Amir (rich) Bombaiya for Muslims and Garib (poor) Bombaiya for temporary migrant labourers of Hindus of Inayat Patti village in Mumbai. It is also found that Chedhabhai was a new form of social identity for migrants, those who lived in chall in Mumbai. These consequences can be analyzed as the role of economic hierarchy in the formation of social identity for migrant labourers of Inayat Patti village in Mumbai where Muslim migrants of Inayat Patti village, lived with Islamic based identity in Mumbai as well as operated Madarsha (religious school) in Mumbai for spreading Islamic ideology in Mumbai. He felt proud of the social identity of Chedhabhai while Hindu migrant labourers of Inayat Patti village lived with their caste-based identities like Aahir (Yadav) and these Aahir (Yadav) were working as manual labourers in a cowshed in the outer area of Mumbai because these migrant labourers were low earning and surviving with principles of Indian philosophy of Santosam Param Sukham (philosophy of economic satisfaction with their economic development) while Muslim migrants of Inayat Patti village were known as Amir Miyan (rich Muslims) among Yadav caste Hindu

---

[51] Information is based on informal interviews and passive observation methods among migrant labourers in the Na Khuda Mohalla of Mumbai in February 2019.

migrant labourers of Inayat Patti village.[52]

> **Box 4.15: Case Study[53]**
> "It is a case study of 56 years old migrant labourer named Abid who belonged to the neighbouring village of Inayat Patti namely Basgit, who worked as a panwala in Mumbai. He said that he considered himself the identity of Bombaiya wala Bhaiya (identity of north Indian migrants) in Mumbai and also said that he was considered rich in his village due to Mumbai-based migration."

It is also observed that Muslim migrants of Inayat Patti village were more aware of the local politics of the village during the Panchayat (local body government) election because Muslims of Inayat Patti village belonged to the upper caste and they decided the politics of backward caste in the election of local body government due to direct interfere in local politics of Inayat Patti village. These Muslim migrants said that they loved the social and cultural traditions of the village as well as played an important role in the formation of the building capacity of diaspora philanthropy through the investment of collective remittances in the construction and reconstruction of a mosque in Dhorhan hamlet of Inayat Patti village. These consequences showed that the culture of Mumbai-based migration gave a separate social identity as Turk Miyan (Turk Muslims) to upper caste Muslim migrants of Inayat Patti village and their boundary of migration was spread and extended from village to Saudi Arabia while Hindu migrants had not option for international migration because Hindus hesitated for migration to Saudi Arabia due to its Islamic based ideology. Muslim migrants of Inayat Patti village said that the culture of Saudi Arabia was based on fundamental Islamic culture and they liked it according to their knowledge about Islam. It is also observed that Muslim migrants of Inayat Patti village were not aware of occurring modernization with vision 2030[54] in Saudi Arabia and the global culture of Mumbai because most Muslim migrants were uneducated as well as did not have any ideas about the occurrence phenomena of modernization in Mumbai and Saudi Arabia.[55]

---

[52] Information is based on informal interviews and passive observation methods among migrant labourers in the Null Bazar areas of Mumbai in February 2019.

[53] Information is based on personal interviews from migrant labourer in the Na Khuda mohalla of Mumbai in February 2019.

[54] Vision 2030 is based on the re-form mechanism in the socio-economic and cultural development of Saudi Arabia in the twenty-first century. Cited from: Nurunnabi, M. (2017). The transformation from an oil-based economy to a knowledge-based economy in Saudi Arabia: the direction of Saudi Vision 2030. Journal of the Knowledge Economy, 8, 536-564.

[55]. Information is based on focus group interviews and passive observation methods among migrant labourers in the Null Bazar area of Mumbai in February 2019

4.4.3. Problem and challenges of nexus of social identity and migration in United Arab Emirates

It is observed that there was a significant social impact of North Indian migrants in the United Arab Emirates due to the huge presence of North Indian migrant labourers in Dubai. There was a different story about the social impact of the presence of migrant labourers of Uttar Pradesh and Bihar in Dubai compared to Mumbai. It is observed that Muslim migrant labourers of Inayat Patti village worked in a disciplined manner in the United Arab Emirates due to strict rules and guidelines of labour laws in the United Arab Emirates because these migrant labourers did not have time for gossip in Dubai like the environment of Inayat Patti village. These migrant labourers were known as "Hindi" due to the social impact of the Hindi language in the environment of the Arabic language in the United Arab Emirates. It is also observed that there was not any presence of Hindu migrants of Inayat Patti village in Dubai while Dubai was a second home for Muslim migrants of Inayat Patti village. It is also observed that these Muslim migrant labourers worked in the bottom segmentation of the labour market as well as known as Ghulam (slave) labourers due to their involvement in the bottom segmentation of the labour market in Dubai. These Muslim migrant labourers were also known as Kafeer (non-Muslims) among Arabians because these Muslims said that Arabians considered unskilled Indian Muslim migrant labourers as inferior due to their involvement in the bottom segmentation of the labour market in the United Arab Emirates. These consequences can be analyzed as the role of Gulf migration in the process of creation of the social identity of migrant labourers of Inayat Patti village as inferior in Dubai compared to the identity of Dabang (powerful), Bhai (brother) and Turkan (aggressive Muslims) in Inayat Patti village.[56]

Box 4.16: Case Study[57]

"It is a case study of 34 years old migrant labourer named Ahamed, who was from Inayat Patti village and worked in Abu Dhabi. He said that he found a different social environment in Dubai compared to the environment of the Dabang (powerful) migration based Muslim community in Inayat Patti village. These consequences can be analyzed as the role of strict guidelines for labourers in the United Arab Emirates, where Indian Muslim migrant labourers found economic space with its social implication compared to social inequality in implication of migration in Inayat Patti village."

It is also observed that there was a crucial role in the social impact of the Arabi language on Hindi-speaking migrant labourers because Indian Hindi-

---

[56] Information is based on informal interviews and passive observation method among Indian migrant labourers in parks of Dubai in December 2019.
[57] Information is based on a personal interview from migrant labourer at Karachi Darbar restaurant in Abu Dhabi in December 2019.

speaking migrant labourers used to frequently speak the Arabic language in Dubai. These consequences showed that the Arabic language was the major tool for measuring the phenomena of assimilation and integration between Arabic and Hindi languages among unskilled migrant labourers. These consequences created a social hybrid diaspora in the Arabic environment of the United Arab Emirates as well as created a linguistic diaspora in the global culture of Dubai.[58]

Flowchart 4.1. Culture and Migration

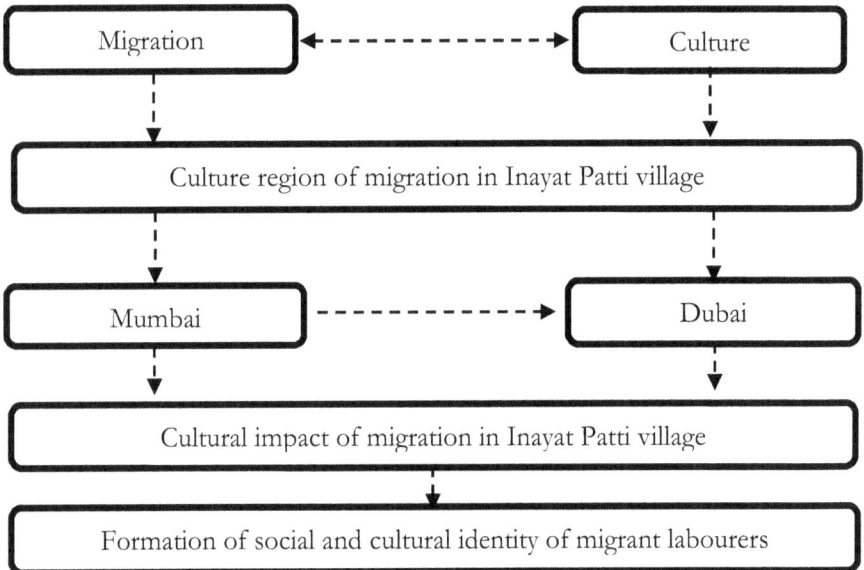

Source: Designed by Author

Flow chart 4.1 shows that there is a cordial nexus between migration and culture in labour migration from Inayat Patti village to Dubai via a culture of internal migration to Mumbai. Consequences of impact of migration paved the route of cultural region of migration from Inayat Patti to Dubai via Mumbai in the consequences of globalization of migration and its reflection in the form of socio-economic and cultural transformation in the village. These consequences are being reflected in the psychological behaviour of migrant labourers in the form of cultural values, norms, beliefs and myths about the process, determinants and consequences of migration. These consequences determined the social and cultural identity of migrant labourers in Inayat Patti village.

---

[58] Information is based on the passive observation methods among migrant labourers in Dubai in December 2019.

CHAPTER 5

MIGRATION AND ETHNICITY

5.1. Migration, Ethnicity and Globalization

According to Choucri (1983), the trend of migration in oil-producing Gulf countries was based on ethnic diversity because the initial phase of labour migration from oil-producing Gulf countries was led by Arabian migrants from non-oil-producing countries namely- Syria and Yemen due to the ethnic homogeneity of races of Arabian migrants in oil-producing Arab countries. These consequences led to huge ethnic migration from non-oil-producing Arab countries to oil-producing Arab countries. A study by Choucri (1986) also shows that the initial phase of labour migration from non-oil-producing Arab countries to oil-producing Arab countries was most welcomed in oil-producing Arab countries due to its Islamic-based labour market under the Arab common labour market in Arab. Still, the increasing trend of labour migration from non-oil producing countries created a homogeneity-based labour migration system where Arabian Muslim migrant labourers migrated to oil-producing Arab countries due to the availability of the Islamic-based labour market in Arab countries. Studies of Seccombe (1983&1986), show that the initial structure of the labour market of oil-producing Arab countries allowed the Muslim-based labour migration from British India to oil petroleum companies of Qatar and Saudi Arabia due to managing the ethnic homogeneity in the Islamic-based labour market in both Saudi Arabia and Qatar. According to Calton (2010), ethnic diversities played a crucial role in the formation of the labour market in oil-producing Arab countries due to the phenomena of Arab- the Israel war in 1973 and these consequences created an incident of the oil boom in Arab as well as increased the price of crude oil due to aggressive role of oil-producing Arab countries in Middle East. These phenomena divided the Arab world into the Islamic world and the Jewish world and developed an Islamic-based labour market in oil-producing Arab countries. A study by Winckler (2010) also shows that the consequences of Arab- the Israel war created incidents of the oil boom with a "rentier state" system under the approach of "no tax no representation system" for Arabians in oil-producing Arab countries as well as created system of dual labour system under Kafala (sponsorship) system where

Kafala system ensured the luxuries working conditions for Arabians in upper segmentation of labour market while non-Arabian migrant labourers work in bottom segmentation of labour market under labour intensive labour market system in Gulf countries. A study by Kapiszewski (2016) shows that these consequences led to the huge trend of labour migration from Asian countries to the bottom segmentation of the labour market in oil-producing Arab countries and these consequences divided the structure of the labour market into ethnic diversities based on Arabian migrants and Asian migrants according to the structure of the labour market system under Kafala system.

In these contexts, the ethnic diversity of the labour market system was based on the occurring political economy of globalization in the Middle East during the invasion of Iraq on Kuwait in 1991, the study of Rahman (2010) shows that the Iraq and Kuwait war created a hurdle situation for oil-producing Arab countries because Iraqi and Palestinian migrants supported the invasion of Iraq on Kuwait due to ethnic homogeneity with Iraq. Therefore, Saudi Arabia deported 1.5 million Arabian migrants, those who supported the invasion of Iraq and these consequences created a vacuum in the labour market of Saudi Arabia and shifted the trend of demand for labourers toward South Asian countries because South Asian countries had surplus labourers, those were favourable according to the occurring political phenomena in Middle east because these South Asian migrant labourers were mute and did not have right to interfere in the political matter of oil-producing Arabian countries. These consequences created an ethnic diversity in the dynamics of the labour market in oil-producing Arab countries due to the inflow of huge migration from South Asian countries. In the context of labour migration from India to oil-producing Arab countries, the study of Khadria (2001) shows that India opened the door of labour migration toward Arab countries because the changing scenario of the political economy of globalization was favourable for Indian migrant labourers according to ethnic homogeneity and diversity based labour market system in oil-producing Arab countries. Likewise, a similar study by Khadria (2006) shows that the consequence of globalization was a major factor behind the labour migration from India to oil-producing Arab countries because the result of globalization plays an important role in creating ethnic diversities in the bottom segmentation of labour market in oil-producing Arab countries with managing ethnic homogeneity in upper segmentation of labour market under Kafala system in oil-producing Arab countries.

In the context of labour migration from Kerala, the study of Zachariah &

Rajan (2012) shows that India to Gulf countries, it is well known that there is a long history of migration from Kerala to Arabian countries before the discovery of oil and after the discovery of oil due to ethnic linkages between Keralities and Arabians from the era of British India to post-independent India. Mostly Christian community of migrants migrated to British oil petroleum companies due to ethnic homogeneity with Britishers as well and Muslim migrants migrated to oil-producing Arab countries due to Islamic-based homogeneity with Arabians. These consequences showed that matter of ethnicity played a crucial role in facilitating labour migration from Kerala to Gulf countries from ancient India to the British era and its reflection in the form of modern Gulf migration in post-independent India. In these perspectives, the study of Kurien (2002) shows that ethnic homogeneity worked as a pull factor in the process of labour migration from Kerala to oil-producing Arab countries with its past experiences to present phenomena of migration from Kerala in the context of globalization of migration. The findings of a study by Zachariah & Rajan (2016) show that both Muslims and Christians are prominent in the formation of building capacity of labour migration from Kerala to oil-producing Arab countries because the entire function of migration from Kerala to oil-producing Gulf countries is based on historical ethnic linkages between Arabian countries and Kerala.

According to annual reports of the overseas employment division, ministry of External Affairs, government of India (2014-15), recent phenomena of labour migration from India to oil-producing Gulf countries is being led by north Indian states namely- Uttar Pradesh and Bihar because the trend of unskilled labour migration from Kerala to oil-producing Gulf countries is shifted toward Uttar Pradesh and Bihar compared to skilled migration from Kerala to oil-producing Gulf countries in Arab world. These consequences can be analyzed as ethnic diversities in the trend of labour migration from South India and North India to oil-producing Gulf countries by economic classification of the migrant labourers in the context of the nexus of ethnicity and migration in the context of globalization of migration. Therefore, the findings of a study by Taukeer (2017) show that trend of labour migration from rural areas namely Inayat Patti village of Uttar Pradesh to oil-producing Gulf countries is being led by Muslims, those considered consequences of Gulf migration as part of their cultural practices of livelihood by ethnic homogeneity between Indian Muslims and Arabians because Muslim migrant labourers considered process of Gulf migration as blessing of Prophet Mohammed on their prosperity at root level in rural Uttar Pradesh. Therefore, it can be realized that matter of ethnic homogeneity and diversity played a crucial role in the function of migration in the context of globalization of migration because findings of the study of Torress (2015) show that the nexus of migration and ethnicity created a cultural phenomenon of migration because migration creates culture and culture leads migration.

Based on the above concise description, the background of this section is based on an explorative analysis of the nexus of migration and culture in the context of the function of ethnicity, culture and globalization of migration from India to oil-producing Gulf countries via the culture of internal migration to Mumbai (Flow chart: 5.1).

5.1.1. Migration, ethnicity and globalization of migration from Inayat Patti to Gulf countries via internal migration to Mumbai

It is observed that there was a significant impact of the ethnic homogeneity in the process of labour migration from Inayat Patti village to oil-producing Gulf countries via a culture of internal migration to Mumbai because Muslim migrant labourers considered oil-producing Gulf countries as a favourable home for Muslims due to explicit visibility of the Islamic based culture in Saudi Arabia. Return migrant labourers said that historical sequences of migration from Inayat Patti village to Saudi Arabia are being led by historical consequences of Muslim-based migration due to the well-developed culture of migration from village to Gulf countries via a culture of internal migration to Mumbai. Therefore, the culture of both internal and international was based on ethnic homogeneity of migration in the village because return migrant labourers said that they felt proud to consider themselves as Gulf migrant due to the Islamic-based ideology in Saudi Arabia. In the context of the gender view of migration, it was observed that it was a total male-based migration because return migrant labourers said that the nature of jobs in the bottom segmentation of the labour market did not allow female migration as well it also observed that Hijab based system was so prominent in the village and these consequences did never allow of women for migrate to Saudi Arabia. In the consequences of globalization of migration, it was observed that the participation of women was increasing in both internal and international migration from villages because wives of migrant labourers were migrating to Mumbai and Saudi Arabia with their husbands. These consequences were the result of the initial phase of gender-based equality in the culture of migration from Inayat Patti village to Gulf countries via internal migration to Mumbai in the context of the feminist perspective of migration. In the case of the religious factor of migration, it is observed that some

Hindus were migrating to Saudi Arabia with the help of Muslim migrant agents but these returned migrant labourers were told that Saudi-based migration was based on Islamic-based migration, therefore, they were not interested in re-migration to Saudi Arabia but interested in Mumbai based internal migration due to well developed social network system of internal migration among Hindus compared to well developed international social network among Muslims in Inayat Patti village.[1]

Flow chart 5.1.

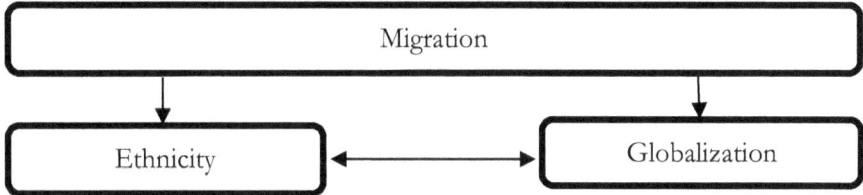

Source: Designed by Author, 2023

Box 5.1: Case Study[2]

"It is a case study of 37 years migrant labourer named Monu Siddique, who said that he worked in Mumbai before migrating to Saudi Arabia and also told that Mumbai-Saudi-based migration is being led by Muslims within well-developed cultural region of migration through well-developed social network system of migration from Inayat Patti village to Saudi Arabia. He also said that his wife also migrated to Saudi Arabia with him. These consequences can be analyzed as the role of depth penetration of globalization of migration on the ground level in Inayat Patti village where ethnicity played a crucial role in the function of migration with aspects of migration, ethnicity and culture by development practices in the periphery of globalization of migration in the twenty-first century in rural India."

5.1.2. Migration, ethnicity and globalization of migration in Mumbai

It is observed that there was a significant impact on the Bhojpuri diaspora in Mumbai, who migrated from rural areas of Uttar Pradesh and Bihar to Mumbai due to well-developed ethnic region of migration within well-developed cultural region of migration. The consequences of the Bhojpuri diaspora were the result of a huge trend of labour migration of North Indian migrants; those were living and working in Mumbai with similar geographical homogeneity of North India as well as had a well-developed ethnic bonding among migrant labourers of Uttar Pradesh and Bihar because these migrant labourers were cordially associated to each other by similar economic and cultural phenomena of migration. These consequences developed ethnic

---

[1] Information is based on passive observation and informal interviews methods among return migrant labourers in Inayat Patti village from February 2015 to March 2015.
[2] Information is based on personal interview from return migrant labourer in Inayat Patti village in October 2023.

cultural diaspora in the context of the confluent of globalization and migration in the perspective of assimilation and integration between economic and cultural perspectives of migration from North India to Mumbai in the twenty-first century. These consequences were helpful in the development of cultural diaspora in the Marathi culture of Mumbai where these North Indian migrant labourers were unified in their linguistics and dialectic similarities with homogenous cultural practices of the Bhojpuri region of Uttar Pradesh and Bihar. These consequences created a homogenous identity of migrant labourers as "Bhojpuri" among Marathis in Mumbai because the identity of Bhojpuri was considered as mute, hard-working and honest labourers of Uttar Pradesh and Bihar and these consequences developed a culture of Bhojpuri ethnic diaspora in Mumbai due to positive role of the Bhojpuri culture in Mumbai based global culture in twenty-first century. It is also realized that the homogenous culture of the Bhojpuri diaspora was the result of long historical sequences of migration from the heartland of indentured migration from Uttar Pradesh and Bihar in colonial India as well as its emerging form as Bhojpuri migration from Uttar Pradesh and Bihar to Mumbai. These consequences can be analyzed in the form of the role of past phenomena of indentured experiences of migration in phenomena of internal migration in the aspect of globalization of migration in the twenty-first century. These consequences developed a homogenous ethnic diaspora of migrant labourers based on historical narratives of migration by transformation of ethnic consequences of migration from one generation to the next generation under its past phenomena to present and its future implication of ethnic migration from Uttar Pradesh and Bihar to Mumbai.[3]

It is also observed that these Bhojpuri north Indian migrant labourers considered themselves as the identity of Chedhabhai with the traditional identity of Bhaiya and both types of identities were associated with similar homogenous economic, cultural and geographic identity of Bhojpuri region as well as developed a psychological bonding among Bhojpuri migrant labourers in Mumbai under similar ethnic homogenous character of migrant labourers. In the context of migration from rural Uttar Pradesh to Saudi Arabia via internal migration to Mumbai, it is observed that the culture of "Bombay- Saudi" migration was characterized by ethnic homogenous migration of the Muslim community because Muslims were willingly involved in both Mumbai and Saudi based migration due to long historical sequences

---

[3] Information is based on informal interviews and passive observation methods among migrant labourers in Na Khuda Mohalla of Mumbai in February 2019.

of migration from Inayat Patti village to Saudi Arabia via culture of internal migration to Mumbai in the consequences of leading role of ethnic homogeneity among Muslim, those considered matter of migration as key of their cultural livelihood practices. These consequences created a pathway of ethnic migration where Muslims migrated from Inayat Patti village to Gulf countries within a well-developed ethnic route of migration within a well-developed cultural route of migration from the village to the Gulf countries.[4]

Box 5.2: Case Study[5]

"It is a case study of 38-year-old Sebu Ahamed, who was from Inayat Patti village and migrated to Saudi Arabia via internal migration to Mumbai. He said that he migrated to Mumbai and Gulf countries due to the well-developed cultural pathway of migration due to the availability of the well-developed social network system of migration. These consequences can be analyzed as the role of ethnic similarities in the process of migration from Inayat Patti village to Saudi Arabia via culture of internal migration to Mumbai in the context of globalization of migration among the Muslim community in Inayat Patti village, where Muslims existed in similar scale of ethnic measurement within well developed cultural and ethnic homogenous Bombay- Saudi based migration."

5.1.3. Migration, ethnicity and globalization of migration in Dubai

It is observed that there was a significant impact of the Bhojpuri migrant labourers in the environment of Arabic culture in Dubai because a huge trend of labour migration from rural Uttar Pradesh and Bihar to Dubai developed a form of ethnic diaspora like ethnic Bhojpuri diaspora of Mumbai. These consequences were the result of the depth penetration of globalization of migration in the perspective of globalization of nexus of migration and culture. The consequences of migration from rural Uttar Pradesh and Bihar to Dubai were based on the nexus of internal and international migration because a well-developed ethnic pathway of migration led to the cultural migration from rural Uttar Pradesh and Bihar. It is also observed that there was ethnic homogeneity among migrant labourers of rural Uttar Pradesh and Bihar by similar linguistics and dialectic patterns of Bhojpuri language with Bhojpuri songs, movies, folks and cultural practices. These consequences developed a form of Bhojpuri ethnic diaspora in the global culture of Dubai. Bhojpuri migrants played an important role in the formation of building capacity of the Bhojpuri ethnic diaspora because Bhojpuri ethnic diaspora maintained their psychological behaviour through their homogenous cultural

---

[4] Information is based on informal interviews and passive observation methods among migrant labourers in Null Bazar area of Mumbai in February 2019.

[5] Information is based on personal interview from migrant labourers at Mumbai in February 2019.

practices of Bhojpuri culture in the environment of Arabic culture in Dubai.[6]

In the context of the globalization of the Bhojpuri diaspora, it is observed that there was a significant impact of social media and telecommunication in the process of digital migration of Bhojpuri culture from rural Uttar Pradesh and Bihar to Dubai where Bhojpuri migrant labourers developed a unique building of ethnic homogenous cultural diaspora in the context of assimilation and integration between Arabic and Bhojpuri culture as consequence of form of hybrid culture where Bhojpuri culture were being re-designed and re-shaped by explicit influences of Arabic culture. These consequences were helpful in the development of a new form of ethnic homogenous diaspora of rural Uttar Pradesh and Bihar in Dubai in the context of globalization of cultural migration in the scale of ethnic homogenous cultural practices of migrant labourers.[7]

It is also realized that there was not an ethnic diversity between Hindu and Muslim migrant labourers because both lived and worked with their homogenous ethnic identity of Bhojpuri among Arabians in Dubai. These migrant labourers were working in similar working conditions as contract labourers under Kafeel with the identity of Ghulam (slave) labourers. These consequences can be analyzed as the emergence of indentured labour migration in the context of experiences of colonial migration and its role in the formation of contract-based labour migration from rural Uttar Pradesh and Bihar to Dubai via internal migration to Mumbai. These consequences were the result of depth penetration of historical sequences of migration of Bhojpuri migration in the twenty-first century. These consequences helped develop an understanding of the process, determinants and consequences of Dubai-based migration in the Bhojpuri region and these consequences also developed an ethnic homogenous migration of rural migrant labourers, those who migrated to Dubai with hopes of a better life for their individual life with the survival of their left behind family members at the root. These consequences developed a form of ethnic economic homogenous migration from rural Uttar Pradesh and Bihar to Dubai for employment.[8]

---

[6] Information is based on informal interviews and passive observation methods among migrant labourers at Deira in Dubai in December 2019.

[7] Information is based on passive observation method among migrant labourers at Deira in Dubai in December 2019.

[8] Information is based on passive observation method among migrant labourers at Deira in Dubai in December 2019

Box 5.3: Case Study[9]

"It is a case study of a 24-year-old migrant labourer, named Guddu, who was from Inayat Patti village, who told that the culture of internal migration led to the culture of international migration within ethnic homogenous migration. He found a cultural space among Bhojpuri migrants in Dubai as well as developed an ethnic Bhojpuri migration in the Arabic environment of Dubai. These consequences can be analyzed as the role of ethnic homogenous Bhojpuri Diaspora in the Arabic environment of Dubai-based diversified global culture."

In the consequences of ethnic homogenous phenomena in migration from Inayat Patti village to Dubai via culture of internal migration to Mumbai, there was a cordial association between economic and cultural phenomena of migration because both factors lead to each other in the sense of the formation of the boundary of ethnicity in process of facilitating migration capacity building. In the context of the present study, it is realized that there were similarities between internal and international migration because both types of migration were led by the Bhojpuri region of Uttar Pradesh and Bihar as well as caused by similar socio-economic and cultural phenomena. These consequences developed the building of ethnic homogeneity among Bhojpuri migrant labourers in both Mumbai and Dubai. These Bhojpuri migrant labourers were identified as unique geographical identity like Bhojpuria migrant labourers in the global working environment of Mumbai and Dubai as well as developed a similar ethnic cultural region of migration from rural Uttar Pradesh and Bihar to Dubai via internal migration to Mumbai. The matter of ethnic homogenous was a core quality of both internal and international migration in terms of similar economic ethnicity because both internal and international Bhojpuri migrant labourers used to work in labour intensive labour market in the bottom segmentation of economic hierarchy and these consequences gave them homogeneous economic identity as cheap hard working labourers in both Mumbai and Dubai. Therefore, the culture of both Mumbai and Dubai were favourite destinations for Bhojpuri migrant labourers because these migrant labourers found similar cultural phenomena by similar races, and similar cultural practices and these consequences developed a form of ethnic homogeneity among Bhojpuri migrant labourers in Mumbai and Dubai. It is also observed that the culture of Bombay- Saudi-based migration was being continuously shifted toward Dubai-based migration because young migrant labourers showed their tendency toward Dubai due to its global culture but these migrant labourers also liked Riyadh and Jeddah cities of Saudi Arabia due to huge presence of migrant labourers of Uttar Pradesh and Bihar in these cities. Apart, it was also found that

---

[9] Information is based on personal interview from migrant labourer at Deira in Dubai in December 2019.

Mumbai base culture was so explicitly visible in Dubai due to its nature of migration where Bhojpuri migrant labourers developed their world based on their values, norms, traditions, beliefs and myths concerning the labour migration from rural Uttar Pradesh and Bihar to Dubai via culture of internal migration to Mumbai. These consequences can be analyzed as the role of similar wishes and abilities of Bhojpuri migrant labourers by race, gender, religion and economic classification of occupation and these perspectives were creating a form of ethnic homogenous among Bhojpuri migrant labourers in the global culture of Mumbai and Dubai because these Bhojpuri migrant labourers considered themselves as Hindi-speaking migrant labourers in culture of Marathi language in Mumbai and diversified linguistic patterns in Dubai. Therefore, the matter of language and dialect was a major key concerning the identification of Bhojpuri migrant labourers as Bhojpuria migrant labourers in Mumbai and Hindi and Bhojpuri migrant labourers in the environment of Arabic culture in Dubai.[10]

It is also observed that migrant labourers of Uttar Pradesh and Bihar were so cordial with migrant labourers of Pakistan in Dubai due to similar ethnic perspectives because their cultural routes were led by similar socio-economic and cultural practices. These consequences developed a form of homogenous similar ethnicity between migrant labourers of the plain area of Punjab state of Pakistan and North Indian migrant labourers because these migrant labourers belonged to similar ethnicities as well as developed similar ethnic diaspora of South Asian migrant labourers in the global diversified culture of Dubai.[11]

Box 5.4: Case Study[12]

"It is a case study of 25 years old migrant labourer named Faraz, who was from the Sargodha district of Punjab of Pakistan, He said that he had a little bit of knowledge about the cultural and economic practices of migrant labourers of Uttar Pradesh and Bihar, due to impact of Bhojpuri language in environment of Arabic culture in Dubai. He also said that he was very impressed with Bhojpuri migrant labourers as well as cordially associated with Bhojpuri migrant labourers due to similar economic and cultural causes of migration from Punjab, Pakistan and North India to Dubai. These consequences can be analyzed as the role of ethnic homogenous considering it as a pull factor in the process, determinants and consequence of migration."

---

[10] Information is based on focus group discussions and informal interviews among migrant labourers at labour apartments, and parks in Dubai in December 2019.

[11] Information is based on focus group interviews and informal interviews among migrant labourers at Diera in Dubai in December 2019.

[12] Information is based on personal interview from Pakistani migrant labourer in Dubai in December 2019.

5.2. Race, Gender based ethnicity and migration

A study conducted by Healey & Stepnick (2019) shows that matter of ethnicity plays a crucial role in building migration capacity by race and gender in the context of globalization of migration. The consequence of race and gender is an important keyword concerning the process of migration within well-developed cultural regions of migration where aspects of homogeneity in race and gender determine the boundary of cultural migration. The importance of race and gender determines the ethnicity of migrants. In contrast, homogeneity in race and gender ensures ethnicity among migrants through similarities in common cultural practices because the study of Zack & Gracia (2007) shows that matters of race and gender play an important role in the process of formation of ethnic homogenous groups of migrants, those have common homogenous cultural practices by the similar function of race and gender in specific region of migration. Likewise study by Healey & Brien (2007) shows that homogenous race and gender determine the ethnic migration community as well as give them a social and cultural identity by the similar function of cultural practices among migration communities. Findings of Fox & Jones (2013) show that the role of ethnicity plays a crucial role in the process of formation of building capacity of migration with ethnic diversification and its role in the creation of ethnic biases because individual values, norms and beliefs of migrants create an ethnic bias among migration based community, these consequences are helpful in the study of the role of ethnicity in process of migration.

In the context of the role of race, and gender-based ethnicity in migration in Gulf-based migration in the Arab world, the study of Taukeer (2019) shows that gender-based ethnicity played a crucial role in the process of migration from rural Uttar Pradesh to the Gulf countries because Muslim women were invisible in male based migration from rural Uttar Pradesh to Gulf countries due to orthodox types of prejudice about women in the Muslim community. These Muslim women were not allowed to work in a male male-based society but these Muslim women were happy with the identities of "Gulf wives" because these Muslim women considered their responsibility to manage the matter of remittances in households in the absence of their husbands. These consequences can be analyzed as the role of gender-based ethnicity among Muslims in the perspective of feminism discourse in male-based migration where these Gulf wives found a space in migrant households with control of their rights through direct intervention of males in households. The findings of the submitted thesis of Taukeer (2020) show that matter of ethnic homogenous among the Muslim community determined the migration from rural Uttar Pradesh to Gulf countries because similar cultural values, norms, beliefs and attitudes determined the ethnic homogenous group migration community in the context of their involvement in Gulf-based Arabian migration within the well developed ethnic region of migration from rural Uttar Pradesh to Gulf countries via internal migration to Mumbai. A study conducted by Nadjmabadi (2010) shows that ethnic homogeneity among Iranian migrants determined the similar ethnic migration-based community in Dubai because these migrant labourers found similar socio-economic and cultural phenomena. These consequences developed the ethnic cultural world of Iranian ethnic migration within a well-developed ethnic migration region of rural Iran to the United Arab Emirates.

Likewise, the findings of the Study of Taukeer (2022) show that the Bhojpuri ethnic group migrated within well developed cultural region of migration from the Bhojpuri region of rural Uttar Pradesh and Bihar to the United Arab Emirates. These consequences were the result of a well-developed social network system of migration by homogenous ethnic values and cultural norms among Bhojpuri migrants in the Arabic environment of the United Arab Emirates. The findings of Gardner (2010) show that linguistic ethnic groups among South Asian migrants, played a crucial role in the development of building capacity of ethnic migration from South Asia to Gulf countries through depth penetration of ethnic similarities among South Asian migrants by common cultural ethnic practices. A study by Segal (2019) shows that the consequences of globalization worked as an important factor in the development of ethnic-based migration because the cultural factor of migration is key word concerning the function of globalization in the process of migration.

In the case of migration from Inayat Patti village to Gulf countries via internal migration to Mumbai, the finding of Taukeer (2017) showed that matter of Arabian based Gulf migration was so popular among Muslim youth because Muslim youth migrated to Gulf countries due to homogenous ethnic values about Gulf migration within the well developed cultural impact of Arabian migration in Hindi belt region of rural Uttar Pradesh. These consequences were the result of the similarities of ethnic Islamic ideology between Indian Muslim youth and Arabians because ethnic homogeneity worked as a pull factor in the process of migration from rural Uttar Pradesh to Gulf countries through the role of ethnic internal migration in Gulf-based Arabian migration. The findings of the study of Majumder & Taukeer (2019) show that there was an interconnection between internal and international migration where the culture of internal and international migration was based on ethnic homogenous values among Muslim youth because the matter of migration was associated with ethnic cultural practices of livelihood for Muslims in Inayat Patti village. Likewise, the study of Majumder (2022) shows that the impact of the pandemic of COVID-19 created a hurdle situation for male-based Muslim migration from Inayat Patti to Mumbai and Saudi Arabia because these consequences started re-verse migration as well as created an ethnic crisis among Muslims, who migrated to Gulf countries within the well developed ethnic cultural route of migration.

5.2.1. Race, Gender based ethnicity and migration in Inayat Patti village

In the case of labour migration from Inayat Patti village to Gulf countries via internal migration to Mumbai, it is observed that there was a cultural consequence of Gulf migration among Muslims because Muslims considered Gulf migration as a matter of ethnic values of Muslims, those found similar racial phenomena in the Arabic environment in Gulf countries. These consequences were the direct result of the Islamic base ethnic values among Muslims, those considered the matter of Gulf migration as a suitable source for their livelihood in the context of similarities between Arabians and Indian Muslims. These consequences paved the role of Islamic-based phenomena in the process of migration from Inayat Patti to Saudi Arabia because Muslim youths desired Gulf migration as Islamic practices of livelihood according to the principles of Islamic ideology about Al-Hijrah[13] (migration). The concept of Al-Hijrah created a common homogenous ethnic value among Muslim youths, those who considered the matter of Arabic base Gulf migration as a sacred space for their values, norms and beliefs about the holy city – Makkah & Madina. It is also observed that Muslim youth expressed their depth belief in Prophet Mohammed and said that the message of Prophet Mohammed created a form of ethnic homogeneity between Indian Muslims and Arabians as well as developed ethnic Islamic community in Saudi Arabia. It is also observed that Muslim youths created their world due to the direct impact of Islamic tradition in the life of the village because these consequences motivated them to involve themselves in Arabian-based Gulf migration. Therefore, Muslim youths were learning the Arabic language for their adjustment in life in Saudi Arabia and these consequences developed a form of an ethnic homogenous group of Muslim migrants, who were familiar

---

[13] Al-Hijrah is Arabic meaning of migration.

with the Arabic language with Arabic culture as well as excluding themselves from the traditional Hindi belt culture of Uttar Pradesh. These consequences developed an ethnic homogenous group of Indo-Arabian migrants, where Hindi culture was being replaced by Arabic traditions in the Hindi belt region of Uttar Pradesh.[14]

Box 5.5: Case Study[15]

"It is a case study of 28 years old returned migrant labourer named Ataullah in Inayat Patti village; he said that he considered Saudi-based migration for the heartland of the Muslim community because Muslim migrant labourers of Inayat Patti village found an Islamic space in Saudi Arabia. These consequences can be analyzed as the role of ethnic Islamic-based norms in the process of facilitating labour migration from Inayat Patti village to Saudi Arabia where Islamic-based ethnicity worked as a pull factor in labour migration in the context of globalization of migration in the twenty-first century. These consequences also developed a cultural region of migration due to the penetration of ethnicity by race and gender in the process of migration."

It is also observed that the huge impact of Gulf remittances created a migration-based community in Muslim hamlets in Inayat Patti village because the trend of huge inflow of Altahwilat almalia[16] (remittances) from Saudi Arabia to Inayat Patti village created Islamic-based ethnic group of migrants in the village but these consequences created an ethnic inequality between Hindus and Muslims because Muslims were cordially associated with Arabian culture by the Arabic language, music, folk song and values. These consequences developed a form of Arabic ethnic cultural community in Inayat Patti village because Muslim migrant households continuously abandoned traditional Indian culture due to the large impact of *Al*-Hijrah (migration), Altahwilat almalia (remittances) of Arabian migration in the periphery of Arabian migration in the village. These consequences developed a mental region of ethnic Arabian migration-based community among Muslim youth in the Hindi belt region of rural Uttar Pradesh. It is also observed that Hindus called Muslims Turka in Inayat Patti village because these Muslims felt proud of the identity of Turka due to their ancestral historical linkages with Turkey because Muslims considered that they belonged to Turkey. These consequences developed an ethnic inequality between Hindus and Muslims because the impact of Arabian-based Gulf migration because impact of Gulf migration created ethnic-based identities like- Miyan (Muslim) and the identity of Miyan (Muslim), was so popular

---

[14] Information is based on informal focus group interviews and passive observation methods among return migrant labourers in Inayat Patti village in October 2023.

[15] Information is based on personal interviews from return migrant labourers in Inayat Patti village in November 2023.

[16] Altahwilat almalia is Arabic meaning of remittances.

among local Hindus because Hindus considered Muslim migrants as Amir Miyan (rich Muslim) compared to poor Hindus as well as these Muslim migrants were known as Katua among Hindus where identity of Katua were being taken as fun among Hindus and Muslims. These consequences can be analyzed as the role of matter of identity in ethnic-based migration whereby the huge impact of Gulf migration created an ethnic homogenous identity among Muslims, those who migrated to Saudi Arabia via internal migration to Mumbai due to the availability of the well-developed ethnic route of migration within the cultural region of migration.[17]

It is observed that matter of feminism discourse was so popular in the process of Arabic-based Gulf migration in the context of the creation of economic mythology about Gulf wives in Inayat Patti village because it is observed that there was invisibility of women in male-based Gulf migration from Inayat Patti village due to depth penetration of masculinity and patriarchal based system paved the culture of Islamic tradition among Muslims. These consequences also created an ethnic inequality between males and females among Muslims in Inayat Patti village where Muslim males were involved in Gulf migration and Muslim women were working as Gulf wives with limited rights of economic decision in households.[18]

Box 5.6: Case Study[19]

"It is a case study of 56 years of Mirza Moid Beg, who considered Gulf wives as Burrak (female horse angels of heaven of Allah) because Gulf wives received huge remittances from Saudi Arabia. These consequences can be analyzed as the role of matter of identity in the perspective of gender-based identity in the context of the ethnicity of Islamic-based migration from Inayat Patti to Saudi Arabia. It also showed the role of Islamic myths about beautiful women among male-based society in Inayat Patti village."

5.2.2. Race, gender based ethnicity and migration in Mumbai

It is observed that there was explicit visibility of the presence of north Indian-based migrant labourers in Mumbai and these consequences developed a world of Bhojpuri region in the environment of Marathi culture in Mumbai. From the perspective of race, it is observed that there was a significant impact of the Bhaiya-based migration in the culture of Mumbai because the term Bhaiya was the symbol of mute and hard-working labourers of Uttar Pradesh and Bihar; those belonged to similar socio-economic and cultural

---

[17] Information is based on informal interviews and passive observation methods among return migrant labourers in Inayat Patti village from February 2015 to March 2015.
[18] Information is based on informal interviews and passive observation methods among migrant households in Inayat Patti village in March 2015.
[19] Information is based on personal interview from respondent in Inayat Patti village in October 2023.

background. It is found that the entire function of Mumbai-based migration was based on matter of social identities of migrant labourers due to depth penetration of matter of caste in rural Uttar Pradesh and Bihar because a vast majority of the migrant labourers were from upper castes like Swarna Jati[20] (upper caste) like, Thakur Brahman in Hindus; Khan and Siddique in Muslims where these upper caste communities belonged to upper segmentation of social hierarchy system of India but worked in bottom segmentation of labour market in economic hierarchy of India. Therefore, there was an adverse relationship between economic hierarchy and social hierarchy from the perspective of caste-based identity in the economic culture of Mumbai. In the case of the role of caste in the economic function of migrant labourers, it was realized that caste-based social identity was positively associated with the economic mobility of the migrant labourers from the rural-based economy of Uttar Pradesh and Bihar to Mumbai where these migrant labourers found themselves a new type of socio-economic and cultural identity of Bhaiya in Mumbai. These consequences showed that the matter of racism was being covered by economic identities as migrant labourers because the matter of upper caste-based identity pushed the labourers from the rural-based economy of Uttar Pradesh and Bihar to Mumbai but it was also realized that both push and pull factors of migration was also functioned due to role of the theory of new economics of labour migration. Upper caste migrant labourers migrated within the well-developed cultural region of migration in the context of confluent economic and social phenomena of migration and these consequences led to phenomena of cultural migration from rural Uttar Pradesh and Bihar to Mumbai due to both economic and non-economic factors of migration where the economic factor of migration included matter of wage differential between rural-based economy of Uttar Pradesh, Bihar and Mumbai because upper caste migrant labourers gained higher wages in Mumbai compared to low wages in rural-based economy of Uttar Pradesh and Bihar. From the perspective of non-economic phenomena of migration, it is realized that the matter of upper caste identity played a crucial role in the function of migration because upper caste migrant labourers did not like to engage themselves in the labour market in the rural-based economy of Uttar Pradesh and Bihar but they migrated to Mumbai due to not any matter of social identities in economic hierarchy of Mumbai as well as glamour of jobs in Mumbai also worked as pull factor

---

[20] Swarna Jati is upper caste community (Brahamin, Thakurs in Hindu, Khan and Siddique in Muslims). Cited from: Quack, J. (2016). Organised atheism in India: An overview. *Secularity and Non-Religion*, 49-67.

among upper caste migrant labourers in rural Uttar Pradesh and Bihar. These consequences can be analyzed in the function of the theoretical perspective of migration including the role of push and pull theory, the theory of new economics of labour migration, and the dual labour market-based theory of migration where these consequences developed a safe zone concept of migration from rural Uttar Pradesh and Bihar to Mumbai because these upper caste migrant labourers found a secure position of guarantee about access jobs in Mumbai. According to Taukeer (2023), the safe zone concept of migration is based on the process of functioning of migration with the expectation of guarantee of jobs in the economic environment of the urban-based economy. Therefore, these consequences can be analyzed as the transformation of the concept of expectation of access jobs into the concept of guarantee of access jobs in Mumbai for upper caste migrant labourers; those were not interested in engaging at root due to economic and non-economic phenomena of migration.[21]

Box 5.7: Case Study[22]

"It is a case study of 37-years old migrant labourer named Bablu Mishra, who was from Santravidas Nagar, Bhadohi district of Uttar Pradesh. He said that Mumbai was the heartland for upper caste migrant labourers because the rural-based economy was not suitable for upper caste youth due to low wages and matter of nexus of social hierarchy and economic hierarchy. After all, upper-caste youth denied their engagement in the rural-based economy due to their upper-caste social status in Uttar Pradesh and Bihar. He also said that he found Mumbai as a safe zone for upper caste youth where these youth found a suitable economic space according to their eligibility of efficiency. These consequences led to the function of labour migration within well-developed safe zones of migration from Uttar Pradesh and Bihar to Mumbai in the consequence of globalization of migration in the twenty-first century."

These consequences can be shown in the form of racism based on upper caste mobility due to the economic consequence of migration in the context of globalization of migration within well-developed cultural regions of migration as safe zone regions of migration from Uttar Pradesh and Bihar to Mumbai.

From the perspective of backward and schedule caste based youth, those who belonged to the lower segmentation of the social hierarchy system of India, also found a suitable economic space in Mumbai because these backward and scheduled caste youths migrated from rural Uttar Pradesh and Bihar to Mumbai due to wage differential between root and destinations with the glamour of jobs in Mumbai. These consequences led to caste-based mobility

---

[21] Information is based on informal interviews and passive observation methods among migrant labourers in Null Bazar areas of Mumbai in February 2019.
[22] Information is based on personal interview from migrant labourer in Mumbai CST in February 2019.

among youths; those who were interested in their engagement in the glamour of Mumbai. These consequences can be analyzed as the role of the economic function of migration where caste-based racism was not any matter of existence in the framework of the economic hierarchy of Mumbai like caste-based economic function in rural Uttar Pradesh and Bihar.

From the perspective of feminism discourse of migration, it is realized that female-based migration was so prominent in the case of labour migration to Mumbai because married women migrated with their husbands and these consequences led to the family-based migration in the framework of rural-urban inter-state of migration through the positive role of the globalization of migration in rural Uttar Pradesh and Bihar.

Box 5.8: Case Study[23]

'It is a case study of 28 years old woman named Afreen Siddique was educated woman who was from Inayat Patti village. He said that he was the victim of a patriarchal system in the village because Afreen married an uneducated boy in the village due to the pressure of her family members. Therefore, Afreen migrated with her boyfriend without informing her family members and settled in Mumbai with her boyfriend, who was also from the upper caste. These consequences can be analyzed as the role of the decision-making process of women in the patriarchal-based system in upper caste Muslims where a woman challenged the patriarchal-based system of Inayat Patti village through the function of migration."

It is also realized that feminism-based discourse was so prominent in caste-based racism in the context of economic mobility of youth because the consequence of economic mobility was continuously fading to a matter of social hierarchy in the form of class-based society in the glamour of Mumbai. These consequences can be analyzed in the framework of globalization of migration by the role of economic culture in the process of replacing the social hierarchy system of rural Uttar Pradesh and Bihar in the context of migration.

5.2.3. Race, gender based ethnicity and migration in Dubai

It is observed that there was a significant impact of the presence of migrant labourers in the environment of Arabic culture in Dubai where upper caste migrant labourers worked in the bottom segmentation of the labour market under the *Kafala* system. It is also observed that there was not any type of discrimination and contradictions in caste-based racism among migrant labourers of Uttar Pradesh and Bihar. These upper caste migrant labourers migrated to Dubai due to the wage differential between Mumbai and Dubai

---

[23] Information is based on personal interview from female migrant labourer in chall of Mumbai in February 2019.

because these upper caste migrant labourers gained higher wages in the glamour of Dubai as well as improve their social and economic status at root in rural Uttar Pradesh and Bihar. These consequences showed that matter of globalization of migration led to economic mobility among upper caste youths, those who considered a matter of migration as a source of their livelihood in rural Uttar Pradesh and Bihar.[24]

These consequences can be analyzed as a nexus of social hierarchy-based caste racism and economic hierarch-based class system in the function of migration because upper caste migrant labourers worked with the identity of class as contract labourers in the bottom segmentation of the labour market in the United Arab Emirates. These migrant labourers were recognized as *Kafeer* (non-Muslims) and *Ghualam* (slave labourers) in Dubai due to their economic activity in the bottom segmentation labour market in the United Arab Emirates. These consequences can be analyzed as the role of nexus of class and caste where migrant labourers lived in the framework of social hierarchy system in rural Uttar Pradesh and Bihar but they lived in an economic hierarchy-based system in the United Arab Emirates and these consequences improved the economic and social status of upper caste migrant labourers in rural Uttar Pradesh and Bihar. It is also observed that there was little presence of backward caste (OBC) and scheduled caste (SC) [25] Indian migrant labourers in Dubai because these castes did not have access to social network system of migration like well developed social network system of migration among upper caste migrant labourers, these consequences determined the economic efficiency of boundary network of migration within safe zone region of migration from rural Uttar Pradesh and Bihar to Dubai via internal migration to Mumbai.[26]

In the case of the tendency of migration from rural Uttar Pradesh and Bihar to Dubai via internal migration to Mumbai, it found that upper caste youth had well developed social network system of migration up to Mumbai and beyond it but backward caste (OBC) and scheduled caste (SC) had limited access of boundary of social network system of migration. These consequences led to the caste-based mobility for upper caste youth from migration to rural Uttar Pradesh and Bihar to Dubai via internal migration to

---

[24] Information is based on informal interviews and passive observation methods among migrant labourers at Deira in Dubai in December 2019.

[25] Other backward caste (OBC) and scheduled caste (SC) is listed caste in Indian constitution according to socio-economic development. Cited from: Kumar, A. (2023). Why Are Some Backward Castes Demanding Scheduled Caste Reservation?. *Dalits in the New Millennium*, 394.

[26] Information is based on informal interviews and passive observation methods among migrant labourers at Deira in Dubai in December 2019

Mumbai while backward caste (OBC) and scheduled caste (SC) youths migrated to Mumbai as well as were unable to migrate to Dubai due to lack of social network system of migration. These consequences showed that the boundary of the social network system of migration led to caste-based racism and its mobility where the matter of identity of caste was being replaced by class-based identity in the economic environment of both Mumbai and Dubai. Therefore, the nexus of caste and class was developing an understanding of racism where the matter of castes was being explained by the class at destinations and the matter of class was being explained by caste in the context of the role of migration in improving the social status as caste and economic status as class in rural Uttar Pradesh and Bihar.[27]

Box 5.9: Case Study[28]

"It is a case study of 34-year-old Shoaib Khan from the Lucknow district of Uttar Pradesh, who worked as an AC technician in Sharjah in the United Arab Emirates. He said that matter of caste played a crucial role in the social hierarchy-based system in India but a consequence of the social hierarchy-based system transformed into an economic hierarchy-based system in the United Arab Emirates because there was not any existence of caste-based racism among migrant labourers of Uttar Pradesh and Bihar in the United Arab Emirates. The class-based system faded the matter of caste-based racism in the United Arab Emirates. These consequences showed that there was an adverse relationship between caste-based racism and class-based function in the global working environment of the United Arab Emirates."

In the case of the feminism-based discourse of migration, it was observed that there was not any space for family-based migration like migration from rural Uttar Pradesh and Bihar to Mumbai because unskilled and semi-skilled migrant labourers were not allowed to live with family in the United Arab Emirates. Apart, migrant labourers said that geographical distance with long-term contract-based migration was a barrier to female migration from rural Uttar Pradesh and Bihar to the United Arab Emirates. These consequences led to masculinity-based male migration from rural Uttar Pradesh and Bihar to the United Arab Emirates. These consequences can be analyzed in the framework of gender-based discourse in the process of labour migration from rural Uttar Pradesh and Bihar to Dubai via internal migration to Mumbai where women migrants were involved in internal migration but these women migrants were unable to migrate to Dubai due to male based labour intensive job market in the bottom segmentation of labour market in

---

[27] Information is based on informal interviews and passive observation methods among migrant labourers at Deira in Dubai in December 2019.
[28] Information is based on personal interview from respondent at Deira in Dubai in December 2019.

the United Arab Emirates.[29]

5.3. Politics, economic, cultural ethnicity and migration

According to the study of Fox & Jones (2013), a matter of migration creates phenomena of politics, economics and cultural ethnicity in the context of development practices of migrants in cultural landscapes of migration in the perspective of globalization of migration. The findings of Sirkeci (1996) show that nexus of migration and ethnically plays an important role in the formation ethnic based migration groups through similar cultural practices of migrants as well as also creates matter of conflicts due to discrimination and contradictions among migrants due to the function of different cultural values, norms, attitudes and cultural belief. The findings of a study of Sahin (2010) give a realistic picture of the role of the nexus of migration and ethnicity in creating a feeling of nationalism among migrants in the Middle East where migrant labourers migrate from different parts of the world with their different cultural values. These consequences developed phenomena of racism in the building capacity of diaspora in the context of spreading nationalism among migrants in the Middle East. In these contexts, a study by Webb (2016) shows that the phenomenon of the development of a diversified ethnic diaspora community in the Middle East is the result of a huge trend of ethnic-based migration from South Asia to the Middle East and these consequences lead to the development of ethnic cultural diaspora by process of similarities and differences in cultural values, norms, beliefs and attitudes of diversified migrant community in Middle East.

In the context of labour migration from India to Gulf countries in the Middle East, a study by Rahman (2010) shows that Indian migrant labourers face the problem of ethnic conflict among Arabians in the context of their national identity in Gulf countries because Arabian Kafeel retains the passport of migrant labourers, those work in the bottom segmentation of labour market in Gulf countries. These consequences create a hurdle situation for Indian migrant labourers, who are considered as Indian but suffer lots of pain due to the crisis of national-based identity in Gulf countries. A study by Taukeer (2020) shows that Indian migrant labourers are known as Kafeer (non-Muslim) and Ghulam (slave labour) among Arabians in Gulf countries because Arabians consider Indian migrant labourers as inferior due to their involvement in the bottom segmentation of the labour market

---

[29] Information is based on informal interviews and passive observation methods among migrant labourers at Deira in Dubai in December 2019.

under Kafeel (sponsor). These consequences created an ethnic conflict in the labour market of Gulf countries as well as led to the matter of ethnic crisis for Indian migrant labourers in oil-producing Gulf countries. A study by Taukeer (2022) shows that the pattern of labour migration from India to Gulf countries via internal migration to Mumbai is realized that migrant labourers of Uttar Pradesh and Bihar face problems of ethnic racism in both Mumbai and Gulf countries due to explicit impact of the Bhojpuri culture in the living and cultural practices of migrants in Mumbai and Dubai in the context of globalization of migration from rural Uttar Pradesh and Bihar to Dubai via internal migration to Mumbai. The findings of a study by Taukeer (2023) show that matter of ethnicity-based migration creates an emotional bonding among migrant labourers due to the explicit impact of Bhojpuri culture-based racism among migrant labourers of Uttar Pradesh and Bihar because these migrant labourers lead the Bhojpuri-based cultural identity in diversified racism based migrant's community in Marathi culture of Mumbai. In the context of ethnic-based discourse, politics and economics matters, the findings of Taukeer (2022) show that the South Asian diaspora are diversified by different cultural values, practices and geographical diversities but these South Asian migrant labourers are recognized as South Asian among Arabians in Dubai. Apart, the study also shows that Indian migrant labourers are known as Hindi due to the impact of the Hindi language in Dubai as well as Pakistani migrant labourers are known as Urdu in the Arabic environment of Dubai. These consequences show that ethnic-based racism is an important phenomenon concerning the diversified South Asian diaspora with contradictions, discriminations and challenges in the framework of homogeneity and diversity.

In the context of the impact of Gulf migration in rural Uttar Pradesh, findings of Taukeer (2022) show that there is a significant impact of the Arabian culture among migrant households in the Hindi belt region of Uttar Pradesh because return migrant labourers and their family members follow the Arabian culture and these consequences developed an ethnic-based migration community as the identity of sheikh of Arab in Hindi belt region of Uttar Pradesh. In these perspectives, the study of Taukeer (2023) shows that there is an explicit impact of the Arabian-based Gulf migration in Inayat Patti village in Uttar Pradesh where traditional Hindi culture is being replaced by the impact of Arabic culture and these consequences developed a form of ethnic homogenous migration community as a sheikh in Hindi belt region of rural Uttar Pradesh in the context of globalization of migration in twenty-first century.

Based on the above concise descriptive based analysis, it is realized that the pattern of migration from Uttar Pradesh to Gulf countries is based on ethnic migration by race, gender and occupation in the context of emerging ethnic discourse concerning the economics and politics of migration in the context of globalization of migration in twenty-first century.

5.3.1. Politics, economic, cultural ethnicity and migration in Inayat Patti village

It is observed that there is a significant impact of Arabian-based Gulf migration in Inayat Patti village in the context of globalization of migration in the twenty-first century because the depth penetration of globalization of migration developed the culture of migration from Inayat Patti village to Dubai via internal migration to Mumbai. These consequences developed a form of ethnic homogenous community among Muslims, who considered the matter of Gulf migration as a source of their economic well-being and social status. Therefore, a consequence of the nexus of economic well-being and social status started a new debate concerning the nexus of class and caste in the context of globalization of migration because the impact of migration improved the economic status of migrant households as well as social status in Inayat Patti village. Therefore, a consequence of the improvement in economic status was positively associated with social status because the economic status of upper-caste Muslim migrant households was being improved by migration and these consequences also enhanced the social status of Muslims as sheikhs among backward caste Hindus because the identity of sheikh was being considered as an economic class for upper caste migrant labourers in the context of Arabian based Gulf migration in Inayat Patti village in the twenty-first century.[30]

It is also observed that the explicit impact of Arabian-based Gulf migration on local politics of the village because Muslim sheikh migrant labourers participated in local politics in the village with the help of the local regional party of Uttar Pradesh namely – Samajwadi party because these sheikh Muslim considered that Samajwadi party as party of Muslim but these sheikh Muslims did not have any ideas about basic principles of socialism and basic principles of Indian democracy. It is also observed that local political leaders of the Samajwadi party gave space to *sheikh* Muslims in local politics because the both economic and social status of Muslims were being improved by the positive role of the Arabian-based Gulf migration and

---

[30] Information is based on passive observation and informal interview methods among return migrant labourers in Inayat Patti village in October 2023.

these consequences led to the re-placing of caste-based politics into class-based politics in Inayat Patti village, there was a significant impact of the Arabian based culture among emerging sheikh community. These consequences can be analyzed as the role of Arabian-based Gulf migration in the process of creating a new type of ethnic group among Muslims, those who considered themselves as sheikh (Arabian Muslim) due to their cordial relationship with Arabians as well as started a new debate concerning around the matter of economics, politics and ethnic phenomena in the environment of Arabian based Gulf migration in Inayat Patti village.[31]

In the context of the impact of internal migration, it is observed that return internal migrant labourers were known as Bhaiya and Bombia in Inayat Patti village and both types of identities created homogenous ethnic identities of Muslim migrant labourers, those migrated to Mumbai with hopes of migration to Gulf countries. These consequences developed a form of migration-based community in Inayat Patti village as well as developed a well-developed pathway of migration from Inayat Patti village to Dubai via internal migration to Mumbai. It is also observed that both upper-caste Muslims like sheikhs and backward-caste Hindus like Yadav were playing important roles in internal migration from Inayat Patti village to Mumbai. These consequences also improved both the economic and social status of Muslim and Hindu migrant households in the village but the economic and social status of Muslim migrant households was more improved than Hindu migrant households because Muslim sheikhs were involved in Arabic-based Gulf migration. These consequences created an ethnic inequality between Hindus and Muslims because Muslim sheikhs were so prosperous compared to Yadav caste Hindus. Therefore, the nexus of class and caste-based discourse of migration gave a new debate on the economic, political and ethnic-based narratives in Inayat Patti village.[32]

It is also observed that the there was significant impact of M-Y (Muslim-Yadav) factor of politics of Uttar Pradesh in Inayat Patti village because both Muslim sheikhs and Yadavs Hindu determined the local politics of Inayat Patti village through the function of diaspora philanthropy in the village. Both Yadav and sheikhs were considered local political leaders of the Samajwadi party with aspects of political ethnic identity of M-Y factors. It is also observed that there was not any influence of the Congress party in Inayat

---

[31] Information is based on passive observation and informal interview methods among return migrant labourers in Inayat Patti village in November 2023.

[32] Information is based on passive observation and informal interview methods among return migrant labourers in Inayat Patti village in November 2023.

Patti village because villagers of Inayat Patti village said that they considered themselves as congressi during the ruling of Congress in Delhi but the increasing role of BJP gave a new type of identity to Muslims as sapai in Inayat Patti village due to politics of Samajwadi party. These consequences gave an ethnic homogenous political identity to Muslims; those entire political functions were moving around internal and international migration in the twenty-first century.[33]

As a consequence of Mumbai-based internal migration, it is observed that both Muslim and Hindu migrants were interested in the politics of Shiv Sena in Mumbai because these Muslim and Hindu migrants considered that *Bhaiya* migrants of Uttar Pradesh and Bihar found a social, political and economic space in Maratha based politics of Mumbai. These consequences were helpful in the creation of homogenous political ethnicity among migrant labourers in Inayat Patti village, those who worked in Mumbai for the survival of their left-behind family members in the village.[34]

It is also observed that these *sheikh* Muslims were considering the politics of BJP as the politics of Hindutava but these *sheikh* Muslims did not have any ideas about philosophical components of Hindutava. These consequences were directly associated with the impact of Arabian-based Gulf migration among Muslims, those who were interested in Muslim-based politics compared to considering Hindutava-based politics of BJP in Inayat Patti and its surrounding village. These Muslims said that they liked the Samajwadi party due to its positive role in Muslim politics compared to the Hindutava politics of BJP toward Hindus in Inayat Patti and its surrounding villages. These consequences created an ethnic conflict in local politics in the context of Arabian-based Gulf migration and Mumbai-based internal migration.[35]

In the case of non-migrant schedule caste –Dalits were also an ethnic homogenous group in Inayat Patti village and these Dalits were involved in Delhi-based internal migration due to well developed social network system of migration from Dalits' hamlets to Delhi but it was realized that entire political ethnic discourse of Dalits was being continuously shifted toward politics of BJP due to agenda of Sabka Sath Sab ka Vikas (Development of

---

[33] Information is based on passive observation and informal interview methods among return migrant labourers in Inayat Patti village in November 2023.
[34] Information is based on passive observation and informal interview methods among return migrant labourers in Inayat Patti village in February 2015.
[35] Information is based on passive observation and informal interview methods among return migrant labourers in Inayat Patti village in March 2015.

all with approach of together). It is also observed that these Dalits were happy and satisfied with the public distribution system (PDS) in Inayat Patti village because PDS based system improved the food rights for poor Dalits, those who did not have agricultural fields like sheikh Muslim migrant households and Yadav Hindu migrant households in village. These consequences created a new scenario of ethnic political discourse about *Dalit* politics in Uttar Pradesh due to the ruling of the BJP in Lucknow and Delhi as well as faded the politics of BSP and *Dalit* woman leader Mayawati. These consequences shifted *Dalit* votes toward the BJP due to the direct implementation of food rights through the PDS[36] (Public distribution system) system in the village. A consequence of the PDS system increased the wages in the local labour market of Inayat Patti village due to the impact of PDS system in *Dalit* households because *Dalits* labourers denied engaging themselves as agricultural labourers in the agricultural farmhouse of upper caste sheikhs in Inayat Patti and its surrounding villages. Therefore, the PDS system increased the labour scarcity due to the economic and political mobility of *Dalits* to form of ethnic homogeneity as identity of Hindus instead of *Dalits* in the periphery of politics of BJP in Uttar Pradesh.[37]

In the context of MGNREGA[38] (Mahatma Gandhi National Rural Employment Guarantee Act) in Inayat Patti village, it is realized that the function of MGNREGA was not properly working due to the depth penetration of culture of migration in Inayat Patti village because *Dalit* migrant labourers gained more wages in Delhi compared to low wages in MGNREGA. It is also observed that upper caste sheikh Muslims and Yadav caste Hindus were not interested in MGNREGA due to low wages and matters of socio-economic and political identities in the village. These consequences can be analyzed as the role of migration and the PDS system in the poor function of MGNREGA because the economic mobility of *Dalits* emerged as barriers in the way of MGNREGA in Inayat Patti and its surrounding villages in the context of globalization of migration in twenty-

---

[36] PDS system is based on food rights provisions for poor Indians being implemented by government of India. Cited from: George, N. A., & McKay, F. H. (2019). The public distribution system and food security in India. *International journal of environmental research and public health*, *16*(17), 3221.

[37] Information is based on passive observation and informal interview methods among return migrant labourers in Inayat Patti village in October 2023.

[38] MGNREGA is rural based employment employment scheme for rural labourers conducted by government of India. Cited from: Ranaware, K., Das, U., Kulkarni, A., & Narayanan, S. (2015). MGNREGA works and their impacts: A study of Maharashtra. *Economic and Political Weekly*, 53-61.

first century. [39]

These consequences developed a socio-economic and cultural transformation among migrants in the aspect of the process, determinates and consequences of ethnic-based racism and its discourse in the socio-economic and politics of Inayat Patti and its surrounding villages in the perspective of globalization of migration in twenty-first century.

5.3.2 Politics, economic, cultural ethnicity and migration in Mumbai

It is observed that there was a significant impact of the Bhojpuri diaspora in Mumbai and these consequences created a matter of politics, economics, and cultural ethnicity in the perspective of migration and globalization in Mumbai. It is also observed that the social aspect of migration created social-based ethnicity among migrant labourers of Uttar Pradesh and Bihar because North Indian migrant labourers developed a form of social region of Bhojpuri in Marathi-based culture in Mumbai. These consequences gave a new sharpness to the matter of politics about Bhojpuri migrants in Maratha-based political culture in Mumbai because the consequence of Bhojpuri migration created an ethnic homogenous group of migrant labourers of Uttar Pradesh and Bihar in Mumbai. It is also observed that these consequences created an ethnic conflict about political values between the Bhojpuri migrant labourers and the Marathi people of Mumbai. Therefore, it is realized that the matter of political ethnic conflict gave a new debate to the politics of Mumbai and the regional politics of Uttar Pradesh and Bihar from the perspective of the role of labour politics. These consequences also determined the psychological and economic behaviour of migrants in the working culture of Mumbai because seasonal and temporary migrant labourers developed their economic cultural world in the culture of Mumbai but Bhojpuri migrant labourers used to live and work in their mental region of "Bhojpuri region" due to similar cultural practices and ethnic homogenous activities in Mumbai. These consequences helped develop an understanding of the study of the political economy of globalization of migration from the perspective of politics of ethnicity among Bhojpuri migrant labourers, those who maintained their homogenous ethnic practices in the global culture of Mumbai. These consequences also determined the economic efficiency of migrant labourers of Uttar Pradesh and Bihar because these migrant labourers were being considered as Bhaiya due to north Indian geographical

---

[39] Information is based on passive observation and informal interview methods among return migrant labourers in Inayat Patti village in October 2023.

identity and Chedabhai due to their settlement pattern in the slum areas of Mumbai. Both types of identities gave an ethnic homogenous identity to migrant labourers of Uttar Pradesh and Bihar, those who worked in Mumbai for a better life with hopes of surviving their left-behind family members at root in rural Uttar Pradesh and Bihar. These consequences showed that matter of ethnicity created phenomena of politics and economic perspective concerning the debate of the role of ethnic-based identical issues among Bhojpuri migrant labourers in Mumbai. These consequences also developed a cultural and ethnic route of migration from rural Uttar Pradesh and Bihar to Mumbai in the context of globalization of migration in the twenty-first century.[40]

It is also observed that Mumbai-based internal migration was led by ethnicity race, and gender because Mumbai-based internal migration was recognized as positive role on the Bhojpuri migrant labourers, who had common values, norms, beliefs, attitudes and perceptions about Mumbai and these consequences developed a building capacity of Bhojpuri ethnic diaspora in Mumbai where consequences of ethnic perspectives were being discussed by the political economy of globalization of migration in twenty-first century of India. Therefore, matter of globalization played a crucial role in the matter of discussing ethnic conflict and its politics as economic phenomena in the global culture of Mumbai.[41]

Box 5.10: Case Study[42]

"It is a case study of 45-year-old migrant labourer named Juber, who was from a neighbouring village of Inayat Patti, namely Basgit village in Prayagraj district, Uttar Pradesh. He worked as Panwala in Nakhuda Mohalla in Mumbai. He said that he was considered as Panwala Bhaiya in Mumbai and felt proud of this identity. He also said that he was known as Chedhbhai because he used to live on rent in the Kolkata building in Nakhuda Mohalla in Mumbai. These consequences showed that there was a crucial role of the political economy of the ethnicity of Bhojpuri migrant labourers of Uttar Pradesh and Bihar in the informal based economy of Mumbai".

5.3.3. Politics, economic, cultural ethnicity and migration in Dubai

It is observed that there was a significant impact of the Bhojpuri diaspora in the Arabic environment of Dubai because huge trend of unskilled and semi-skilled labour migration from Uttar Pradesh and Bihar developed a Bhojpuri

---

[40] Information is based on informal interviews of migrant labourer in Null Bazar area of Mumbai in February 2019.

[41] Information is based on informal interviews of migrant labourers in Bhindi Bazar area of Mumbai in February 2019.

[42] Information is based on personal interview from respondent in Bhindi Bazar area of Mumbai in Febraury 2019.

world in Dubai. These consequences created a form of ethnic homogenous identity for Bhojpuri migrant labourers in Dubai. It is also observed that there were diversified socio-economic and cultural practices in Dubai but migrant labourers of the Bhojpuri region of Uttar Pradesh and Bihar were being recognized as "Hindi" due to the explicit impact of the Hindi language in the environment of the Arabic language in United Arab Emirates. Therefore, ethnic homogenous identity as Hindi gave a feeling of similarity to Bhojpuri migrant labourers as well as led to psychological bonding among migrant labourers of Uttar Pradesh and Bihar; those migrated to Dubai with hopes of their better life with the survival of their left behind family members at root in rural Uttar Pradesh and Bihar. It is also observed that Bhojpuri migrant labourers of Uttar Pradesh and Bihar felt proud of Bhojpuri dialect, folk song-like Birha, and Bhojpuri cuisines like Litti and Chokha where these consequences minimized the psychological panic conditions of long-term migration in Dubai as well as developed an ethnic homogeneity among Bhojpuri migrant labourers in Dubai.[43]

These consequences showed that there was prominent importance of ethnic-based identical issues in the economic performance of migrant labourers of Uttar Pradesh and Bihar, those who worked in the bottom segmentation of the labour market in the United Arab Emirates. Therefore, these consequences developed an ethnic homogenous identity in the form of economic perspective as contract-based labourers. Therefore, the economic characteristic of migrant labourers of Uttar Pradesh and Bihar were being recognized as "guest workers" due to their participation in the bottom segmentation of the labour market in labour intensive labour market under the *Kafala* (sponsor) system dual labour market system in United Arab Emirates. These migrant labourers said that Arabians called contract-based unskilled and semi-skilled migrant labourers Ghulam (slave labourers) because Arabians considered unskilled and semi-skilled migrant labourers as inferior due to their engagement in bottom segmentation of the labour market. These consequences can be analyzed as the role of the economic ethnic homogenous identity of migrant labourers of Uttar Pradesh and Bihar with the matter of ethnic crisis in the system of the dual labour market of Kafala system in the United Arab Emirates.[44]

It is also observed that there was not any matter of politics or ethnic conflict

---

[43] Information is based on informal interviews and passive observation methods among migrant labourers at Deira in Dubai in December 2019.
[44] Information is based on informal interviews and passive observation methods among migrant labourers at Deira in Dubai in December 2019.

in Dubai like matter of ethnic conflict of migrant labourers in Mumbai because there was not any conflict matter among migrant labourers in the perspective of religion in Dubai. These migrant labourers worked in a very friendly way in the global economic culture of Dubai as well as being considered as Hindi instead of the diversified culture of India. Therefore, these consequences developed a form of "Hindi Diaspora" in the Arabic culture of the United Arab Emirates as well as gave a similar socio-economic and cultural ethnic-based identity to migrant labourers of Uttar Pradesh and Bihar, those led to their Bhojpuri culture in Dubai. Therefore, these migrant labourers of Uttar Pradesh and Bihar were being recognized as "Bhojpuriya" migrant labourers in Dubai as well as developed a mental region of Bhojpuri culture in the environment of Arabic culture in Dubai.[45]

Box 5.11: Case Study[46]

"It is a case study of 50 years -old migrant labourer named Ram Virxa, who was from the Kushinagar district of Uttar Pradesh. He said that he worked as a carpenter in Jalandhar City of Punjab, India before migrating to Dubai. He also said that he felt proud of the identity of a Bhojpuri migrant labourer in the Arabic culture of the United Arab Emirates. These consequences showed that there was an inter-connection between internal and international migration in the perspective of migration from rural Uttar Pradesh to Dubai as well as developed ethnic-based Bhojpuri migration due to the explicit impact of the Bhojpuri culture among Bhojpuri language-speaking migrant labourers in the environment of Arabic language in Dubai."

---

[45] Information is based on informal interviews and passive observation methods among migrant labourers at Deira in Dubai in December 2019.
[46] Information is based on personal interview from migrant labourer at Deira in Dubai in December 2019.

CHAPTER 6

SAFE ZONE CONCEPT OF MIGRATION AND GLOBALIZATION

6.1. Introduction

According to Cohen & Sirkeci (2011), the culture of migration plays a crucial role in facilitating migration across the globe because depth penetration of the culture of migration is positively associated with the function of globalization of migration around the world where migration creates a culture and culture leads migration. The consequences of a culture of migration are an important factor in building the capacity of labour migration because the findings of the study of Kesici (2021) show that the historical consequences of migration are the result of the cultural aspect of migration. After all, the migration community migrates within the well-developed cultural region of migration through the positive role of the social network system of migration from root to destinations in the context of globalization of migration. A study by Demir et al. (2021) shows that depth penetration of the culture of migration leads the process of migration from Asian countries to Europe through documented and un-documented migration because migrants find a better way in the context of migration where the function of migration works as a safe zone for migrants. After all, migrants find migration as a safe zone for their livelihood. Other findings show that the culture of migration from Turkey to Europe is the result of the globalization of cultural migration where migrants migrate through the cultural route of migration with their cultural beliefs, values, norms, and beliefs and these consequences lead to the building capacity of the cultural diaspora of migration. A study by Amuedo et al. (2023) shows that the consequences of cultural migration work as a safe zone for migrants within specific cultural regions of migration in the context of the role of innovative approach in the function of migration regarding leads the phenomena of cultural migration from root to destinations through transit destination between root and destinations. The findings of a study by Molland (2022) show that depth penetration of cultural migration is positively associated with the function of a safe zone where migrants find matter of migration as a source of their livelihood as well as do not think about another source of livelihood instead of migration because consequences of a culture of migration determine the safe zone of migration within well developed cultural region of migration.

The findings of the study of Taukeer (2022) show that the current phenomena of labour migration from Uttar Pradesh and Bihar are based on the colonial experiences of indentured labour migration during the rule of British India. In the context of labour migration from India to Gulf countries, a report of the overseas employment division, Ministry of External Affairs Government of India (2014-15) shows that there is a long history of labour migration from India, especially from southern Indian states namely – Kerala to oil-producing Gulf countries but recent phenomena of labour migration are shifted toward north Indian states namely- Uttar Pradesh and Bihar in the context of globalization of international Gulf migration in both Uttar Pradesh and Bihar. Findings of Zachariah & Rajan (2012) show that the trend of labour migration from Kerala to oil-producing Gulf countries is being led by skilled labour migration compared to unskilled and semi-skilled labour migration from Uttar Pradesh and Bihar to oil-producing Gulf countries. These consequences are the result of the role of vocational training institutions, in Kerala where migrant labourers get training in skills and these consequences lead to skilled migration compared to Uttar Pradesh and Bihar, where the absence of such kinds of vocational training institutions, leads to unskilled labour migration.

In these perspectives, the findings of a study by Khadria (2001) show that the consequence of the globalization of migration works as a pull factor in the process of unskilled and semi-skilled labour migration from India to oil-producing Gulf countries because the function of globalization opened the door for unskilled and semi-skilled migrant labourers in oil-producing Gulf countries in the twenty-first century. Likewise, a similar study by Khadria (2006) shows that the trend of labour migration from India to Gulf countries is a new phenomenon of the role of globalization of migration in the twenty-first century because the result of the consequence of globalization paved the route for unskilled and semi-skilled labour migration toward oil-producing Gulf countries. A study by Rajan & Kumar (2010) shows that the consequence of globalization is a major trigger factor in the process of labour migration from Uttar Pradesh and Bihar to oil-producing Gulf countries in the twenty-first century of migration in India. Historical consequences of migration play a crucial role in the function of migration because findings of a study by Kumar (2016) show that there is a significant role of the historical facts in the process of labour migration from India to Gulf countries with the paradigm of nexus of economy and migration. After all, the discovery of oil opened the door for labour migration from India to oil-producing Gulf countries as well as oil-based economy is working as a pull factor in the process for Indian labour migration from India to Gulf countries.

Based on the above concise introduction background this chapter explores to unfold facts about the process, determinates and consequences of labour migration from Uttar Pradesh to Gulf countries in the twenty-first century. In the consequences, the present chapter analyzes the role of the safe zone concept of migration in the consequence of depth penetration of cultural migration in the context of globalization of international migration in rural Uttar Pradesh. Therefore, the present chapter better advocates the formation function and consequences of the safe zone mechanism of migration from the perspective of labour migration from rural Uttar Pradesh to Gulf countries via internal migration to Mumbai (Flow chart: 6.1).

Flow chart 6.1. Safe Zone of Migration from rural Uttar Pradesh to Gulf Countries via Mumbai

Boundary of Social Network

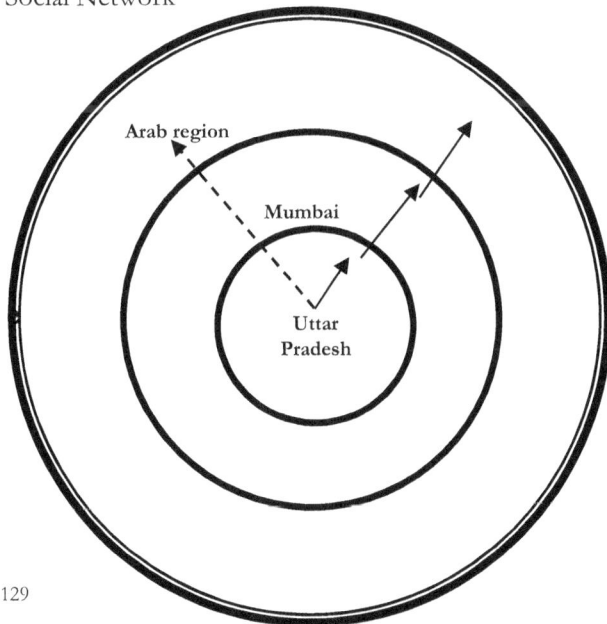

Taukeer, 2023, p.129

Therefore, the present study covered rural Uttar Pradesh as the root, Mumbai as the transit destination and the United Arab Emirates as the international destination. Therefore, the findings of this chapter conceptualized the consequences of cultural migration from the perspective of livelihood where the matter of migration works as a major source of livelihood because Gulf-based international migration is being led by a guarantee of access to better jobs with higher wages in Gulf countries compared to low wages of jobs in cities of India. Therefore, the fact of access guarantee of jobs in Gulf countries is key for the formation of the safe zone concept of migration because depth penetration of the culture of migration transfers the mechanism of expectation about access jobs into a guarantee of access to jobs.

6.1.1. Migration from India to Gulf countries in current phenomena

The findings of the study of Taukeer (2021) show that there is a culture of both internal and international migration from Uttar Pradesh where unskilled and semiskilled migrant labourers migrated to Gulf countries via a culture of internal migration to Mumbai. Therefore, the consequences of the connection between internal and international migration are positively associated with the depth penetration of culture of migration in the context of globalization of cultural migration in the twenty-first century. The findings of a study by Sasikumar & Thimothy (2015) show that the trend and tendency of international labour migration from Uttar Pradesh to Gulf countries is being led by wage differentials between cities of India and Gulf countries because migrant labourers get higher wages in Gulf countries as well as well developed social network system of migration also work as pull factor in the process of migration. These consequences lead to cultural migration as a positive role of the globalization of migration in rural Uttar Pradesh. A study by Azeez & Begum (2009) shows that the consequences of international Gulf migration ensured the huge inflow of remittances in rural Uttar Pradesh and these consequences leads the culture of migration from Uttar Pradesh to Gulf countries in the twenty-first century. A study by Taukeer (2017) shows that the consequences of aculture of migration lead to the labour migration from Inayat Patti village to oil-producing Gulf countries via internal migration to Mumbai. These consequences led to internal to international migration within well-developed cultural regions of migration.

In the context of labour migration to Mumbai, the findings of Bhagat (2011) show that Mumbai is a dream city for seasonal and temporary migrant labourers of Uttar Pradesh due to availability of the jobs in Mumbai. These perspectives of the study of Gavaskar (2010) show that Mumbai is a hub for north Indian migrant labourers; those migrate from rural Uttar Pradesh and Bihar to Mumbai with hopes of surviving their individual life with their left behind family members at root. A study by Kumar et al. (2012) shows that Mumbai works as glamour for seasonal and temporary migrant labourers of Uttar Pradesh and Bihar. A study by Jha & Kumar (2016) shows that Mumbai-based internal migration developed a cultural region of migration in Mumbai where Mumbai-based economy works as a backbone for seasonal and temporary migrant labourers in Mumbai. Findings of Taukeer (2023) show that Mumbai-based internal migration opened the door for international Gulf migration from rural Uttar Pradesh because the culture of internal migration leads the culture of international migration to oil-producing Gulf countries within well-developed cultural regions of migration from rural Uttar Pradesh to Gulf countries via Mumbai.

6.1.2. Safe zone concept in migration from Inayat Patti village to Gulf countries via Mumbai

It is observed that there is a well-developed cultural region of migration from rural Uttar Pradesh to Gulf countries via internal migration to Mumbai because the consequences of a culture of migration developed a safe zone region of migration where migrant labourers migrate with a guarantee of access to jobs in Mumbai and Gulf countries. In the case of labour migration from Inayat Patti village to Saudi Arabia, it is realized that there was an inter-connection between internal and international migration because the culture of internal migration paved the route of international migration in the consequence of long journey of migration from Inayat Patti village to Gulf countries. It is also observed that depth penetration of globalization of migration developed a safe zone for migrant labourers because migrant labourers found better jobs with higher wages in Mumbai and Gulf countries due to the availability of the well-developed social network system of migration in the context of globalization of migration in Inayat Patti village. From the perspective of the function of the culture of migration in Inayat Patti village, it is found that historical consequences of migration developed a cultural route of migration from Inayat Patti village to Gulf countries through the positive role of the internal migration in the process of facilitating international migration.[1]

---

[1] Information is based on informal interviews and passive observation methods among return migrant labourers in Inayat Patti village in February 2015.

> **Box 6.1: Case Study[2]**
>
> 'It is a case study of 39 years old return migrant labourer named Shonu; he said that he worked in Mumbai before migrating to Saudi Arabia. He said that he migrated to Mumbai and Saudi Arabia due to the long historical consequences of migration in the context of globalization of migration in the twenty- first century. He also said that Inayat Patti village was known for its journey of migration based on colonial experiences of migration and the consequences of colonial experiences of migration led to the culture of internal and international migration. These consequences can be analyzed in the form of a culture of migration among youths of the village, who considered a matter of Gulf migration as a source of livelihood because they did not think of another source of livelihood instead of migration due to the deep impact of migration in development practices of village.'

It was found that a well-developed mechanism of culture of migration led to a well-developed social network system of migration from Inayat Patti village to Gulf countries via internal migration to Mumbai. Therefore, the social aspect of the consequences of the culture of migration created a safe zone for migrant labourers because the well-developed social network system of migration worked as a pull factor in the process of building the capacity of migration. These consequences were helpful in the determination of the social well-being of migrant labourers because migrant labourers found the matter of migration as a safeguard for their livelihood as well as a key for social development. It is also observed that the consequences of the social network system of migration were being led and functioned by social values, norms, beliefs, myths and attitudes and these consequences determined the social psychological behaviour of migrant labourers in the periphery of the village. It is also observed that the social function of migration created a safe zone concept of migration where depth penetration of the social network system of migration gave a platform to migrant labourers with the guarantee of jobs in both Mumbai and Gulf countries and these consequences worked as pull factor in the process of migration from village to Gulf countries via culture of internal migration to Mumbai within well developed safe zone region of migration.[3]

From the perspective of the economic concept of a safe zone of migration, it is observed that the economic impact of both internal and international migration created a form of economic region of migration from Inayat Patti village to Gulf countries via internal migration to Mumbai. It is also observed that the matter of wage differential played a crucial role in the process of economic migration because the mechanism of the safe zone concept of

---

[2] Information is based on personal interviews from return migrant labourer in Inayat Patti village in March 2015.

[3] Information is based on informal interviews and passive observation methods among return migrant labourers in Inayat Patti village in March 2015.

migration was led by the economic factor of migration where a migrant labourer had in-depth information about the availability of the jobs with higher wages based on his/her cost and benefit analysis. Therefore, it is realized that the safe zone concept of migration was led by the mechanism of wage differential between rural-based economies and destinations where migrant labourers developed their economic perception about migration in the context of economic valuation of migration in the context of wages and the nature of jobs. These consequences were helpful in the building and formation of a safe zone of migration from Inayat Patti village to Gulf countries via a culture of internal migration to Mumbai. Therefore, both internal and international migration were assimilated and integrated into each other in the aspect of the safe zone concept of migration where the economy of migration led to the process of migration within the safe zone of migration.[4]

From the perspective of the cultural aspect of the safe zone concept of migration in the village, it is observed that there was a well-developed culture of migration in the sense of internal to international migration because internal migration led to the international migration in Inayat Patti village. Therefore, it is found that the culture of migration from Inayat Patti village to Mumbai and Gulf countries was based on long historical consequences of migration from colonial India and its emerging form as organized migration in the village in twenty-first century. It is also observed that both internal and international migration functioned by common cultural values about migration among migrants in villages because migration created a culture and culture led migration in the consequences of the globalization of migration. It was found that the cultural aspect of migration was more widespread compared to the social and economic aspects of migration because the function of both social and economic aspects of migration ensured the pathway of the culture of migration within the well-developed culture region of migration from Inayat Patti village to Gulf countries via internal migration to Mumbai. Therefore, the consequence of depth penetration of the culture of migration created a safe zone of migration where migrant labourers were ensured about their cultural engagement in migration in the aspect of cultural livelihood practices of migration based on the cultural evolution of migration from its past to present with future implication of migration.[5]

---

[4] Information is based on informal interviews and passive observation methods among return migrant labourers in Inayat Patti village in March 2015

[5] Information is based on informal interviews and passive observation methods among return migrant labourers in Inayat Patti village in March 2015

> **Box 6.2: Case Study[6]**
> "It is a case study of 34 years return migrant labourer named Aftab Ahamed, who said that there was a well-developed culture of migration in Inayat Patti village due to its long historical consequences of migration from village to Gulf countries via culture of internal migration to Mumbai. He also said that youths never think about another source of livelihood instead of migration because both internal and international migrations were deeply rooted in their livelihood practices. These consequences can be analyzed as the role of long historical consequences of the culture of migration in Inayat Patti village in the context of globalization of migration as a function of the safe zone concept in migration in twenty-first century."

6.1.3. Component of safe zone concept of migration

Both economic and non-economic phenomena worked as components in the mechanism of the safe zone concept in migration where economic and non-economic factors of migration were correlated and assimilated to each other and the function of the culture of migration worked as a pull factor in the process of migration. It is also observed that the wishes and abilities of migrant labourers were moving around the function of cultural migration because the impact of migration plays an important role in the improvement of the wishes and abilities of migrant labourers in the consequence of migration. Therefore, it is observed that there was a significant impact of the safe zone concept of migration where both culture and globalization were important components of migration because the boundary of culture was widespread by the direct impact of globalization of migration on the cultural behaviour of migrants. Both culture of migration and globalization were important factors because the nexus of migration and culture was being led by the function of globalization of migration in the environment of the cultural periphery of the village. It is also observed that the matter of migration was deeply rooted in the cultural practices of migrant labourers because migrant labourers used to take matters of migration as key to their livelihood and economy. These consequences developed a safe zone of migration from villages to Gulf countries via a culture of internal migration to Mumbai. These consequences were helpful in the socio-economic and cultural transformation in Inayat Patti village in the context of the culture of migration from the perspective of globalization of migration.[7]

It is also realized that the cultural landscape of migration was a direct result of the nexus of migration and culture in the context of the impact of

---

[6] Information is based on personal interviews from return migrant labourer in Inayat Patti village in March 2015.

[7] Information is based on informal interviews and passive observation methods among migrant labourers from India to United Arab Emirates from February 2015 to December 2019.

globalization in Inayat Patti village. These consequences paved the route of migration from villages to Gulf countries through the positive role of internal migration because it is also observed that region of both internal and international migration was being designed by the boundary of the social network system of migration in the context of globalization of migration in the twenty-first century. Therefore, it is also found that the boundary of social networks system of migration was widespread to Gulf countries because Muslim youth were not aware of southeast Asian and European countries due to depth penetration of Arabian-based Gulf migration where Arabian-based migration was suitable according to Islamic ideology of Muslim youths, those considered Saudi Arabia as holy country as well as a safe country for Muslims. It is also observed that these Muslim youth did not have any idea of current phenomena in Saudi Arabia like Vision 2030. These consequences showed that these Muslim youths were living in darkness world due to the existence of safe zones of migration where these Muslim youths used to see the dream of Saudi-based migration from their childhood, therefore, these Muslim youths were not interested in modern education but they gave priority to Islamic based education due to Saudi based migration. These consequences were the direct result of the consequence of safe zone of migration in the context of the globalization of the culture of migration among Muslim youths in Inayat Patti village.[8]

Box 6.3: Case Study[9]

"It is a case study of 42 years return migrant labourer named Lalle, in Inayat Patti village, He said that he was not educated but had information about Islamic principles because Islamic principles were an important factor in Saudi-based migration. He also said that he dreamt in his childhood of migrating to Saudi Arabia, therefore, he excluded himself from the modern education system of India. These consequences showed that the depth penetration of globalization of culture of migration developed a safe zone of migration in Inayat Patti village where Muslim youths found matter of migration as a source of the safeguard for their livelihood because the impact of Saudi-based migration was prominent for them and they were willingly involved in Saudi based migration by the inter-generational journey of migration."

Based on the above concise description and analysis, it can be finalized that depth penetration of globalization of culture migration designed the safe zone of migration through the positive function of the social network system of migration from Inayat Patti village to Mumbai and Gulf countries. The consequences of the social network system of migration led to the entire

---

[8] Information is based on informal interviews and passive observation methods among migrants from India to United Arab Emirates from February 2015 to December 2019.
[9] Information is based on personal interviews from return migrant labourer in Inayat Patti village in October 2023.

function of migration where Mumbai worked as a transit cultural destination between Inayat Patti and Saudi Arabia. Therefore, both cultures of internal and international migration existed in the framework of safe zones where the boundary of the safe zone of migration was designed by the social network system of migration from Inayat Patti village to Mumbai and later to Saudi Arabia. Therefore, the consequences of the safe zone of migration led to the step-wise migration from Inayat Patti to Mumbai and Saudi Arabia where the culture of short-term Mumbai-based internal migration led to the long-term Saudi-based international migration through the way of a well-developed social network system of migration. In these consequences, it is realized that long historical sequences of the journey of migration from Inayat Patti village to Mumbai were based on colonial experiences of migration and its emerging form in the aspect of Saudi-based international migration in the twenty-first century of migration. These consequences were helpful in the formation of building capacity of a safe zone of migration due to the impact of the culture of migration on the ground level as the consequence of the globalization of migration among Muslim youths in Inayat Patti village. Therefore, the social network system of migration, the culture of migration and globalization were important factors in the formation of a safe zone of migration in Inayat Patti village.

Box 6.4: Case Study[10]

"It is a case study of 49-years- old return migrant labourer named Kallu, in Inayat Patti village. He said that he migrated to Saudi Arabia with the help of their kinship network system of migration due to the well-developed culture of migration as the consequence of the globalization of migration in Inayat Patti village. These consequences can be analyzed as a positive role of the dynamics of the social network system of migration where both cultures of internal and international migration were being led by the social network system of migration in twenty-first century."

6.2. Function of safe zone concept of migration from root to destinations

According to Singh (2021), the tendency of labour migration from India to oil-producing Gulf countries is based on the long historical consequences of migration in the context of globalization of international migration in rural India. The findings of a study by Taukeer (2020) show the function of unskilled and semi-skilled labour migration from rural Uttar Pradesh to Mumbai and Gulf countries worked within the safe zone region through the positive role of the social network system of migration. Therefore, these

---

[10] Information is based on personal interview from return migrant labourer in Inayat Patti village in November 2023.

consequences developed the culture of migration from rural areas of Uttar Pradesh to Gulf countries as a consequence of globalization of the culture of migration in rural Uttar Pradesh in the twenty-first century. These consequences developed migration-based communities, which considered matters of migration as their source of livelihood due to the depth of penetration of the inter-generational culture of migration. The findings of Naufal & Ali (2010) show that unskilled and semi-skilled labourers are important sources for ensuring a huge inflow of remittances from Gulf countries to rural Uttar Pradesh because these unskilled and semi-skilled migrant labourers work as temporary migrant labourers and these consequences determined the huge inflow of remittances from Gulf countries to rural Uttar Pradesh. Likewise, the study of Rajan et al. (2017) shows that Uttar Pradesh receives India's largest remittances from Gulf countries because Uttar Pradesh is the leading state in unskilled and semi-skilled labour migration from India to Gulf countries in the context of globalization of international migration in rural Uttar Pradesh.

In these contexts, the study of Magliveras (2019) shows that Saudi-based migration was deeply rooted among Indian Muslims due to the depth of penetration of Islamic-based culture among Indian Muslim migrant labourers. These consequences developed a culture of migration from India to Saudi Arabia in the context of globalization of Saudi-based migration among Indian Muslim migrant labourers because these Muslim migrant labourers considered Saudi Arabia as a holy space for their cultural practices of livelihood. Likewise, findings of the study of Rahman (2001) show that there is a well-developed culture of migration among Muslims in rural India because Muslim migrant labourers consider the matter of Saudi based migration as a source of their livelihood due to the positive role of the Islamic ideology among Muslim youths about migration. These consequences developed a culture of migration from rural India to Saudi Arabia where Muslim youth considered a matter of migration as a safeguard for their livelihood practices in the sense of globalization of migration. In these consequences, the findings of Ali (2007) show those Indian Muslim youths find the perspective of migration as part of their culture and these consequences are positively associated with their cultural perception of Saudi-based migration because Muslim youths entered a safe zone of migration where they think only about migration due to its swift earning in Saudi Arabia. These consequences developed a culture of migration among Muslim youths toward migration to Saudi Arabia in the context of globalization of migration in the twenty-first century.

In the case of labour migration from Inayat Patti village to Saudi Arabia via the culture of internal migration to Mumbai, findings of the study of Majumder & Taukeer (2019) show that the culture of both Mumbai-based internal and Saudi-based international migration developed a cultural region of migration where migrant labourers used to take matter of migration as source of their livelihood because Saudi based migration was positively associated with their cultural practices of livelihood in the sense of globalization of migration in twenty-first century in Inayat Patti village. Recent findings of a study by Taukeer (2023) show that a well-developed culture of migration from Inayat Patti village to Mumbai and Gulf countries developed a safe zone region of migration because the matter of migration worked as a safeguard for Muslims. After all, Muslim youths did never think about another source of employment, instead of migration due to the depth penetration of inter-generational consequences of migration in the culture of Muslims in Inayat Patti village. These consequences paved the route of labour migration from Inayat Patti to Saudi Arabia via internal migration to Mumbai within well-developed culture of migration in the context of globalization of Saudi-based migration among Muslim youths.

The findings of a study by Gardner (2010) show that South Asian migrant labourers find a suitable cultural space in Gulf countries and these consequences develop a form of cultural diaspora in Gulf countries as well as leads to the cultural migration from India to the Gulf countries because Indian migrant labourers considered the matter of migration as part of their culture because migration is working as a safeguard for their livelihood. These consequences developed an economic bonding among Indian migrant labourers in the perspective of diaspora philanthropy because findings of a study by Afsal & Reshmi (2023) show that there is a significant role of the Gulf-based remittances in socio-economic and cultural development in migration-abundant zones in India and these consequences created a socio-economic and cultural transformation where the cultural impact of migration gave a safeguard to migrant labourers about engaging themselves in matter of Gulf migration.

Based on the above concise analysis of the review of literature, it can be realized that there is a significant impact of both internal and international migration in rural Uttar Pradesh because Saudi-based international migration is a new phenomenon in the context of development practices concerning migration in the twenty-first century. Analysis of the selected review of literature gives realistic based phenomena about the penetration of culture of migration among Muslims because the matter of migration is deeply rooted with cultural livelihood practices of migrant labourers, those willingly involved in the process of the inter-generational journey of migration from rural Uttar Pradesh to Gulf countries via culture of internal migration in Mumbai. Therefore, the culture of the consequence of internal migration is leading to the process of international labour migration from rural Uttar Pradesh to Gulf countries because the consequences of globalization of international migration opened the door for Saudi-based Gulf migration in rural Uttar Pradesh. These consequences developed a form of safe zone of migration within well developed cultural region of migration from rural Uttar Pradesh to Saudi Arabia via internal migration to Mumbai because the function of the safe zone concept of migration gives a guarantee of better jobs with higher wages in both Mumbai and Saudi Arabia. Therefore, migrant labourers find themselves in a better secure position in the context of their development practices concerning migration due to the increasing role of the globalization of the culture of migration in the rural-based economy of rural Uttar Pradesh. These consequences are leading to a shifting of the labour force from a rural-based economy to an urban-based economy in the case of inter-state rural-urban migration as well as internal to international migration in the case of migration of rural migrant labourers from Mumbai to Saudi Arabia in the perspective of assimilation and integration between internal and international migration in process of labour migration from rural Uttar Pradesh to Gulf countries via internal migration to Mumbai.

In the case of labour migration from Inayat Patti village to Gulf countries via internal migration to Mumbai, a selected review of the literature shows that the impact of migration led to the function of a safe zone of migration due to the depth penetration of cultural migration in Inayat Patti village. A selected review of the literature also shows that long historical consequences of migration in Inayat Patti village developed a safe zone of migration in the context of the depth nexus between the culture of migration and globalization among Muslims. These consequences play an important role in the function of a safe zone of migration because Muslim youths find the matter of migration as a guarantee of the source of livelihood with access to better jobs with higher wages in both Mumbai and the United Arab Emirates. Consequences of both Mumbai-based internal and Dubai-based international migration developed a form of safe zone of migration within well-developed cultural region of migration from Inayat Patti village to the United Arab Emirates via a culture of internal migration to Mumbai. Therefore, it is realized that long historical consequences of migration paved the route of migration as well as functioned as a safe zone of migration where Muslims have their own developed beliefs, values, norms and myths about migration and these consequences are giving an important role in the function of the safe zone of migration from Inayat Patti village to Dubai via internal migration to Mumbai. These consequences are also leading to cultural migration as well as replacing the hopes of expectation of jobs with a guarantee of access to better jobs with higher wages in both Mumbai and the United Arab Emirates.

In these consequences, the present section of this chapter analyzes the function of a safe zone of migration from root to destinations where Inayat Patti village is selected as the root due to its long historical journey of migration from colonial India to recent phenomena of migration in the twenty-first century. These consequences developed a safe zone region of migration in Inayat Patti. Apart, Mumbai urban agglomeration is selected as the internal destination for the study of the function of the safe zone of migration among migrant labourers of Inayat Patti village as well and Dubai is selected as the international destination for the study of the function of safe zone of migration among migrant labourers of Inayat Patti village. Therefore, the findings of the present section of this chapter try to better advocate the function of a safe zone of migration through the role of both economic and non-economic phenomena of migration from Inayat Patti village to the United Arab Emirates via internal migration to Mumbai. Therefore, these consequences developed a safe zone of migration within the well-developed cultural region of migration from village to Dubai via internal migration to Mumbai due to the large impact of the globalization of the culture of migration among Muslims in Inayat Patti village according to dynamics of globalization in the twenty-first century. Therefore, the findings of the present chapter help develop an understanding of critical analysis of the traditional theory of migration as well as give a new lens to observing phenomena of migration through the function of the safe zone concept of migration where depth penetration of cultural migration is being re-formed and re-designed by both economic and non-economic factors of migration because assimilation and integration between economic and non-economic factors of migration developed safe zone of migration due to long historical consequences of cultural migration from Inayat Patti to Mumbai and Gulf countries. These consequences are leading to the function of a safe zone of migration.

6.2.1. Function of safe zone of migration in Inayat Patti village

It is observed that there was a socio-economic and cultural function of the safe zone of migration from Inayat Patti village to Dubai via the culture of internal migration to Mumbai in the context of globalization of migration in the twenty-first century. The social function of the safe zone of migration was based on the social perception of the long historical journey of migration from Inayat Patti village to Dubai because Muslims developed their social perception of migration as a source of safeguard for their social cultural and economic practices concerning migration. These Muslims said that they considered matters of Saudi and Dubai-based migration with the availability of the guarantee of jobs with higher wages in both Mumbai and Dubai within well well-developed social region of migration from Inayat Patti village to Dubai via internal migration to Mumbai. The social aspect of the function of the safe zone of migration was also functioned by a well-developed social network system of migration in the context of the economic function of the safe zone of migration. Muslim youths migrated to both Mumbai and Dubai based on their social values, norms, beliefs and myths about migration in the village because long historical consequences of migration developed a migration-based community, those considered the culture of migration as part of their economic practices. These Muslims migrated to Saudi Arabia due to the significant impact of the Islamic-based *zakat* economy on the economic development of the village and these consequences developed a safe zone for Muslims, those who considered the Islamic-based economy for their economic practices. These consequences developed a specific Islamic region in the village where Saudi-based migration created an economic culture and the consequence of economic culture led to a safe zone of migration in the context of globalization of migration among Muslims in Inayat Patti village. Therefore, these consequences developed a specific Islamic economic community in the context of depth penetration of Saudi-based migration among Muslims; that entire economic function was based on the culture of internal and international migration. These consequences paved the way for the cultural function of a safe zone of migration because the nexus of social and cultural perspectives created a cultural transformation among Muslims in the context of Saudi-based migration. After all, both the wishes and abilities of Muslim migrant labourers were being improved by consequences of the Islamic impact of Saudi-based migration in the economic environment of the village. These consequences developed a form of the cultural region of migration where migrant labourers migrated with the help of myths about Saudi-based migration because Muslim youths considered Saudi Arabia as the "Tree of riyal" due to the mechanism of collecting zakat from sheikhs of Saudi Arabia. These consequences were helpful in the function safe zone of migration for Muslims because Muslim youths also considered a matter of Saudi-based migration as an important part of their cultural practices due to their consideration of the blessing of Prophet Mohammed on their economic activities in Saudi Arabia. These consequences played giving important role in the design of a safe zone for migration and its function in the context of migration from Inayat Patti to Saudi Arabia due to the mentality of sacred space about holy cities of Makkah and Madina among Muslims; those had little bit information about Islamic economy in the context of Saudi based migration.[11]

Box 6.5: Case Study[12]

"It is a case study of 34 years old return migrant labourer, named Gulam Gaus, who worked in an Iranian tea restaurant in Madinah city in Saudi Arabia. He said that he considered his economic activities in Saudi Arabia as a blessing of Prophet Mohammed because he never thought about his existence without the blessing of Prophet Mohammed he also said that he was not educated according to the Indian education system but used to feel proud with Islamic knowledge about consequences of zakat based economy in village. These consequences can be analyzed as the role of the Islamic-based economy in the function of a safe zone of migration among Muslim youths; those were not benefited from modern Indian education due to the long historical consequences of Saudi-based migration in Inayat Patti village. Therefore, Islamic-based migration was the major trigger in the function of a safe zone of migration among Muslim youth in Inayat Patti village."

6.2.2. Function of safe zone of migration in Mumbai

It is observed that Muslim youths of Inayat Patti village developed their Asiyana (cultural settlement pattern) in Mumbai due to the long historical journey of migration. These consequences developed a mental region of Inayat Patti in Mumbai due to the huge presence of Muslim migrant labourers; those migrated to Mumbai with hopes of migrating to Dubai and Saudi Arabia. These consequences were the result of the culture of migration among Muslims because Muslim youth found a secure social and economic space in Mumbai due to the availability of the well-developed social network system of migration. These consequences were helpful in the function of a safe zone of migration among Muslims in Inayat Patti village, those considered Mumbai as the dream city as well as the door for migration to Saudi Arabia and Dubai. These consequences led to the huge trend of labour migration from Inayat Patti to Mumbai the consequences of the first step of

---

[11] Information is based on informal interviews and passive observation methods among return migrant labourers in Inayat Patti village in October 2023.

[12] Information is based on personal interviews from return migrant labourer in Inayat Patti village in October 2023.

migration whereby the second step of migration was being led by the first step of internal migration. These consequences developed a mechanism of step-wise migration within the socio-economic region of migration covered by a safe zone of migration where both internal and international migration was being functioned within the socio-economic region of migration as safeguard for matters of livelihood among Muslims. It is also observed that Muslim youth used the term "Bombay-Saudi" for their culture of migration because Mumbai-based migration was positively associated with Saudi-based migration based on their common social and economic values about migration. Consequences of common social and economic values were based on oral history about the journey of migration among Muslim youths, those willingly involved in the intergenerational mechanism of migration due to the culture of migration in Inayat Patti village. These consequences functioned as the components of a safe zone of migration through the positive role of the dual step migration within the cultural region of migration from Inayat Patti village to Saudi Arabia and Dubai via internal migration to Mumbai. It is also observed that Muslim youths of Inayat Patti developed their Gav (village) in Mumbai where these Muslim youths found socio-economic support for finding jobs in Mumbai as well as motivated to migrate to Saudi Arabia and Dubai. These consequences were working as meal stones for the function of a safe zone of migration within the cultural region of migration from Inayat Patti to Saudi Arabia and Dubai via the culture of internal migration to Mumbai.[13]

Box 6.6: Case Study[14]

"It is a case study of 65 years old Muslim, named Akhter, who was never involved in migration, and told that his sons were working in Mumbai and Saudi Arabia. He also told that the youths of the village never preferred modern Indian education but also liked Islamic education due to the culture of Saudi-based migration in Inayat Patti village. He said that Utnai padhe, jitna ki Bambai aur Saudia jai ke kam karai , ka hoi padh ke (there is not any importance of education in life of youth because Bombay-Saudi migration is a safeguard for Muslim youths). These consequences can be analyzed as the role of the culture of Bombay- Saudi migration in the function of a safe zone of migration in the village."

6.2.3. Function of safe zone of migration in Dubai

It is observed that there was a huge presence of Muslim youths of Inayat Patti and its surrounding villages in Dubai, those who worked as unskilled and semi-skilled migrant labourers in Dubai. These consequences developed a mental region of Inayat Patti in Dubai because Muslim youths of the village considered Dubai as their Gav (village). These consequences developed as

---

[13] Information is based on informal interviews and passive observation methods among migrant labourers in Mumbai in February 2019.
[14] Information is based on personal interview from migrant labourer in Mumbai in February 2019.

Dubai's model of migration among Muslim youths who dreamt about Dubai-based migration in their childhood due to the explicit visibility of the Islamic-based economy in Inayat Patti village. It is also observed that the Dubai-based model was a major trigger factor in the function of a safe zone of migration because the glamour of jobs in Dubai motivated Muslim youths to migrate to Dubai. It is also found that Saudi-based migration was being continuously shifted toward Dubai-based migration due to the global image of Dubai but it is realized that traditional Muslim youths liked Saudi Arabia due to sacred spaces like Makkah and Madinah. These consequences were working as a leading factor in the process of migration within the cultural region of migration from Inayat Patti village to Saudi Arabia and Dubai. These Muslim youths said that they were not worried about their future because they easily accessed the jobs in Dubai and Saudi Arabia. These consequences gave a safeguard to Muslim youths, who always used to think about migration because the matter of migration was deeply rooted in their cultural and economic practices of livelihood concerning migration. Therefore, these consequences were being led by the depth penetration of the culture of migration from Inayat Patti to Saudi Arabia and Dubai in the context of globalization of the long historical journey of migration among Muslims in Inayat Patti village. Therefore, the desires of Muslim youths were being functioned by a safe approach to migration among Muslim youths; those were considering the matter of migration as a guarantee of jobs in Dubai and Saudi Arabia. These consequences were replacing the concept of expectation about access jobs into a guarantee of jobs in Saudi Arabia and Dubai. Therefore, the function of the safe zone of migration was moving around through the positive role of the socio-economic and cultural function of migration among Muslim youths, those who had common socio-economic and cultural values about the history of migration in Inayat Patti village and these consequences determined the psychological behaviour of the Muslim youths regarding the investment of their wishes and abilities in the formation of building capacity of the function of safe zone of migration in Inayat Patti village.[15]

---

[15] Information is based on informal interviews and passive observation methods among migrant labourers in Dubai in December 2019.

6.3. Consequences and challenges of safe zone of migration from root to destinations

According to Sirkeci (2003), the consequences of depth penetration of culture of migration is a major trigger factor in the formation of building capacity of cultural migration among migrants in the context of globalization of culture of migration in the twenty-first century. In the case of migration from India to Gulf countries via internal migration to Mumbai, findings of the study of Taukeer (2023) show that consequences of a safe zone of migration paved the route of cultural migration from rural Uttar Pradesh to Dubai via culture of internal migration to Mumbai. These consequences developed a migration-based community in a specific region; those considered the matter of migration as a source of their cultural livelihood practices but these consequences created both economic and non-economic challenges in migration abundant zone in rural Uttar Pradesh, where the impact of Gulf migration created socio-economic and cultural transformation. Consequences of socioeconomic and cultural transformation gave both advantages and disadvantages of migration in the context of the culture of migration among Muslims in rural Uttar Pradesh. Therefore, the consequences of Gulf migration diverted Muslim youths toward migration to Saudi Arabia because findings of the study of Taukeer (2023) show that the culture of both internal and international migration created a migration-based community among Muslims and these migration-based communities find themselves in secure position because these migration based community does not think about another source of livelihood, instead of migration. These consequences created a form of cultural inequality between migrant and non-migrant Hindu households because non-migrant Hindu households were unable to migrate to Gulf countries. These consequences led to economic inequality between migrations-based Muslims and non-migrant Hindu communities because non-migrant Hindu communities are less affected by Gulf migration. Therefore, these consequences created a hurdle situation for

---

[16] Information is based on personal interview from migrant labourer in Dubai in December 2019.

non- migrant Hindu community, those who do not think about Gulf migration due to its Muslim-based identity. Apart, the study also shows that the consequences of the safe zone of migration created a neighbour effect of migration on the economic behaviour of non-migrant Muslim households because the tendency of economic mobility of non-migrant Muslim households is being continuously shifted toward Mumbai-based internal migration and Dubai based international migration. The findings of the study of Taukeer (2022) show that the consequence of the impact of Gulf migration developed a safe zone of migration among Muslims in the Hindi belt region of Uttar Pradesh. The consequences of Saudi-based migration created a socio-economic and cultural transformation among Muslims and these consequences are being reflected in the socio-economic and cultural behaviour of Muslims in rural Uttar Pradesh. Therefore, these consequences developed linguistic diversities among Muslims in the Hindi belt region because Muslims used to speak in the Arabic language with their native Hindi language. These consequences created a crisis for the Hindi language due to the large impact of Saudi-based migration among Hindi-speaking Muslim migrants in the Hindi belt region of Uttar Pradesh. A study conducted by Zachariah & Rajan (2016) shows that Muslims of Kerala are the leading factor in labour migration to Gulf countries due to a well-developed culture of migration among Muslims. These consequences developed a form of socio-economic and cultural inequality between Muslims and non-Muslims in Kerala in the context of labour migration from Kerala to Gulf countries in the twenty-first century.

In the context of the study of consequences and challenges of the safe zone of migration at the destination in the United Arab Emirates, the findings of the study of Taukeer (2022) show that there is socio-economic and cultural inequality between South Indian migrant labourers and north Indian migrant labourers because both South Indian and north Indian migrant labourers follow their traditional norms as well as existed least communication between north Indian and south Indian migrant labourers. In these consequences, the findings of Nadjmabadi (2010) show that ethnic diversity created a form of challenges among the diaspora in the United Arab Emirates due to the existence of different values, norms, and cultural beliefs among migrants. These consequences created challenges for the Indian diaspora in Dubai as well as created a crisis for ethnic identical issues for the Indian diaspora. A study by Rahman (2010) shows that there is a problem of identity before Indian migrant labourers, are engaged as unskilled and semi-skilled migrant labourers in the bottom segmentation of labourers because these unskilled and semi-skilled Indian migrant labourers are deprived of basic human rights in Gulf countries. A study by Zachariah et al. (2004) shows that there are huge numbers of Indian migrant labourers in the United Arab Emirates and these Indian migrant labourers created challenges for the local labour market due to the problem of wage inequality among Indian migrant labourers in the working environment of United Arab Emirates.

The findings of Taukeer (2022 & 2022) show that migrants face the problem of cultural inequality due to the huge trend of migration from South Asia to the Middle East because these South Asian migrants work in different economic segmentation and these consequences developed a line of socio-economic and cultural differences among South Asian migrants in Middle East. Therefore, these consequences created a form of crisis among South Asian migrants because the findings of the study of Farooq (2021) show that diversity among South Asian migrants created an ethnic crisis and cultural inequality among South Asian migrants. After all, there is ethnic diversity among South Asian migrants and these consequences developed a linguistic crisis among South Asian migrants.

In the context of the impact of COVID-19 in Inayat Patti village, the findings of a study by Majumder (2022) show that the consequences of the pandemic of COVID-19 and the lockdown created a form of economic uncertainty among Muslims, those taken the matter of migration as source of their livelihood but pandemic of COVID-19 started re-verse migration to village as well as created an economic phobia of COVID-19 among Muslim return migrants in Inayat Patti village.

Based on the above concise analysis of the review of literature, it is realized that depth penetration of culture of migration created a safe zone of migration in the case of labour migration from India to Gulf countries but findings of the selected review of the literature show that consequences of safe zone of migration created a socio-economic and cultural inequality between migrant and non-migrant community in migration abundant zone in India. In the case of Uttar Pradesh, a selected review of the literature shows that recent phenomena of labour migration from rural Uttar Pradesh to Saudi Arabia and the United Arab Emirates via culture of internal migration to Mumbai, created a hurdle situation of socio-economic and cultural development among Muslims and Hindus because Muslims are benefited from Gulf migration compared to least benefit of migration among Hindus. These consequences created socio-economic and cultural inequality between migration and non-migration communities in the context of reflection of

Gulf migration among migration-based communities; those follow the traditional norms of Arabic culture as well as excluding themselves in the traditional Hindi culture of rural Uttar Pradesh. These consequences are working as a crisis for the traditional Hindi culture of rural Uttar Pradesh due to the increasing role of the influence of Arabic culture among migration-based Muslim communities in rural Uttar Pradesh.

In the context of the impact of labour migration from India to the United Arab Emirates, findings of the selected review of literature show that there is a crisis of identity before Indian migrant labourers in the United Arab Emirates due to ethnic diversity among Indian migrant labourers by different languages and dialects pattern with differ cultural values, norms, beliefs and attitudes. These consequences created a form of ethnic crisis among the diversified Indian diaspora. These consequences are creating phenomena of identical issues among the diversified Indian diaspora in the United Arab Emirates. Apart from this, the selected review of literature also shows that there is also existence of economic inequality among Indian migrant labourers according to their skill variations and these consequences determine their working and living conditions in the Arabic environment of the United Arab Emirates. These consequences also determined the economic psychological behaviour of migrant labourers as well as determined the pattern of inflow of remittances from Gulf countries to India and its reflection in the socio-economic performance of migrant households in the migration-abundant zone in India.

Based on the above concise summary of the review of literature, the present section of this chapter broadly advocates the consequences and challenges of safe zones of migration from rural Uttar Pradesh to Mumbai and the United Arab Emirates. The findings of the chapter show that there is a significant impact of the safe zone of migration in Inayat Patti village due to its long historical consequences of Gulf migration and consequences of depth penetration of Gulf migration determined the socio-economic and cultural behaviour of migrant labourers in the village. These consequences are also leading to socio-economic and cultural inequality between migrant Muslim households and non-migrant Hindus as well as creating a form of Islamic-based ideology among Muslims in the context of Saudi-based migration. These consequences can be realized as the role of function of Saudi-based migration in the formation of common social perception about Islamic-based ideology and its reflection among Muslims, those who consider themselves as sheikh of Saudi Arabia in India. This chapter also presents the role of

Gulf migration in building the capacity of changing the scenario of political mobility among uneducated Muslims in Inayat Patti village; those are giving their participation in the local politics of the village without knowledge about basic principles of Indian democracy. Therefore, these consequences are deeply associated with the impact of Gulf migration among Muslims where Hindus are findings themselves as an isolated community because these Hindus are not being affected by Gulf migration due to the Islamic-based image of Gulf migration. These perspectives are changing the socio-economic and cultural scenario of Inayat Patti village due to the depth penetration of the culture of migration among Muslims where consequences of the culture of migration developed a safe zone of migration for Muslims; those are taking the matter of Gulf migration as a socio-economic and cultural symbol. These consequences are leading to huge migration from Inayat Patti to the United Arab Emirates via internal migration to Mumbai within the safe zone of migration but a consequence of the safe zone of migration is creating panic conditions for non-migrant Hindus, those are suffering to problem of economic inequality in village. These consequences develop an understanding of the phenomena of migration in the context of dynamics of the political economy of globalization of migration in Inayat Patti village where a long historical journey of migration paved the route of Islamic-based migration toward Saudi Arabia and the United Arab Emirates as well as excluded to Hindus in process of modernization of globalization in the twenty-first century.

6.3.1. Consequences of safe zone of migration in Inayat Patti village

It is observed that there was a significant impact of the culture of migration in Inayat Patti village in the consequences of depth penetration of the long journey of historical consequences of migration where Arabian-based Gulf migration created a socio-economic and cultural transformation in the development of the village through investing of *zakat* based remittances in Muslim households. These consequences worked as a safeguard for Muslims, those who considered the matter of migration as a source of their livelihood and the result consequences of the nexus of migration and culture developed a safe zone for Muslims, those willingly involved in the inter-generational process of Arabian-based Gulf migration. These consequences gave an isolated socio-economic and cultural image to Muslims because *zakat*-based remittances improved the socio-economic status of Muslims as well as paved the route of migration from Inayat Patti to Saudi Arabia and the United Arab Emirates in the form of cultural migration where migration created culture and culture led migration in the context of globalization of migration. The impact consequences of the globalization of cultural migration created both challenges and crises for both migration-based community Muslims and non-migration-community Hindus because the impact of Arabian-based migration created a form of cultural economic inequality with the silent social crisis between migrant and non-migrant-based communities in Inayat Patti and its surrounding villages. It is also observed that Muslims were so confused about the matter of the National Register of Citizens (NRC) due to the explicit impact of Arabian-based Gulf migration in Inayat Patti village.[17]

Box 6.8: Case Study[18]

"It is a case study of 70 years old named Kevali in Dhorhan, Inayat Patti, who lived with their own development practices but there was not any person was involved in Gulf migration in households of Kevali. Therefore, Kevali lived in very precarious conditions compared to prosperous Muslim migrant households. These consequences can be analyzed as negative impact of Gulf migration in creating inequality in development in Inayat Patti village in the context of nexus of migration and development."

It is observed that consequences of safe zone of migration created economic inequality where Muslim migrant households accessed better life compared to poor living conditions of non-migrant Hindus due to the deep penetration of the culture of Arabian-based Gulf migration among Muslims where Muslim youths desired jobs in Gulf but Hindu youths hesitated and did not like to Arabian based Gulf migration due to Islamic based reflection of Gulf migration in the village as well as lack of social network system of migration was major barrier for migration of Hindu youth to Saudi Arabia but these Hindu youths migrated to Indian cities like- Surat and Daman. Therefore, there was a different existence of trajectories and routes of migration in villages where Arabian-based Gulf migration gave huge *zakat*-based remittances to Muslim migrant households compared to a low inflow of remittances in Hindu households, which were involved in internal migration. These consequences created a gap in economic function by religion in the sense of migration because the mechanism of the safe zone of migration gave a dress to Saudi-based migration as Islamic-based migration in Inayat Patti and its surrounding villages due to Islamic-based socio-economic and cultural behaviour among Muslim youths. These consequences sketched a line of socio-economic and cultural differences between Muslims and Hindus in the

---

[17] Information is based on informal interviews and passive observation methods among return migrant labourers in Inayat Patti village from October 2023 to November 2023.
[18] Information is based on personal interview of Kevali named woman in Inayat Patti village in October 2023.

context of the implication of a safe zone of migration in the village.[19]

Box 6.9: Case Study[20]

It is a case study of 35 years old return migrant labourer named Gyas, who worked in Madinah in Saudi Arabia. He said that he considered Saudi-based migration as part of Islamic culture and he felt proud of Islamic culture but it is realized that he did not have any specific knowledge about the culture of Saudi Arabia as well as Indian secularism. These consequences can be analyzed as an implication of safe zone of migration created both crisis and challenges for both India and Saudi Arabia because uneducated Muslim youths were creating an environment of Islamic culture in Inyat Patti village as well as created Islamic phobia in the village in the context of Saudi based migration.

It is also observed that consequences of Gulf migration led to the tendency of internal migration from tribal areas of central India to local brick kilns in surrounding villages of Inayat Patti because a huge trend of out-internal and international migration created a labour scarcity in local brick kilns and these consequences gave a way to tribal migration of "Parosee"[21], those worked in local brick kilns in surrounding villages of Inayat Patti. These consequences can be analysed as the role of international migration in leading internal migration due to the gap in local labour markets as well as higher wages also led to the tribal migration in Inayat Patti and its surrounding villages. These consequences were also the result of the matter of social identity of Muslims, those who could never think about their engagement in local brick kilns due to the glamour of Mumbai and Dubai due to the function of a safe zone of migration in the context of globalization of migration. It is also observed that these consequences were leading to air pollution due to the increasing role of brick kilns because Muslim migrant labourers invested *zakat*-based remittances in the constriction and re-construction of houses, mosques, and religious schools and these consequences led to the demand for raw materials like bricks, soils from local brick kilns. These consequences motivated local Mafias to operate brick kilns in the surrounding villages of Inayat Patti.[22]

6.3.2. Consequences of safe zone of migration in Mumbai

It is also observed that the culture of migration from Inayat Patti to Gulf countries via internal migration to Mumbai developed a safe zone of

---

[19] Information is based on informal interview and passive observation method among return migrant labourers in Inayat Patti village from October 2023 to November 2023.

[20] Information is based on personal interview from return migrant labourer in Inayat Patti village in October 2023.

[21] "Parosee" is tribal identity of those types of tribal migrants, who work in brick kilns in rural eastern Uttar Pradesh. *Ibid.* pp. 115-131.

[22] Information is based on informal interviews and passive observation methods among return migrant labourers in Inayat Patti village from October 2023 to November 2023.

migration among Muslim youths of Inayat Patti village in Mumbai due to the long history of labour migration from Inayat Patti to Mumbai. These consequences gave a specific route of migration to Muslim youths, where the culture of both internal and international migration was deeply rooted in the cultural and economic practices of Muslim youths. These consequences also led to the culture of migration to Saudi Arabia and the United Arab Emirates via Mumbai due to the availability of the well-developed social network system of migration among Muslims. Therefore, the implementation of well developed social network system of migration developed a safe zone of migration within the cultural region of migration from Inayat Patti to Gulf countries via Mumbai-based internal migration where both internal and international migration were being taken under similar phenomena of image of migration among Muslims because Muslims considered Mumbai, Riyadh and Dubai as their Gav (village) like Inayat Patti. These Muslim youths found socio-economic and psychological support in these cities due to the well-developed social network system of migration in the context of a safe zone of migration from Inayat Patti village to Gulf countries via internal migration to Mumbai. These consequences were the result of the function of a safe zone of migration in the context of globalization of the culture of migration among Muslims in Inayat Patti village.[23]

These consequences created a specific migration-based Muslim community in North India in Mumbai, those considered Mumbai a door for Saudi-based migration due to the consequence of interconnection between internal and international migration where the culture of internal migration led to a culture of international migration. These consequences led to the huge migration from Inayat Patti village to Mumbai but it is realized that the consequence of Gulf migration was leading to Islamic-based culture in the glamour culture of Mumbai due to Islamic-based reflection of socio-economic and cultural behaviour of Muslim youths, those were affected the *zakat* based remittances and Islamic culture of Inayat Patti village and their considerable understanding about culture of Saudi Arabia as Islamic culture. These consequences were the result of the safe zone of migration because the consequence of the culture of migration blocked the mentality of Muslim youths about the beauty of Islam and the beautiful aspect of democracy of India. These consequences led to the form of Islamic phobia in Mumbai as well as confusion among both Muslims and non-Muslims about the core of Islam due to the inflow of social remittances from Saudi Arabia to Mumbai

---

[23] Information is based on passive observation and informal interview among migrant labourers in Mumbai in February 2019.

in the form of "J"[24] term migration where international migrant labourer returned from Saudi Arabia to Mumbai as well as engaged in economic and cultural practices of the village through "U" term migration. Therefore, the consequence of both "J" term and "U"[25] term migration was leading to an inflow of social remittances and *zakat*-based remittances in both Mumbai and Inayat Patti village. These consequences led to the dynamics of migration with its complexity in the context of the socio-economic and cultural return of Saudi-based migration in both Mumbai and Inayat Patti village.[26]

Box 6.10: Case Study[27]

"It is a case study of 56-year-old Mumtaz Ahamed urf Phul Babu, who was from Dhorhan, Inayat Patti village. He operated an Islamic school namely Qadri public school in Dhorhan as well as a Madarsha (religious school) in Mumbai. He said that he worked in Mumbai before migrating to Saudi Arabia but recently, he worked as a retired migrant labourer in a village. In these consequences, it can be analyzed that both the "J" term and "U" term migration were leading to Islamic-based phenomena in both Mumbai and Inayat Patti village."

6.3.3. Consequences of safe zone of migration in Dubai

It is observed that the safe zone of migration created a form of ethnic crisis between north Indian and South Indian migrant labourers because a huge trend of labour migration from rural Uttar Pradesh to Dubai developed a form of north Indian Bhojpuri diaspora in Dubai. Therefore, trajectories of migration from India to Dubai are new phenomena in the context of labour migration from rural Uttar Pradesh and Bihar to Dubai compared to long historical phenomena of labour migration from South India. These consequences created ethnic diversities with challenges among the Indian diaspora because it is observed that there were explicit differences between South Indian and North Indian diaspora because there was not any soft communication between South Indian and North Indian migrants in Dubai due to different cultural practices. These consequences worked as a crisis for the diversified Indian diaspora in Dubai. In the case of migrant labourers of Inayat Patti village in Dubai, it is observed that these Muslim youths were unified with North Indian migrant labourers of Punjab, Haryana and Bihar

---

[24] "J" term migration is reverse migration from international destination to internal destination at root. Cited from: Wltshire, R. (1979). Research on Reverse Migration in Japan: (I) Reverse Migration and concept of 'U-turn'. *Science reports of Tohoku University ,7th series* , 63-68.

[25] " U" term migration is reverse migration from international destination to their roots. Cited from: Cerase, F. P. (1974). Expectations and Reality: A Case Study of Return Migration from the United States to Southern Italy . *International Migration Review* , 245-262.

[26] Information is based on passive observation and informal interviews among migrant labourers in Mumbai in February 2019.

[27] Information is based on personal interviews from return migrant labourer in Inayat Patti village in October 2023.

as well as used to keep their distance from South Indian migrant labourers. Apart from, Muslim migrant labourers of Inayat Patti village were so cordial with Pakistani migrant labourers because these Muslim migrant labourers considered Pakistani as brothers because they used to easily understand the languages of Hindi and Urdu due to ethnic homogeneity between North India and Pakistan. These consequences created a form of discrimination and challenges for the diversified Indian diaspora in the global diversified environment of Dubai in the context of a safe zone of migration in the twenty-first century.[28]

Box 6.11: Case Study[29]

"It is a case study of 34 years old Aniket Singh, who was from Punjab India and worked in Dubai. He said that he loved his Punjab and north Indian migrant labourers due to his cordial relationship with the north Indian migrant labourers. These consequences can be analyzed as the role of a safe zone of migration in Dubai where North Indian migrant labourers developed their world in Dubai and these consequences were the result of the perception of North Indian migrants according to their values, norms, beliefs about north India and north Indians in Dubai."

---

[28] Information is based on informal interviews and passive observation methods among migrant labourers in Dubai in December 2019.

[29] Information is based on personal interviews from migrant labourer at restaurant in Dubai in December 2019.

CONCLUSION

7.1. Sustainable development goals and migration

According to the United Nations, Sustainable Development Goals (SDGs) report (2022), the agenda of SDGs ensures the well-being of the world community through the removal of poverty, hunger, and inequality by improving better quality of education, health and eco-friendly economic function in the context of better utilization of nexus globalization and development across the globe with the lesson of past to present function of the economy and its implication in well being of future. In this context, the World Development Report (2023) gives a realistic picture of the scenario of the world's development pattern in the context of the nexus of migration and development because the consequences of the nexus of migration and development are the core of sustainable development regarding ensuring the socio-economic and cultural development in both migrants sending and receiving countries.

According to recent reports of the United Nations, Department of Economic and Social Affairs (2020)[1], there are a total 281 million of migrants across the globe and accounts for a total of 3.5 per cent of the world's population. According to the international migration report of the United Nations, the Department of Economic and Social Affairs (2019)[2], there was a total of 30.0 million migrants in GCC[3] states, among them South Asian countries accounted for 60.4 per cent of the total migrants where the proportion of Indian migrants was accounted 31.08 per cent of total migrants in GCC states. According to the World Bank (2023)[4], GCC states are major remittances sending countries to India due to huge numbers of Indian migrant labourers in GCC states. These migrant labourers sent near about 58.0 per cent of the total remittances of India. Among the GCC states, the Kingdom of Saudi Arabia and the United Arab Emirates are major remittances-sending countries to India. From the perspective of economic

---

[1] Source: https://www.un.org/en/global-issues/migration
[2] International migration report, UNDESA 2019. Accessed from: https://www.undesa.org
[3] GCC states are based on the Gulf Cooperation Council of six oil-producing countries of the Arabian Peninsula including Saudi Arabia, United Arab Emirates, Oman, Bahrain, Kuwait and Qatar. Cited from: https://www.gcc-sg.org/en-us/CognitiveSources/GulfDatabases/Pages/GulfInformationwithCategorization.aspx
[4]Source:https://www.worldbank.org/en/news/press-release/2023/12/18/remittance-flows-grow-2023-slower-pace-migration-development-brief

re-building and sustainable development goals in Saudi Arabia, the agenda of Vision 2030[5] gives broad issues about the economic well-being of migrants under the Sustainable Development Goals (SDGs) 2030 of the United Nations. These consequences can be analyzed as the role of sustainable development goals in building the capacity of the well-being of migrants through the nexus of migration and development in the context of globalization of migration and development under Sustainable Development Goals (SDGs) 2030 of the United Nations.

Therefore, the findings of Singh et al. & Elzein et al. (2022 & 2016) show that there is a significant impact of sustainable development goals on the well-being of migrants through the positive role of migration in development in the context of globalization in the twenty-first century. A study by Holliday et al. (2019) shows that gender equality and the well-being of left-behind family members are major cores of the nexus of migration and development in the context role of migration in the well-being of migrants and their family members. These perspectives give a base for developing an understanding of the role of sustainable development goals in ensuring the well-being of migration-based communities in migration-abundant zones in Uttar Pradesh. It is well known that the north Indian state- Uttar Pradesh is the leading state in labour migration from India to oil-producing Gulf countries in the twenty-first century.[6] In the context of Uttar Pradesh, it is well known that there are diversified socio-economic and cultural practices in Uttar Pradesh and these consequences are leading to the role of sustainable development goals in the well-being of the economy and society of Uttar Pradesh.[7] Both internal and international Gulf migration plays an important role in the economy of rural Uttar Pradesh. In the context of labour migration from rural Uttar Pradesh, India to Saudi Arabia via internal migration to Mumbai, the finding of the study shows that there was a cordial nexus of migration and development in both roots and destinations. Therefore, the statistical report of the Uttar Pradesh Department of Economic and Social Affairs (2022)[8] shows that there is gender-based inequality in the socio-economic development in rural Uttar Pradesh, India and these consequences are major barriers to the way of implementation of sustainable development goals of the United Nations.

Based on the above concise introduction part, the major points of this chapter are based on conceptualizing the findings chapters under points of

---

[5] Source: http://www.vision2030.gov.sa/en
[6] Source: www.mea.gov.in
[7] Source: https://epariyojana.up.gov.in/sdg/
[8] Source: : http://www.updesa.nic.in

Sustainable Development Goals (SDGs) 2030 of the United Nations.

7.2. Economic well being and migration

According to Melzer (2011), there is an important role of the migration in economic well-being of migration-based communities because migration plays an important role in improving health quality, education and quality of life. These consequences promote sustainability in the context of the nexus of migration and development. A study conducted by Jones (2014) shows that the implementation of economic well-being creates a way of happiness in a family of migrants. Based on the above concise description of the study of the nexus of economic well-being and migration, the present section of this paragraph conceptualizes the findings of chapters from the perspective of economic well-being and migration from root to destination.

It is realized that there was a significant impact of Arabian-based migration and zakat-based remittances in economic transformation in rural Uttar Pradesh, India where migration created structural changes in development practices of rural development. These consequences led to the well-being of the economy through improvement in income and expenditure patterns but findings show that the impact of Arabian-based Gulf migration created an economic inequality in rural Uttar Pradesh from the perspective of the migration-based Muslim community and non-migration-based Hindu community as well as also created a gender-based inequality of development between Muslim women and Hindu women. These consequences also generated problems in the implementation of the agenda of Sustainable Development Goals (SDGs) in rural Uttar Pradesh because a huge inflow of zakat-based remittances is promoting an Islamic-based economy where the increasing role of fundamentalism of Islam is a major barrier in the context of ensuring agenda of Sustainable Development Goals (SDGs) 2030 of United Nations.

These consequences are also a barrier to the implementation of the agenda of Vision 2030 of Saudi Arabia because return migrant labourers were promoting the Islamic ideology of fundamentalism through the investment of zakat-based remittances in Islamic economic function in Inayat Patti village. These consequences are also a barrier to the well-being of the society of India as well as to democracy of India where the government of India is promoting an agenda of sustainable development goals in ensuring economic well-being but the findings of chapters show that zakat-based remittances created a large gap in economic development as well as promoted the isolated economy of zakat according to Islamic ideology in rural Uttar Pradesh. Therefore, it is realized that Arabian-based Gulf migration is generating challenges in the way of implementation of sustainable development goals in ensuring economic well-being. In these consequences, the conceptualization of chapters gives a broad aspect about the role of the agenda of sustainable development goals in the formation building of the function of the economy in the context of migration and development in the perspective of globalization of migration in the twenty-first century.

7.3. Social sustainability and migration

According to Wickramasekara (2016), the consequences of Gulf migration work as a safety valve for migrant labourers in South Asia because the impact of Arabian-based Gulf migration plays an important role in social well-being through social investment of remittances. These consequences lead to the mechanism of social well-being of migrants and their left behind family members at the root and create a social transformation in development from root to destinations under sustainability. A study by Chowdhury and Rajan (2018) shows a significant social impact of the Gulf migration in India because remittances create socio-economic development and structural changes in development practices. These consequences lead to social well-being through improving health quality, education quality and quality of life from the perspective of social sustainability. These consequences help develop an understanding of the phenomena of the nexus of migration and development in sustainable development practices.

In these consequences, findings of the chapters show that there was a significant impact of the Arabian-based Gulf migration on the social development of both root and destinations because the consequences of migration created social well-being in the form of social reproduction of human values, norms and its reflection in psychological behaviour of migrants. It is realized that the impact of Arabian-based Gulf migration played an important role in the formation of building capacity for social development. *Zakat*-based remittances played an important role in the social development in Inayat Patti village because zakat-based remittances played an important role in improving health quality, quality of education, and quality of life among Muslims and these consequences were leading the sustainability in development practices among migration-based community in Inayat Patti village. It is also observed that these consequences were playing an important role in the formation of building capacity of social well-being in the aspect of the nexus of migration and development in the context of globalization of migration in the twenty-first century. From these perspectives, Muslim-based Gulf migration created an inequality in social well-being between migration-based Muslims and non-migration-based Hindus. The social economy of migration-based Muslims was based on a huge inflow of zakat-based remittances where non-migration-based Hindus did not benefit from Arabian Gulf migration and these consequences were creating a large gap in the implementation of social sustainability in the context of migration and development. Apart from that, it is also observed that Muslim women were less benefited from modern education due to the impact of male-based migration because Arabian-based Gulf migration promoted Islamic biases about women due to the prominence of Islamic tradition among migration-based Muslim communities. Therefore, these consequences were promoting gender inequality among Muslims due to the patriarchal system in Inayat Patti village. The consequence of Arabian-based Gulf migration was promoting a form of rigid belief about Islam among Muslims; those excluded themselves from the modern educational framework because Muslims were following Islamic education due to the tendency of Gulf migration. These consequences were major barriers to the implementation of modernity in the aspect of the approach of sustainability because migration-based Muslim communities were failing to promote a balance between modernity and Islamic education as well as creating a form of traditional Islamic values in the place of modernity in sustainable development. These consequences were creating a traditional Muslim community in Inayat Patti village, where the approach of sustainability like the function of social well-being was being promoted by traditional Islamic ideology and these consequences were diverting the major principles of sustainability and Sustainable Development Goals (SDGs) of the United Nations. In Mumbai, Muslim migrant labourers of Inayat Patti village were promoting Islamic ideology through the investment of their beliefs, values and norms in the implementation of Islamic phenomena in the glamour of Mumbai and these consequences were working as a major barrier in the implementation of nexus of sustainability and development because the impact of Arabian based Gulf migration was promoting traditional form of Islamic ideology among Muslims in Mumbai. These consequences were also major barriers in balancing social development and social well-being due to rigid Islamic tradition among Muslim migrants of Inayat Patti and its surrounding villages in Mumbai. Therefore, these consequences were creating a problem in developing an understanding of the nexus of sustainability and development in the context of migration. In Dubai, it is observed that there was a balanced relationship between modernity and Islamic culture in the context of globalization of development in Dubai in the twenty-first century. In the case of migrants of Inayat Patti, these migrants were enjoying their life in the glamour of Dubai but they were following the traditional form of Islamic culture at the root. These consequences created a confused Muslim society about the balanced relationship between modernity and Islamic culture. Therefore, these consequences were major barriers in the way of sustainable development under the Sustainable Development Goals (SDGs) 2030 of the United Nations as well as emerging as barriers to Vision 2030 of the Kingdom of Saudi Arabia; like the traditional form of Islamic culture among traditional Indian Muslims without knowing facts of modernity and Islam in development practices.

7.4. Human rights and sustainability in the context of migration

According to Sater (2017), the impact of Arabian-based Gulf migration is generating the problem of human rights at the root because the consequence of remittances is generating problems in the way of balance development in the aspect of implementation of sustainability in development practices regarding nexus of migration and development. These consequences are major barriers in the aspect of the well-being of migrants and non-migrants due to a pattern of imbalance development. According to Mburu (2020), a matter of human rights is the subject of discussion in the aspect of the nexus of migration and development from the perspective of sustainability and development.

In these consequences, the findings of the chapter show that the matter of human rights is a core subject in the study area of sustainable development because the investment of zakat-based remittances was generating an imbalance in development where the traditional form of Islamic culture was promoting gender inequality as the inferiority of Muslim women in decision-making process in Inayat Patti village as well as Muslim youths were exploiting themselves in framework of safe zone of migration because these Muslim youths preferred to traditional Islamic education as well as not interested in modern education of India. Therefore, these consequences were raising a question about the human rights of Muslim migrants because the impact of zakat-based remittances and Arabian-based Gulf migration was changing the perception of Muslim youths about politics of development through the demand for human rights under Islamic tradition in democratic India. These consequences were generating an environment of fear among non-migrant Hindus in Inayat Patti village because these non-migrant Hindus were being mentally exploited by the huge impact of zakat-based remittances. Therefore, inequality was raising questions of economic, social and political rights from the perspective of religion where Muslims were prominent in development practices due to Gulf migration compared to least mobility among Hindus. These consequences also promoted the exploitation of Hindus, those who worked as labourers in agro farms of Muslim migrant households because these poor Hindu labourers were deprived of basic human rights in Inayat Patti village due to the huge explicit impact of zakat-based remittances in development practices of village.

In the case of Mumbai, it is observed that unskilled Muslim labourers were deprived of basic human rights in their living and working conditions because these unskilled labourers worked in the bottom segmentation of the labour market. In the case of Dubai, it is also observed that unskilled and semi-skilled labourers lived in barrack-like apartments but these semi-skilled and unskilled labourers found better social and economic rights provisions in the labour laws of the United Arab Emirates but these migrant labourers faced problems of identity in Dubai. Therefore, both unskilled and semi-skilled migrant labourers found a better space in Dubai than in Mumbai but encountered difficulties with identities in both destinations.

These consequences can be analyzed as a form of imbalance development in the context of sustainability and migration where consequences of migration created a diversified pattern of nexus of sustainable development and migration with its discriminations, contradictions and challenges.

7.5. Cultural sustainability and migration

A study conducted by Gryshova et al. (2019) shows that there is a significant association between culture and migration because the culture of migration leads to the process of migration in the context of globalization of migration in the twenty-first century. The findings of the study of Adger et al. (2024) also present a realistic picture of the nexus of migration and sustainable development because the consequence of migration creates a pathway of development in the context of sustainability of cultural values in the well-being process of migrants and their family members at the root. In these consequences, it can be conceptualized that there are cordial linkages between migration and sustainability of cultural development in the context of globalization of the nexus of migration and culture in the twenty-first century. Therefore, the findings of the chapters show that there was a cordial linkage between migration and culture where migration created culture and culture led migration in the context of globalization of migration in the twenty-first century. It is also realizing that there was an explicit impact of the Arabian-based Gulf migration on the cultural practices of migrants in the context of the impact of the Arabian language, cultural values, norms and cultural practices of migrants in the Hindi belt region of Uttar Pradesh. These consequences were also leading the formation of a mixed cultural landscape where the nexus of Hindi and Arabic cultures determined the cultural behaviour of migrants and their family members at root in India as well as leading the phenomena of cultural well-being because migrants were promoting the consequence of "Hybrid' culture by confluent of two different cultures like Arabic and Hindi culture. These consequences were also improving the cultural skills and efficiency of migrants regarding their wishes and abilities because it is observed that both wishes and abilities of migrants were being improved by Arabian-based Gulf migration in the context of migration within the cultural region of migration from rural Uttar Pradesh to Dubai via culture of internal migration to Mumbai. These consequences were symbols of culturalization of migration where migration was creating culture and culture was leading migration with an aspect of sustainability of nexus of migration and culture under Sustainable Development Goals (SDGs) of the United Nations. Apart, it is also observed that the impact of Arabian-based Gulf migration was also giving a new dimension to Vision 2030 of the Kingdom of Saudi Arabia because return migrant labourers played an important role in the formation of a "Hybrid" and culturalization of nexus of Hindi and Arabic culture where Muslim migrants loved and liked Islamic culture due to sacred space of Saudi Arabia in their individual life. These consequences were leading the extreme levels of spirituality among Muslims without basic knowledge about the facts of the principles of Islam. These consequences were leading to wrong phenomena about Islam among Muslim youths as well as presenting a negative aspect of rigid Islam before non-migrant Hindus in Inayat Patti village. These consequences were generating cultural inequality between migration-based Muslims and non-migration-based Hindus where Hindus were being feared by showing the aggressive form of Islamic culture of Muslim migrants in Inayat Patti village as well as not involved in Arabian-based Gulf migration due to Islamic phobia. Apart from this, it is also observed that Muslim women and girls were living in isolated cultures in their households because male-based Muslim culture did not allow to them present their decisions about development practices due to rigid Islamic tradition in Inayat Patti village due to long historical consequences of Arabian based Gulf migration and explicit impact of zakat based economy. These consequences were generating problems of gender inequality in the process of cultural sustainability and working as barriers in the way of women's empowerment under the Sustainable Development Goals (SDGs) 2030 of the United Nations. Apart, these consequences present a negative aspect of Vision 2030 of the Kingdom of Saudi Arabia because return Muslim migrant labourers were presenting rigid traditional views about Muslim women and girls in Inayat Patti village in democratic India. These consequences are major barriers in the way of implementation of sustainable development on the ground level in democratic India where the government of India is implementing reform steps in sustainable socio-economic and cultural development in the context of globalization of development in the twenty-first century. Therefore, imbalance development is a major barrier in the way of ensuring a sustainable approach to the implementation of development on the ground level under the Sustainable Development Goals (SDGs) 2030 of the United Nations.

Conclusion

Based on the above concise description of findings in the aspect of sustainability, it can be concluded that there is a long history of migration from India to Gulf countries from the perspective of colonial phenomena and its reflection in the form of post-modernity of migration in post-colonial phenomena. In the context of labour migration from India to Gulf countries, the initial phase of labour migration from India to Gulf countries was led by Kerala and other South Indian states but recent phenomena of labour migration from India to Gulf countries are being led by North Indian states namely- Uttar Pradesh. It is well known that Uttar Pradesh is also the leading state in internal and international migration in the twenty-first century from the perspective of colonial experiences of internal and international indentured migration in colonial India. Therefore, there is a colonial reflection in recent phenomena of migration from Uttar Pradesh to Gulf countries via Mumbai. Therefore, the findings of the study show that colonial experiences of migration are reflected as modern migration in the post-colonial era in India. These consequences can be analyzed as colonial sustainability of migration where past experiences of migration are being reflected in the form of post-colonial labour migration in twenty-first century. Both colonial and post-colonial migrations are positively associated with each other by the positive role of internal migration in international migration from colonial India to post-colonial India. These consequences are cordially associated with internal to international migration where migrant labourers migrated to Gulf countries via internal migration to Mumbai in the context of long historical consequences of colonial experiences of migration. The entire function of internal and international migration was prominently led by Muslims due to the depth penetration of the colonial cultural paradigm of migration and its reflection in the form of migration from rural North India to Gulf countries via internal migration to Mumbai within a well-developed social region of migration. These consequences can be analyzed in that social network systems work as a pull factor in the process of migration but a matter of wage differential also plays a crucial role in the function of migration as a "push-pull" factor of migration. In the case of Inayat Patti village, both economic and non-economic factors of migration led to the migration within well developed social region of migration in the context of long historical consequences of colonial experiences of migration. It is also important to conclude that there was a significant impact of Gulf migration with positive and negative impacts with the implementation of Islamic-based education in modern India as well as the creation of an isolated Islamic culture in Inayat Patti village. These consequences are major barriers to the way of implementation of the Sustainable Development Goals (SDGs) 2030 of the United Nations. The *zakat*-based economic system presented a scattered picture of the Indian democratic system in Inayat Patti village. Muslims did not know the principles of Indian democracy because these Muslims lived in the mental region of Arabs in the Hindi belt region of Uttar Pradesh. These consequences also promoted the concept of a safe zone of migration where Muslims were positively associated with Gulf migration due to its long historical consequences of migration in Inayat Patti village. Therefore, the entire function of Islamic-based Gulf migration created a form of socio-economic and cultural inequality by religion, caste and gender where depth penetration of Gulf migration created an imbalance development pattern in the context of globalization of Gulf migration among Muslims as well as promoted Islamic agenda according to principles of Islam in democratic India. These consequences developed a form of isolated socio-economic and cultural economy in the framework of Arabian Islamic culture where non-Muslims found themselves excluded in the framework of Gulf migration due to explicit visibility of the Gulf migration among Muslims in Inayat Patti and its surrounding villages. These consequences created contradiction; discrimination and challenges in the way of achieving the agenda of Sustainable Development Goals (SDGs) 2030 of the United Nations.

References

Adger, W. N., Fransen, S., Safra de Campos, R., & Clark, W. C. (2024). Migration and Sustainable Development. *Proceedings of the National Academy of Sciences, 121*(3).

Ali, S. (2007). 'Go West Young Man': The Culture of Migration among Muslims in Hyderabad, India. *Journal of Ethnic and Migration Studies, 33*(1), 37-58.

Amuedo-Dorantes, C., Bucheli, J. R., & Martinez-Donate, A. P. (2023). Safe-Zone Schools and the Academic Performance of Children in Mixed-Status Households: Evidence From the 'Between the Lines' Study. *Migration Studies, 11*(1), 143-173.

Azeez, A., & Begum, M. (2009). Gulf Migration, Remittances and Economic Impact. *Journal of Social Sciences, 20*(1), 55-60.

Basu, S. (2016). Diasporas Transforming Homelands.Nuancing Collective Remittance Practices in Rural Gujarat . *Economic and Political Weekly , 51* (41) 54-62.

Bhagat, R. B. (2011). Migrants '(denied) Right to the City. *Urban Policies and the Right to the City in India: Rights, Responsibilities and Citizenship.* UNICEF, 48-57. https://www.shram.org/uploadFiles/20131010115811.pdf

Bhugra, D. (2004). Migration, Distress and Cultural Identity. *British Medical Bulletin, 69*(1), 129-141.

Birks, J. S., & Sinclair, C. A. (1980). *International Migration and Development in the Arab Region.* Geneva : International Labour Organisation .

Colton, N. A. (2010). The International Political Economy of Gulf Migration. *Migration and the Gulf .Middle East Institute, ,* 34-36.

Carter, R. (2005). The History and Prehistory of Pearling in the Persian Gulf. *Journal of the Economic and Social History of the Orient, 48*(2), 139-209.

Chandramalla, C. B. (2022). Trends in Indian Labour Migration to Gulf Countries from 1990 to 2019: An Assessment of Literature. *Journal of Production, Operations Management and Economics (JPOME) ISSN 2799-1008, 2*(01), 1-9.

Chowdhury, M., & Rajan, S. I (Ed.). (2018). *South Asian Migration in the Gulf* (pp. 35-59). Basingstoke: Palgrave Macmillan

Choucri, N. (1983). Migration in the Middle East:Transformation and Change. *Middle East Review , 2* (4), 16-27.

Choucri, N. (1986). Asian in the Arab World :Labour Migration and Public Policy. *Middle Eastern Studies , 22*(2), 252-273.

Cohen, J. H., & Sirkeci, I. (2011). *Cultures of Migration: The Global Nature of Contemporary Mobility.* Texas: University of Texas Press.

Colton, N. A. (2010). The International Political Economy of Gulf Migration. *Migration and the Gulf .Middle East Institute, ,* 34-36.

Datta, A. (2016). Migration, Remittances and Changing Sources of Income in Rural Bihar (1999-2011): Some Findings from a Longitudinal Study. *Economic and Political Weekly, 51* (31), 85-93.

Demir, Z., Guerer, C., Rottmann, P., & Ghráinne, B. N. (2020). A Safe Zone for Displaced Populations in Northern Syria: Interdisciplinary Perspectives. In *3rd Conference of The German Network of Forced Migration Researchers" Contexts Of Displacement, Refugee Protection And Forced Migrants' Lives".*

Edwards, M. B. (2015). LSE:Global Governance-Labour Immigration and Labour Market in GCC Countries: National Pattern and Trends. *Kuwait Programme on Development, Governance and Globalization in the Gulf States ,* pp. 1-71.

El-Zein, A., DeJong, J., Fargues, P., Salti, N., Hanieh, A., & Lackner, H. (2016). Who's been left behind? Why sustainable development goals fail the Arab world. *The Lancet, 388*(10040), 207-210.

Ewald, J. J. (2000). Crossers of the Sea: Slaves, Freedmen, and Other Migrants in the Northwestern Indian Ocean, c. 1750-1914. *The American Historical Review,105*(1) , 69-91.

Farooq, D. Y. G. (2021). Forging a Linguistic Identity, Overseas-Trained South Asian Doctors in the UK. *Border Crossing, 11*(1), 93–108.

Fox, J. E., & Jones, D. (2013). Migration, Everyday Life and the Ethnicity Bias. *Ethnicities, 13*(4), 385-400.

Gardner, A. M. (2010). City of Strangers: Gulf Migration and the Indian Community in Bahrain. Cornell: Cornell University Press.

Gavaskar, M. (2010). Mumbai's Shattered Mirror. *Economic and Political Weekly, 45* (7), 17-22.

Gentry, J. W., & Mittelstaedt, R. A. (2010). Remittances as social exchange: The critical, changing role of family as the social network. *Journal of Macromarketing, 30*(1), 23-32.

Gilbert, E. (2002). Coastal East Africa and the Western Indian Ocean: Long-Distance Trade, Empire, Migration, and Regional Unity, 1750-1970. *The History Teacher,Vol 36.No.1 / accessed from http://www.jstor.org/stable/1512492* , 7-34.

Grutz, J. W. (1999, Vol.50 January/February). *Saudi Aramco World : Prelude to Discovery.* Retrieved Decmber 2016, from archive.aramcoworld.com/issue/199901/ prelude.to. discovery.htm

Gryshova, I., Kofman, B., & Petrenko, O. (2019). Migration cultures and their outcomes for national security. *Journal of Security & Sustainability Issues, 8*(3), 233-258.

Healey, J. F., & Stepnick, A. (2019). *Diversity and society: Race, ethnicity, and gender.* Sage Publications.

Healey, J. F., & O'Brien, E. (Eds.). (2007). *Race, ethnicity, and gender: Selected readings.* Pine: Forge Press.

Holden, D. (1971). The Persian Gulf: After the British Raj. *Foreign Affairs, 49* (4),721-735.

Holliday, J., Hennebry, J., & Gammage, S. (2019). Achieving the sustainable development goals: surfacing the role for a gender analytic of migration. *Journal of Ethnic and Migration Studies, 45*(14), 2551-2565.

Jha, M. K., & Kumar, P. (2016). Homeless Migrants in Mumbai: Life and Labour in Urban Space. *Economic and Political Weekly, 51* (26), 69-77.

Jain, P. C. (February 1982). Indians Abroad A Current Population Estimate . *Economic and Political Weekly , 17* (8), 299-304 .

Jain, P. C. (1989). Emigration and settlement of Indians abroad. *Sociological bulletin 38* (1), 155-168.

Jones, P., & Krzyzanowski, M. (2008). Identity, Belonging and Migration: Beyond Constructing 'others'. *Identity, Belonging and Migration, 17*, 38-53.

Jones, R. C. (2014). Migration and Family Happiness in Bolivia: Does Social Disintegration Negate Economic Well-being?. *International Migration, 52*(3), 177-193.

K, Afsal., & R. S., Reshmi. (2023). Motives and Areas of Diaspora Philanthropic Donation; A study on Diaspora Community from Kerala, India. Migration and Diversity, 2(3), 343–365. https://doi.org/10.33182/md.v2i3.2982

Kapiszewski, A. (2016). Arab verus Asian migrants workers in the GCC countries. In P. C. Jain, & G. Z. Oommen, *South Asia Migration to Gulf Countries* (pp. 46-70). New York : Routledge Tylor and Francis Group.

Kaur, A. P. (2021, November). Typology of remittances and transnational ties: Study of Punjabi families in Netherlands, Gulf and Punjab (India). In *The Migration Conference 2021 Selected Papers* (pp. 287-290). Transnational Press London.

Kesici, M. R. (2021). The History of Migration from Turkey to Western Europe: A Multi-theoretical Analysis of the Routes to Germany and the United Kingdom. *Border Crossing, 11*(2), 175-192.

Khadria, B. (2001). Shifting Paradigm of Globalisation:The Twenty First Century Transition towards Generics in Skilled Migration from India. *International Migration 39* (5), 46-71.

Khadria, B. (2006). India: Skilled migration to developed countries, labour migration to the Gulf. *Migración y desarrollo*, (7), 4-37.

Koser, K. (2007). *International migration: A very short introduction.* New York: Oxford University Press.

Kumar, K. (2016). Indian labour in the Gulf . In P. C. Jain, *South Asian Migration to Gulf Countries* (pp. 84-85). New York : Routledge.

Kumar, A., Mathur, R., & Hatekar, N. (2012). Paanwalas in Mumbai: Property Rights, Social Capital and Informal Sector Livelihood. *Economic and Political Weekly, 47*(38), 90-96

Kurien, P. A. (2002). Kaleidoscopic Etnicity: International Migration and the Reconstruction of Community Identites in India . Rutgers University Press.

La Barbera, M. (2014). Identity and migration: An introduction. In *Identity and migration in Europe: Multidisciplinary perspectives* (pp. 1-13). Cham: Springer International Publishing.

Levitt, P., & Nieves, D. L. (2011). Social Remittances Revisited. *Journal of Ethnic and Migration Studies* , *37* (1), 1-22.

Magliveras, S. S. (2019). Filipino Guest Workers, Gender Segregation, and the Changing Social/Labour-Scape in the Kingdom of Saudi Arabia. *Migration Letters, 16*(4), 503-512.

Majumder, B., & Taukeer, M. (2019). Dual- Step Migration from a Village in Uttar Pradesh: Causes, Process and Consequences . *Productivity* , *60* (2), 162- 174.

Majumder, B. (2022). Impact of Lockdown on Returnee Migrant Workers: A Study in Two Villages in Uttar Pradesh. *Productivity, 62*(4), 421-429.

Malpass, D. (2023). *World Development Report: 2023.* Retrieved January Tuesday, 2023, from World Bank Group: https://www.worldbank.org/en/publication/wdr2023

Mburu, A. N. (2020). Human Rights Challenges for Migrant Workers: a Case of Returning Kenyans From the Gulf Region (Doctoral dissertation, University of Nairobi).

Mckinley, B. (2003). *Labour Migration : Trends,Challenges and Policy Responses in Countries of Origin* . Geneva, Switzerland : International Organisation for Migration .

Mehra, S., & Singh, G. (2014). Migration: A Propitious Compromise. *Economic and Political Weekly* , 24-25.

Melzer, S. M. (2011). Does Migration Make You Happy? The Influence of Migration on Subjective Well-Being. *Journal of Social Research & Policy, 2*(2), 73-80.

Mili, D. (2011). Migration and healthcareo: access to healthcare services by migrants settled in Shivaji Nagar Slum of Mumbai, India. *The Health, 2*(3), 82-85.

Ministry of External Affairs, Government of India . (2015). *Annual Report* . Retrieved 2018, from Emigration Clearences: http://www.mea.gov.in

Molland, S. (2022). Safe migration and the politics of brokered safety in Southeast Asia (p. 228). Taylor & Francis.

Nadjmabadi, S. R. (2010). Iraninan Migrants in the Arab Countries of the Persian Gulf . *Migration and Gulf , Middle East Institute View Point* , 52-54.

Naidu, K. (1991). Indian Labour Migration to Gulf Countries. *Economic Political Weekly* , *26* (7), 349-354.

Nair, P. (1983). Asian Emigration to the Middle East: Emigration From India. *Working Paper no.180. Centre for Development Studies, Kerala* , 1-110.

Narayana, D., & Rajan, S. I. (2012). The Financial Crisis in the Gulf & Its Impact On South

Asian Migration & Remittances. In S.I.Rajan, *Indian Migration Report 2012. Global Financial Crisis,Migration and Remittances* (pp. 74-93). New delhi: Routledge Taylor and Francis Group.

Naufal, G., & Ali, T. (2010). Remittances from GCC Countries: A Brief Outlook. *Migration and Gulf :Middle East Institute View points* , 37-41.

Naufal, G., & Genc, I (Eds.). (2012). History of Labour Migration to the Gulf. New York: Palgrave Macmillann.

Naweed, N. (2023). Indian Female Migrant Workers and Human Rights Violations in the Gulf: A Case Study of Kuwait. In A. Rahman, S. Babu, & A. PA, *Indian Migration to the Gulf: Issues, Perspectives and Oppurtunites* (pp. 203-204). 4 Park Square, Milton Park, Abingdon, Oxon OX14 4RN: Routledge India.

Onley, J. (2009). Britain and the Gulf Shaikhdoms, 1820–1971: The Politics of Protection. Occasional Paper No. 4 ,Center for International and Regional Studies Georgetown University School of Foreign Service in Qatar , 1-44.

Onley, J. (2005). Britain's Informal Empire in the Gulf, 1820–1971. *Journal of Social Affairs* , 22 (87), 29-45.

Peterson, J. E. (2009). Britain and the Gulf : At the Periphery of the Empire. In L. Potter, *Persian Gulf in History* (pp. 277-293). New York: Macmillan .

Prakash, B. (1978). Impact of Foreign Remittances: A Case Study of Chavakkad Village. *Economic & Political Weekly* , 13 (27), 1107-1111.

Prakash, B. (1998). Gulf Migration and Its Economic Impact- The Kerala Experiances. *Economic and Political Weekly* , 33 (50), 3209-3213.

Rahman, A. (2001). *Indian Labour Migration to Gulf* . New Delhi: Rajat Publication.

Rahman, A. (2010). Migration and Human Rights in the Gulf. *Middle East View Points: Migration and Gulf* , 16-18.

Rahman, A., M, S. B., & PA, A. (2023). COVID-19 and its Impact on Gulf Returnees: A Study of Kerala. In A. Rahman, S. B. M, & A. PA, *Indian Migration to the Gulf:Issues, Perspectives & Oppurtunites* (pp. 28-44). 2023: Routledge: Taylor & Francis Group: New York.

Rajan, S. I., 'Sami, B. D., & Raj, S. S. (2017). Tamil Nadu Migration Survey 2015. *Economic and Political Weekly* , 52 (21), 85-94.

Rajan, S. I., & Kumar, P. (2010). Historical Overview of International Migration. In R. S.Irudaya, *India Migration Report 2010.Gevernance and Labour Migration* (pp. 1-30). New Delhi: Routledge ,Tylor & francis Group.

Rajan, S. I. (Ed.). (2020). India migration report 2010: Governance and labour migration. Taylor & Francis.

Sahin, Z. (2010). Ethnicity, Nationalism, and Migration in the Middle East. In *Oxford Research Encyclopedia of International Studies*.

Sasikumar, S. K. (2021). India–Gulf labour migration in the aftermath of the COVID-19 pandemic. *Economic and Political Weekly*, 56 (34), 22-26.

Sasikumar, S. K. (2019). Indian Labour Migration to the Gulf: Recent Trends, the Regulatory Environment and New Evidences on Migration Costs. *Productivity*, 60(2), 111-125.

Sasikumar, S. K., & Thimothy, R. (2015). From India to the Gulf region: Exploring Links between Labour Markets, SkIlls and the Migration cycle. Geneva: International Orgainsation for Migration.

Sater, J. (2017). Migration and the marginality of citizenship in the Arab Gulf Region: human security and high modernist tendencies. In *The crisis of citizenship in the Arab world* (pp. 224-245). Brill.

Seccombe, I. J. (1983). Labour Migration to the Arabian Gulf:Evolution and Characteristics

1920-1950. *Bulletin (British Society for Middle Eastern Studies), 10 (*1), 3-20.

Seccombe, I. J., & Lawless, R. (1986). Foreign Workers Depenidnece in the Gulf and the International Oil Companies 1910-50. *International Migration Review, 20*(3),548-574.

Segal, U. A. (2019). Globalization, migration, and ethnicity. *Public health, 172*, 135-142.

Shah, N. M. (2006, May). Restrictive labour immigration policies in the oil-rich Gulf: Effectiveness and implications for sending Asian countries. In *UN Expert Group Meeting on International Migration and Development in the Arab Region: Challenges and Opportunities, Beirut* (pp. 1-20).

Shah, N. M. (2013). Labour migration from Asian to GCC countries: Trends, patterns and policies. *Middle East Law and Governance, 5*(1-2), 36-70.

Shirras, G. F. (1931). Indian Migration. In W. F. Willcox, *International Migrations, Volume II: Interpretations* (pp. 591-616). National Bureau of Economic Research. URL: http://www.nber.org/chapters/c5120.

Singh, D. P. (2007). Migration in Mumbai: Trends in fifty years. *Demography India, 36*(2), 315-327.

Singh, R. (2021). International migration from India: an historical overview. In *Handbook of Culture and Migration* (pp. 168-174). Edward Elgar Publishing.

Singh, H. P., Singh, A., Alam, F., & Agrawal, V. (2022). Impact of sustainable development goals on economic growth in Saudi Arabia: Role of education and training. *Sustainability, 14*(21), 14119.

Sirkeci, I. (1996). *Migration, ethnicity and conflict* (Doctoral dissertation, Doctoral dissertation, University of Sheffield).

Sirkeci, İ. (2003). Migration from Turkey to Germany: An ethnic approach. *New Perspectives on Turkey, 29*, 189-207.

Srivastava, R. (2020). Labour migration, vulnerability, and development policy: The pandemic as inflexion point?. *The Indian Journal of Labour Economics, 63*(4), 859-883.

Suksomboon, P. (2008). Remittances and 'Social Remittances': Their Impact on Livelihoods of Thai Women in the Netherlands and Non-migrants in Thailand. *Gender, Techonology and Development 12(3)* , 461-482.

Taukeer, M. (2022). Trend, pattern and analysis of internal labour migration in colonial India to post colonial India. *IASSI-Quarterly, 41*(1and2), 61-74.

Taukeer, M. (2022). Nexus of Social Remittances and Social Change: An Ethnographic Study of Impact of Gulf Migration on Linguistic Pattern of Migrants in Uttar Pradesh. In *India Migration Report 2021* (pp. 292-305). Routledge India.

Taukeer M. (2021). An Analysis of Impact of Occupation on Income, Remittances and Expenditure of International Return Migrant Labourers of Uttar Pradesh in Gulf Countries. *Productivity, 62*(3), 313-329.

Taukeer, M. (2020). Process and Determinants of Labour Migration from Selected Rural Areas of Uttar Pradesh to Gulf Countries. *Man and Development , 40* (4), 123-138.

Taukeer, Mohammed. (2017). Nature and Consequences of Migration to Gulf Countries: A Study of Selected Rural Areas of Allahabad District in India. *The Migration Conference 2017 Proceedings* (pp. 561-574). London: Transnational Press.

Taukeer, M. (2023). An Analysis of the Living and Working Conditions of Migrant Labourers in Mumbai. *Productivity, 64*(1), 95-106.

Taukeer, M. (2022). Migration from India to Gulf Countries: An Analysis from Root to Destinations. *Productivity, 63*(3), 365-373.

Taukeer, M. (2022). "Donki" Migration of Refugees from South Asia to Greece. *Border Crossing, 12*(1), 33-43.

Taukeer, M. (2022). Study of Process, Determinants and Consequences of" Donkey" Migration from South Asia to Greece in Europe. *Refugee Watch Journal: A South Asian Journal on Forced Migration, 59,*(1), 48-62.

Taukeer, M. (2023). Nature, Process, and Consequences of Migration: A Case Study of Migration from India to the Gulf. In *Indian Migration to the Gulf* (pp. 45-58). Routledge India.

Taukeer, M. (2023). Ethnographic Analysis of Nexus about Migration and Culture in Global Perspective. *Border Crossing, 13*(2), 115-131.

Taukeer, M. (2022). South Asian Migrants in United Arab Emirates: Impact and Challenges. *Pakistan Journal of Humanities and Social Sciences, 10*(3), 942-951.

Taukeer, M. (2024). Phenomena of Migration: An Empirical Survey. *Productivity, 65*(2), 198-217.

Taukeer, M. (2024). Ethnographic Analysis of "Safe Zone" Concept in Migration in Global Perspective. *Migration and Diversity, 3*(1), 71-87.

Taukeer, M. (2024). An Analysis of In-Migration of "Parosee" Tribal in Rural Uttar Pradesh, India in the Context of International Gulf Migration. *Migration and Diversity, 3*(3), 269-284.

Taukeer, M. (2024). Migration and Global Culture: An Ethnographic Survey in the Context of Migration to the Middle East. *Productivity, 64*(4), 442-452.

Torres, S. (2015). Ethnicity, culture and migration. In *Routledge handbook of cultural gerontology* (pp. 277-284). Routledge.

United Nation, (2022). *The Sustainable Development Goals Report.* Retrieved January Tuesday, 2023, from United Nation Statistics Division: https://unstats.un.org/sdgs/report/2022/

Webb, P. (2016). The origin of Arabs: Middle Eastern ethnicity and myth-making. *British Academy Review, 27,* 34-39.

Wickramasekara, P. (2016). South Asian Gulf migration to the Gulf: a safety valve or a development strategy?. *Migration and Development, 5*(1), 99-129.

Winckler, O. (2010). Labor Migration to the GCC States: Patterns, Scale, and Policies. *Migration and the Gulf. Middle East Institute Viewpoints* , 9-12.

Wolf, M. (2008). The Market Crosses Borders : from Why Globalisation Works. In S. C. Corbridge, *Development Reader.* New York: Routledge- Taylor & Francis Group.

Zachariah, K. C., & Rajan, S. I. (2016). Kerala migration study 2014. *Economic and Political Weekly, 51*(6), 66-71.

Zachariah, K. C., & Rajan, S. I. (2018). *Emigration from Kerala: End of An Era* . Kochi: RedInk: Nalanda Books.

Zachariah, K. C., & Rajan, S. I. (2022). *Researching International Migration* . Milton Park, Abingdon, UK: Routledge

Zachariah, K. C., & Rajan, S. I. (2012). *Kerala's Gulf Connection , 1998-2011 . Economic and Social Impact of Migration.* New Delhi: Orient Blackswan Private Limited.

Zachariah, K. C., Prakash, B. A., & Rajan, S. I. (2004), "Indian workers in UAE: employment, wages and working conditions", *Economic and Political Weekly, 39*(22),2227-2234.

Zachariah, K. C., Mathew, E. T., & Rajan, I. S. (2014). *Dynamics of Migration in Kerala: Dimensions, Differentials, and Consequences* . Noida : Orient Black Swan

Zack and Gracia, J. J. (Ed.). (2007). *Race or ethnicity?: On Black and Latino identity.* Cornell University Press.

www.ingramcontent.com/pod-product-compliance
Lightning Source LLC
Chambersburg PA
CBHW071103280326
41928CB00051B/2772